DAYS OF

DESTRUCTION

DAYS OF

REVOLT

CHRIS HEDGES
JOE SACCO

BOOKS BY CHRIS HEDGES

War Is a Force That Gives Us Meaning
What Every Person Should Know About War
Losing Moses on the Freeway
American Fascists
I Don't Believe In Atheists
Collateral Damage
Empire of Illusion
Death of the Liberal Class

BOOKS BY JOE SACCO

Safe Area Goražde: The War in Eastern Bosnia 1992–95
Palestine
The Fixer: A Story from Sarajevo
Notes from a Defeatist
War's End: Profiles from Bosnia 1995–96
But I Like It
Footnotes in Gaza
Journalism

DAYS OF
DESTRUCTION

DAYS OF
REVOLT

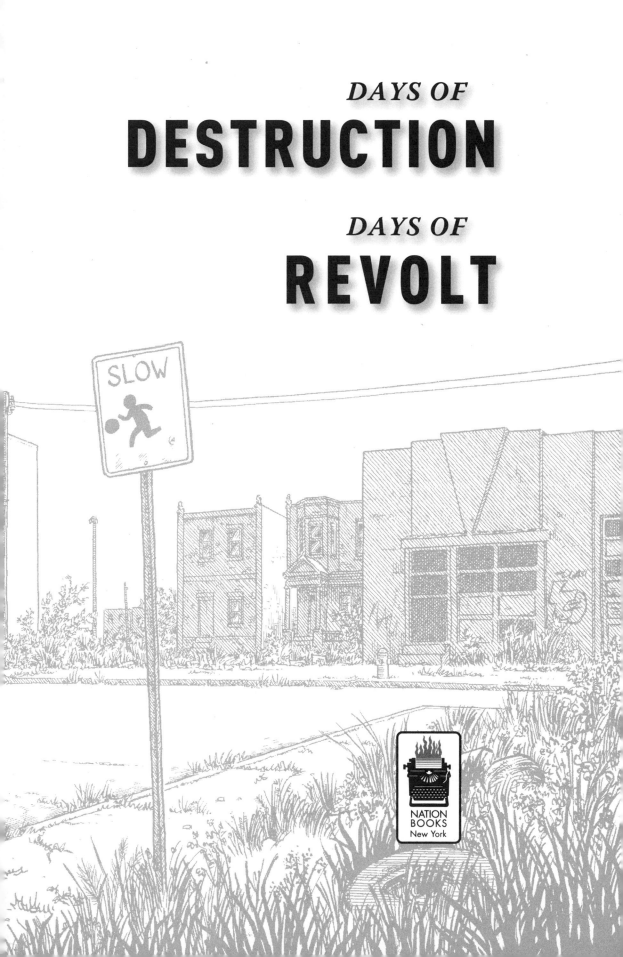

NATION BOOKS
New York

Copyright © 2012 by Chris Hedges and Joe Sacco

Published by Nation Books, A Member of the Perseus Books Group
116 East 16th Street, 8th Floor
New York, NY 10003

Nation Books is a co-publishing venture of the Nation Institute and the
Perseus Books Group

Books published by Nation Books are available at special discounts for bulk purchases
in the United States by corporations, institutions, and other organizations. For more information, please contact the Special Markets Department at the Perseus Books Group,
2300 Chestnut Street, Suite 200, Philadelphia, PA 19103, or call (800) 810-4145, ext.
5000, or e-mail special.markets@perseusbooks.com.

Designed by Jeff Williams

Library of Congress Cataloging-in-Publication Data
Hedges, Chris.
     Days of destruction, days of revolt / Chris Hedges and Joe Sacco.
        p. cm.
     Includes bibliographical references and index.
     ISBN 978-1-56858-643-4 (hardback) — ISBN 978-1-56858-710-3 (e-book) 1. Poor—
United States. 2. Social classes—United States. 3. Crime—United States. 4. United
States—Social conditions—20th century. I. Sacco, Joe. II. Title.

HC110.P6H43 2012
305.5'60973—dc23
                                                                                2012004701

10 9 8 7 6 5 4

CONTENTS

For Amalie and Eunice

For they have sown the wind,
and they shall reap the whirlwind

—HOSEA 8:7

INTRODUCTION

JOE SACCO AND I SET OUT TWO YEARS AGO TO TAKE A LOOK AT THE SACRIFICE zones, those areas in the country that have been offered up for exploitation in the name of profit, progress, and technological advancement. We wanted to show in words and drawings what life looks like when the marketplace rules without constraints, where human beings and the natural world are used and then discarded to maximize profit. We wanted to look at what the ideology of unfettered capitalism means for families, communities, workers and the ecosystem.

The rise of corporatism began with the industrial revolution, westward expansion, and the genocide carried out in the name of progress and Western civilization against Native Americans. It does not denote simply an economic system but an ideology, a way of looking and dealing with each other and the world around us. This ideology embraces the belief that societies and cultures can be regenerated through violence. It glorifies profit and wealth. This is why we went to Pine Ridge, South Dakota. It was there that the disease of empire and American exceptionalism took root. The belief that we have a divine right to resources, land, and power, and a right to displace and kill others to obtain personal and national wealth, has left in its wake a trail of ravaged landscapes and incalculable human suffering, not only in Pine Ridge but across the country and the planet. What was done to Native Americans was the template. It would be done to people in the Philippines, Cuba, Vietnam, Iraq, and Afghanistan, and it is now finally being done to us. This tyranny and exploitation have become our own.

The ruthless hunt for profit creates a world where everything and everyone is expendable. Nothing is sacred. It has blighted inner cities, turned the majestic Appalachian Mountains into a blasted moonscape of poisoned water, soil, and air. It has forced workers into a downward spiral of falling wages and mounting debt until laborers in agricultural fields and sweatshops work in conditions that replicate slavery. It has impoverished our working class and ravaged the middle class. And it has enriched a tiny global elite that has no loyalty to the nation-state. These corporations, if we use the language of patriotism, are traitors.

The belief that human beings and human societies should be ruled by the demands of the marketplace is utopian folly. There is nothing in human history or human nature that supports the idea that sacrificing everything before the free market leads to a social good. And yet we have permitted this utopian belief system to determine how we structure our economy, labor, education, culture, and our relations with foreign nations, as well as how we treat the ecosystem on which we depend for life.

All the airy promises of unfettered capitalism are starkly contradicted in the pockets of despair we visited. The hollow protestations of the courtiers in the media, the government, and the universities, who still chant the official mantra of free markets, have little substance when they are set against reality. Corporate capitalism will, quite literally, kill us, as it has killed Native Americans, African Americans trapped in our internal colonies in the inner cities, those left behind in the devastated coalfields, and those who live as serfs in our nation's produce fields.

The game, however, is up. The clock is ticking toward internal and external collapse. Even our corporate overlords no longer believe the words they utter. They rely instead on the security and surveillance state for control. The rumble of dissent that rises from the Occupy movements terrifies them. It creates a new narrative. It exposes their exploitation and cruelty. And it shatters the absurdity of their belief system.

This book, from its inception, was called *Days of Destruction, Days of Revolt*. But when we began, the revolt was conjecture. The corporate state knows only one word: *more*. We expected a beleaguered population to push back, but we did not know when the revolt would come or what it would look like. We found pockets of resistance, courageous men and women who stood up before the gargantuan forces before them in Pine Ridge; in Camden, New Jersey; in southern West Virginia; and in the nation's agricultural fields. But the nation-wide revolt was absent. It arose on September 17, 2011, in Zuccotti Park in New York City, as we were in the final months of the book. This revolt rooted our conclusion in the real rather than the speculative. It permitted us to finish with a look at a rebellion that was as concrete as the destruction that led to it. And it permitted us to end our work with the capacity for hope.

CHRIS HEDGES
Princeton, New Jersey

AMONG INDUSTRIALIZED NATIONS, THE UNITED STATES HAS THE

- highest poverty rate, both generally and for children;
- greatest inequality of incomes;
- lowest government spending as a percentage of GDP on social programs for the disadvantaged;
- lowest average number of days for paid holiday, annual leaves, and maternity leaves;
- lowest score on the United Nations index of "material well-being of children";
- worst score on the United Nations gender inequality index;
- lowest social mobility
- highest public and private expenditure on health care as a percentage of GDP.

THESE TRENDS ARE ACCOMPANIED BY THE

- highest infant mortality rate;
- highest prevalence of mental-health problems;
- highest obesity rate;
- highest proportion of population going without health care due to cost;
- second-lowest birth-weight for children per capita, behind only Japan;
- highest consumption of antidepressants per capita;
- third-shortest life expectancy at birth, behind only Denmark and Portugal;
- highest carbon dioxide emissions and water consumption per capita;
- second-lowest score on the World Economic Forum's environmental performance index, behind only Belgium;
- third-largest ecological footprint per capita, behind only Belgium and Denmark;
- highest rate of failure to ratify international agreements;
- lowest spending on international development and humanitarian assistance as a percentage of GDP;
- highest military spending as a portion of GDP;
- largest international arms sales;
- fourth-worst balance of payments, behind only New Zealand, Spain, and Portugal;

- third-lowest scores for student performance in math, behind only Portugal and Italy, and far from the top in both science and reading;
- second-highest high-school dropout rate, behind only Spain;
- highest homicide rate
- largest prison population per capita.[1]

1

DAYS OF THEFT

Pine Ridge, South Dakota

❧❀❧

I did not know how much had ended. When I look back now from this high hill of my old age, I can still see the butchered women and children lying heaped and scattered all along the crooked gulch as plain as when I saw them with eyes still young. And I can see that something else died there in the bloody mud, and was buried in the blizzard. A people's dream died there. It was a beautiful dream . . . the nation's hoop is broken and scattered. There is no center any longer, and the sacred tree is dead.

—*BLACK ELK SPEAKS*

But you have there the myth of the essential white America. All the other stuff, the love, the democracy, the flourishing into lust, is a sort of by-play. The essential American soul is hard, isolate, stoic, and a killer. It has never yet melted.

—D. H. LAWRENCE, *STUDIES IN CLASSIC AMERICAN LITERATURE*

GROUP OF FIVE MEN AND THREE WOMEN ARE SEATED CROSS-LEGGED in a small circle, in the shade of a flat-roofed brown building in Whiteclay, Nebraska. They are drinking 24-ounce cans of malt liquor. Three other men are passed out on the sidewalk, one alone and two lying next to each other. One of the pair is on his back. The other is on his side. We look at the soles of their shoes. More drinkers sit in pairs or sleep in the weeds and trash-filled lots. Abandoned cars lie junked behind the buildings. Garbage, empty beer cans, and plastic containers litter the ground.

Whiteclay, an unincorporated village that exists for only a block and a half before vanishing into the flatlands of the surrounding prairie, has only five or six permanent residents. It exists to sell beer and malt liquor. It has no town hall, no fire department, no police department, no garbage collection, no municipal water, no town sewer system, no parks, no benches, no public restrooms, no schools, no church, no ambulance service, no civic organizations, and no library. The main street, Nebraska Highway 87, is the only street in Whiteclay. A few of the buildings on the street, many of which once served as saloons, are boarded up and padlocked shut. Several are wooden, with high false fronts and sloping porches that extend over the dirt sidewalks.

The four boxy liquor stores—Jumping Eagle Inn, D&S Pioneer Service, State Line Liquor and Arrowhead Inn—are little more than oversized beer coolers. They have heavy steel doors, and clerks work inside metal cages. The Arrowhead Inn, a former filling station that is kept at a chilly forty degrees, has stacks of beer that are nine feet high. The liquor stores dispense the equivalent of 4.5 million 12-ounce cans of beer or malt liquor a year, or 13,500 cans a day.[1]

Whiteclay's primary business venture brings in an estimated $3 million a year in revenue. Whiteclay's clients, however, are some of the poorest people in the country. They are Native Americans from the Pine Ridge reservation that is less than 200 feet away, just over the state line in South Dakota. Most of those who live on the reservation earn between $2,600 and $3,500 a year. Dedicated drinkers must often beg, as many do outside the liquor stores, buy on credit, trade food stamps for alcohol, or offer sexual services to get money. Alcoholism on Pine Ridge, although the sale of liquor is banned on the reservation, is estimated to be as high as eighty percent.[2]

On the main street of Whiteclay, Nebraska.

Whiteclay is an extension of the long night of ethnic cleansing, degradation, and murder stretching back more than a century and a half, to the U.S. Cavalry charges on Indian encampments, where screaming women and children were shot down as they fled, and the systematic eradication of food sources by the white colonizers, who soon reduced bands of ragged Indians to destitution. Fights, brawls, and shootings eventually shut down the bars and saloons of Whiteclay. All sales are now carryout. But Whiteclay still provides the liquid fuel for the car wrecks, diabetes, heart attacks, domestic abuse, divorces, joblessness, violence, early deaths, and suicides: one in five Indian girls and one in eight boys attempts suicide by the end of high school. The average male life expectancy on Pine Ridge is forty-eight, the lowest in the Western Hemisphere outside of Haiti.[3]

The poison pouring out of these little shrines of death and profit, erected by tidy white capitalists, greases old, familiar cogs. The genocide that came close to obliterating Native Americans; the Indian boarding schools that ripped children away from their families, forbade them to speak their language, or practice their religious or cultural customs; the eighty percent unemployment on the reservation;[4] the racism by the neighboring white ranchers and law enforcement; the frequent lack of running water and electricity in overcrowded trailer homes and sod huts, and the horrific violence are numbed or forgotten in drunkenness. The fury of self-destruction sweeps across Pine Ridge like the Black Plague. Whiteclay is the modern-day version of the old Indian agencies. It is where Indians surrender. It is where they hand over their self-esteem and autonomy and wait passively in line for a bag of flour, a piece of lard, a few blankets, and the firewater that blunts the pain of what many have become.

Families, wracked by alcoholism, poverty, despair, and domestic violence, living lives in which tenderness and security are grabbed in desperate snatches, disintegrate swiftly under the onslaught on the reservation. The violence imposed on Indian culture has become internalized. Despair and pain of this magnitude lead to lives dedicated to self-immolation. The agony is expressed in self-defeating and self-destructive urges that shred what is left of dignity and hope.

Verlyn Long Wolf is sixty-two, with silver wire-frame glasses and salt-and-pepper hair pulled back into a ponytail. She works at a drop-in center for the homeless in Rapid City. Most of her life, including her childhood, has been colored by alcoholism, and the verbal, physical, and sexual abuse that drunkenness brings with it.

When she was a child, she and her brothers and sisters, terrified of the alcoholic rages of their parents, dug a small cave overlooking a creek near where they lived. The children would flee to the hiding spot when the parents, who were physically abusive to each other and the children, drank heavily. Her father's alcoholism was exacerbated by the trauma of his time in World War II in Europe.

"He was in the Army five years, six months, twenty-nine days, ten hours," Long Wolf says, laughing. "I could tell when he was getting high because he used to say that. 'Been in the military, five years, six months, twenty-nine days, ten hours.' He was in infantry.

"You couldn't even, like, touch him, especially when he was sleeping," she says. "If you touched his foot, boy, he'd be nipping you where's you gonna end up . . . he'd jump up. He'd start swinging at you. There were times when he'd get up three or four in the morning. He'd wake us all up and have us march up the hill, come back down. If our beds, even in the tent, if we didn't fold our quilts right, then he'd tear it apart and make us do it again.

"My brother and I, when we were ten and twelve years old, we picked fields of tomatoes and saved our monies," Long Wolf says. "Forty-two dollars. That was what divorce costed back then on the reservation. So we save all that money and then we gave it to [our mom]. She went out and got drunk with my dad."

The family, impoverished and in need of work, traveled to ranches and farms where her father could find seasonal employment. They camped out in tents or lived out of their car. Long Wolf did not have a permanent place to live until she was in eighth grade. As Indians in rural, white farm towns, the family endured racist taunts and abuse. When she was eight and her sister was four, they were each raped by a gas station owner in Hot Springs. Her father at the time was in prison for a forged check, although she says it was her mother who forged it and her father who claimed responsibility to serve the jail time. Her mother, destitute without her father's meager income, moved to her brother's house on the reservation. Here Long Wolf was repeatedly raped by four of her cousins. When she was eighteen an uncle raped her "down by the river." Rape became a persistent problem, perpetrated by male relatives and casual acquaintances, many of whom were drunk.

"From that district where I grew up, I know that every family along that river, there was sexual abuse," Long Wolf says.

"And most of these cases were among family members?" I ask.

"Yeah," she says.

Long Wolf was sent away, like many of her generation, to an Indian boarding school. One of her classmates, when she was in fourth grade, was killed by four other students. The girl's body was discovered in a nearby creek beneath a large tractor tire.

"They only stayed in prison until they were twenty-one and then they let 'em out," Long Wolf says of the four girls. "They just beat her to death. When I was working at the treatment center . . . two of them walked in and I was like, 'OK, God, help me!' So, I asked them what they wanted. They were selling beadwork. I said, 'No, I don't have any money.' "

By the 1960s the boarding schools began to shut down, and she and several of her siblings returned home. Her parents abandoned them. It would be two and a half years before her parents were located by the Department of Social Services in Denver. During this time as a young teenager, she ran the house, cooking, cleaning, and getting her younger brothers and sisters to school. Once her parents returned she left home. She began to drink heavily and ended up on the street, drifting from one city to the next, with prolonged stays in Denver, Dallas, and Albuquerque.

She was married and divorced seven times, gravitating to Vietnam veterans who replicated her father's rigidity, alcoholism, and struggles with trauma. One of her husbands was white, the others Indians.

"They're all dead," Long Wolf says, "except for the one who wasn't in the military. The longest one I had was four years."

She quietly lists the ways her ex-husbands died.

"Car wreck. Fight. Suicide."

She stops, coughs, and adds softly: "Two of them to suicide."

Long Wolf adds that the husband in the car crash "didn't die from the car wreck itself. He got stuck underneath the truck, so then the coyotes went and killed him."

"How many of these relationships were physically abusive?" I ask.

"All of them," she says, "Except for the one that I had two sons with."

She began to have prolonged blackouts, often not remembering where she had been for days and even weeks. She frequented the liquor stores in Whiteclay. She panhandled for money and burglarized houses, selling the stolen items to buy alcohol.

"There's places you can hide," she says of the tracts of land around White-clay. "If you're with a group of people, you kinda claim a territory. You all stay there, drink until the money runs out."

"In one period of my life, there was nothing but females," she says:

There was eight, ten of us females. When I reflect back then, we all had a hatred for . . . just being born, or something . . . the thing we had in common was the rapes, the sexual abuse. It didn't matter. It's like nothing matters. I mean, here we are, already dead anyway. I used to think that. And then on top of that, growing up in a Catholic school, the Ten Commandments. It's like, you look at that list and then by the time you're eighteen, nineteen, twenty, it's like, you've already committed most of them. It's like, "I'm going to hell anyways, might as well live it up."

Verlyn Long Wolf.

She got sober, she says, on August 3, 1981, when she started attending Alcoholics Anonymous. She had by then lost custody of all her children, most of them living with their grandmothers. She had given up her oldest for adoption to a white Christian minister. Her brothers, trying to pull their own lives together, had found solace and meaning in the old Lakota rituals, including sweat lodges, healing ceremonies, and the traditional four-day Sun Dances, in which participants fast, dance, chant, and make small offerings of flesh. She attended a Sun Dance after she got sober and watched her brothers circle the ceremonial cottonwood tree festooned with colored ribbons. She broke down. It brought back "all the pain we grew up with." It reconnected her with her vanquished culture and religion, she says, and saved her. Those who come out the other end of the hell that can be Pine Ridge almost always endure by turning away from white culture and reviving the traditions and religion the white invaders attempted to destroy. She has listened to old recordings of her great-grandfather Lone Wolf, who toured with Buffalo Bill's Wild West show in Europe and died of pneumonia in England, speaking about the life her ancestors led on the open plains before the Indian Wars. For the first time, she says, she feels rooted.

She and a friend recently visited the abandoned buildings of her old boarding school. She walked alone around the empty dormitory where she had lived as a small girl. She said she could hear the cries and screams of children. And then she stops speaking to us. She buries her face in her hands and begins to sob.

"If that building is there, my ghost is not gonna be there no more," she says through her tears. It's not gonna be stuck there no more."

We wait as she struggles to speak again.

"I'll say about three-quarters of the people I've grown up with are dead," Long Wolf says, her voice wavering. "Very few still alive. Alcohol. Drugs. Violence."

⚘

Rape and indiscriminate violence are the legacies of the white conquest. Soldiers on the western frontier, who passed captive squaws from tent to tent, joked that "Indian women rape easy." Ben Clark, General George Armstrong Custer's chief of scouts, told the historian Walter M. Camp when speaking about Custer's 1868 Washita raid: " . . . many of the squaws captured at Washita were used by the officers . . . Romero was put in charge of them and on the march Romero would send squaws around to the officers' tents every night.

[Clark] says Custer picked out a fine-looking one and had her in his tent every night."[5] Major Scott Anthony witnessed the murder in the Washita raid of a terrified three-year-old child: "I saw one man get off his horse at a distance of about seventy-five yards and draw up his rifle and fire. He missed the child. Another man came up and said, 'Let me try the son of a bitch. I can hit him.' He got down off his horse, kneeled down, and fired at the little child, but he missed him. A third man came up, and made a similar remark, and fired, and the little fellow dropped."[6]

Joe, my son Thomas, and I stand on a bleak, rainy day on the small hilltop in Montana where Custer, his two hundred and sixty-three soldiers, and other army personnel from the Seventh United States Cavalry were wiped out by Lakota, Arapaho, and Northern Cheyenne warriors on the afternoon of June 25, 1876. The decimation of Custer's unit was quick, by most estimates no more than twenty or thirty minutes once they were surrounded.[7] White stone markers behind a low iron fence are clustered on the hillside where the doomed troopers desperately fought and died, including Custer, whose stone is marked in black. Most of the small rectangular stones around him are marked "unknown."

Acquiring the Black Hills, although they had been promised in perpetuity to the Lakota under the Treaty of Fort Laramie of 1868, became a government priority when an expedition in 1874, led by Custer, discovered gold. Miners flooded the Black Hills.[8] The 1868 treaty stated that "no white person or persons shall be permitted" to "enter" the Black Hills, but the lust for profit led the administration of Ulysses S. Grant to pressure the Lakota to sell the Black Hills—the equivalent in the Lakota religion of Jerusalem or Mecca. The Indians refused. Washington, determined to seize the land anyway, launched a prolonged military campaign on behalf of mining companies and land speculators to decimate Indian bands that resisted and refused to resettle on Indian agencies.[9]

Custer, and the commercial interests he sought to protect and advance, set out to obliterate the Indians who stood in the way of the acquisition of buffalo herds, timber, coal, gold, and later minerals such as uranium, commodities they saw as sources of power and enrichment. Land was increasingly sliced up into parcels—usually by the railroad companies—and sold. Sitting Bull acidly suggested they get out scales and sell dirt by the pound. The basic elements that sustain life were reduced to a vulgar cash product. Nothing in the eyes of the white settlers had an intrinsic value. This dichotomy of belief between white man and Native American was so vast that those who held on to animism and mysticism, to ambiguity and mystery, to the centrality of the human imagination, to communal living and a concept of the sacred, had to be extinguished. The belief system encountered on the plains, and in the earlier indigenous communities in New England destroyed by the Puritans, was antithetical and hostile to capitalism, as well as to the concepts of technological progress and empire, and to the ethos of the industrial society. The honoring of the mystery of life, the embrace within native cultures of something very close to the Socratic dictum to know thyself, was pitted against the blind lust for empire, wealth, and power. The allegorical was pitted against the prosaic. The premodern view of the world as a living and sacred entity was violently vanquished, to be replaced by a culture that knelt before the power of the machine and a wage economy. This idolatry of efficiency, rationalism, capitalist expansion, and empire was later summed up by the sociologist Max Weber as the "disenchantment of the world"—a disturbing characteristic, Weber argued, of Western culture.

Custer, whose tireless self-promotion, outsized vanity, lust for fame and power, and incapacity for empathy—most of his soldiers detested him—presaged the sickness of the modern celebrity culture, embodied the cult of the self. He was the quintessential American hustler. Contracts that presented impediments to material and national advancement, defined as progress, were nullified or ignored. Force rather than trust determined relationships. Nature was a commodity to make human beings wealthy. And there was no limit to the amount of human suffering and death, environmental contamination, and extinction of species one could inflict on the road to glory, wealth, and power.

A society in which respect was achieved by the redistribution of wealth and rank was earned by merit, in which the natural and human worlds were intimately connected and revered, in which there was no real concept of personal property and life was communal, was pitted in the final Indian Wars against a society in which meaning was artificially constructed through the amassing of goods, power, social status, and money, a society run by an efficient and impersonal bureaucracy, a society dedicated to exploitation and profit, a society that believed in the twisted notion of regeneration through violence.

The effect of this physical and moral cataclysm, this clash of civilizations, is being played out a century and a half later, as the whole demented project of endless capitalist expansion, profligate consumption, and imperial conquest implodes. Corporate hustlers, the heirs of Custer, are fervently rolling the dice ⟨…⟩ poison us all in the last deadly chapter. They are as blind to ⟨…⟩ heir self-destructive fury as were Custer, the gold specula- ⟨…⟩ agnates, all of whom grew rich by seizing Indian land, ⟨…⟩ od in their way, extinguishing the buffalo herds, and cut- ⟨…⟩ . It is our sad fate, and the fate of our children, to pay for

⟨…⟩ ecame the rallying cry throughout the nation for a system- ⟨…⟩ mpaign of genocide against Native Americans. It led to a ⟨…⟩ d military campaign of extermination, justified by the pop- ⟨…⟩ ne of revenge, and led by the Grant administration.[10] The ⟨…⟩ e celebration of Custer as an American hero, were nearly

⟨…⟩ e Indian Wars—which had erupted more than two cen- ⟨…⟩ th the Pequot War in the eastern North American conti- ⟨…⟩ nd 1638, and raged on the western plains from the end of ⟨…⟩ 890—hundreds of distinct indigenous cultures had been ⟨…⟩ ed. An estimated two million indigenous people in the ⟨…⟩ reduced, through slaughter, starvation, and disease, to less ⟨…⟩ million people by 1900.[11] By the late nineteenth century, ⟨…⟩ rrived in a single year in New York City's slums, the fertile ⟨…⟩ for the U.S. Army during the Indian Wars, than the total ⟨…⟩ Americans left alive across the continent.

⟨…⟩ gh, they have a mind to till the soil, and the love of posses- ⟨…⟩ hem," Sitting Bull said. "These people have made many rules ⟨…⟩ break, but the poor may not. They have a religion in which ⟨…⟩ but the rich will not! They even take tithes from the poor and ⟨…⟩ e rich and those who rule. They claim this mother of ours, the Earth, for their own use, and fence their neighbors away from her, and deface her with their buildings and their refuse.[12]

"We cannot dwell side by side," Sitting Bull said. "Only seven years ago we made a treaty by which we were assured that the buffalo country should be left to us forever. Now they threaten to take that from us also. My brothers, shall we submit? Or shall we say to them: 'First kill me, before you can take possession of my fatherland!'"[13]

Trust in the Lord with all your heart and lean not on your own understanding; in all your ways acknowledge Him, and He will make your paths straight.

Proverbs 3:5-6

The assault on Native American culture did not end with the forced settlement of Indians into what were, in essence, prisoner of war camps. In 1887, Congress passed Senator Henry Dawes's General Allotment Act, usually called the Dawes Severalty Act.[14] By the time Congress ended the allotment program in 1934, Indian lands had decreased from 136.3 million acres to 34.2 million acres. More than ninety thousand Indians had become landless.[15] Hunting as a means of subsistence had ended.

The language of paternalism, used by slave owners in the South to justify the bondage of African Americans, was also employed to justify turning Native Americans into imprisoned and impoverished wards of the state. The Dawes Act banned the practice of Native American culture, language, traditions, and religion. White Christian missionaries descended on the reservations and erected churches. Children were forcibly taken from their families and sent to Christian boarding schools. Many were not allowed to return home for the summer, but were sent to live with white families.

"The Indians must conform to the white man's ways . . . " Thomas J. Morgan, the Commissioner of Indian Affairs, said in 1889. "The tribal relations should be broke up, socialism destroyed, and the family and autonomy of the individual substituted."[16]

A visit to the Smithsonian National Museum of the American Indian, located on the Mall in Washington, D.C., makes our nation's willful forgetting painfully evident. I walked through the museum and thought its closest parallel in fiction was George Orwell's memory hole in the novel *1984*, housed in a cubicle at the Ministry of Truth. In that ministry, newspapers, government documents, and reports that chronicled or detailed unpleasant or inconvenient truths were stuffed into a chute and incinerated. "Who controls the past controls the future," says party leader O'Brien in the novel. "Who controls the present controls the past."

The museum makes no mention of the genocide, starvation, burning of Indian villages, rape, or forced death marches such as the 1838 Trail of Tears, which resulted in the death of most of the Cherokee population. Vague euphemisms gloss over the suffering of Native Americans on government reservations and in Indian boarding schools. A video on the third floor equates Indian "suffering," which is never specified, with a storm or natural disaster:

The storm is powerful and unceasing. It creates and destroys. It offers life and death, hope and despair. It is never simply one thing. The storm is an opportunity. The storm teaches. We have learned much.

The museum skims over some four hundred treaties Washington signed and then violated as it appropriated three billion acres of Indian land. And there is no mention of the series of brutal government massacres of unarmed women, children, and the elderly, including the December 1890 slaughter at Wounded Knee, near Wounded Knee Creek, South Dakota. The museum fails to explain that by 1889 the buffalo population of North America had been reduced to one thousand from more than fifty million in 1830, wiping out the primary food source for the western Indian tribes and reducing them to beggars. And it ignores the heroic resistance of Indian leaders such as Sitting Bull, Geronimo, and Crazy Horse.

The museum has the audacity to display, in large black letters on a glass case of copies of old treaties, an 1829 quote from President Andrew Jackson, one of the country's most fervent proponents of the extermination of Indians:

Your Father [the term denoting the U.S. president] has provided a country large enough for all of you, and he advises you to remove to it. There your white brothers will not trouble you; they will have no claim to the land, and you can live upon it, you and all your children, as long as the grass grows or the water runs, in peace and plenty. It will be yours forever. [17]

⚜

Pine Ridge, the vast and impoverished residue of the Indian Wars in South Dakota, is a monument to a defeated ethic. The reservation, known colloquially as "the rez," is crisscrossed with long, solitary roads that undulate up and down over the rolling hills of the prairie. We drive for hours and see only a few cars, most of which clock speeds well over seventy miles an hour. The roads pass marooned trailers, often with junk cars and discarded appliances out front, and sweep into dusty and forlorn towns, including Pine Ridge itself, and then out again into the vast expanse of grasslands. The open plains, the absence of

Pine Ridge Reservation, South Dakota.

commercial activity, including billboards, the silence that surrounds us when we stop at the crest of the Badlands, gives to Pine Ridge a stillness. Violence does not oppress you on every street corner. It does not stare out at you in the menacing looks of hustlers, pimps, drug dealers, and cops. On the rez there is much death and violence, but they come upon you like a lightning bolt. They devour their victims in fiery car wrecks, in barroom brawls, in suicides, in random shootings, and in overdoses set against a backdrop of wind, sweeping vistas, hills, and grasslands.

Charlie Abourezk, a lawyer and the son of former U.S. Senator James Abourezk, takes three days off from his law practice in Rapid City to take us around Pine Ridge. Charlie, a large, affable man with a moustache and greying hair, has spent his life fighting for Indian rights. He stayed in Washington for one high-school semester when his father was elected senator—and then hitchhiked home to South Dakota. A year later, he moved into a log house on Pine Ridge among Crazy Horse's clan, few of whom spoke English, and immersed himself in the Lakota language, which he now speaks fluently. He also attended the Oglala Lakota College as an undergraduate student. He was involved in the struggle for civil and human rights of traditional tribal members on the Pine Ridge Indian Reservation and worked with them, sometimes alongside members of the American Indian Movement (AIM). During the violent civil conflict in the 1970s between then-tribal chairman Dick Wilson's rogue paramilitary force known as GOONs—Guardians of the Oglala Nation—who traveled the reservation in armed caravans and were charged by critics with frequent beatings, shootings and killings, and the Bureau of Indian Affairs (BIA) police on one side, and traditional people and members of AIM on the other, Charlie survived one of a series of goon squad shootings on January 31, 1976. They had come to the village where Charlie resided because people there had been active in the election campaign against Wilson. A series of shootings over the previous twenty-four hours had claimed the life of Charlie's close friend Byron DeSersa, great-grandson of the spiritual leader Black Elk. A year later, Charlie married DeSersa's widow, Lloydelle Big Crow, and raised DeSersa's two children.

Life on Pine Ridge, he says, has become steadily bleaker and more difficult.

"The vast majority of Indian tribes and tribal members are extremely vulnerable, both to the dissolution of government—upon which they have largely been forced to depend—as well as the tremendous disparities in income and resulting joblessness," he says:

> This has essentially dried up the ability to leave the reservation to work in order to be able to support families back home, who suffer from extreme poverty and unemployment that hovers between seventy and eighty percent. I think it is more true this year than at any time in the past that tribal members are literally going to the government-funded Indian Health Service to die with greater frequency. [Such services] are, even by the government's admission, underfunded by about fifty percent. A recent example is Delle Big Crow, the mother of my children, who was diagnosed with congestive heart failure in July, and who was referred by her IHS physician to a non-IHS cardiologist, but as of September, she had been denied the referral three times because IHS was "out of money." She died in the Pine Ridge Indian Health Service Hospital ER in September [2011] at age fifty-five. She is of no greater or lesser importance than the multitude of others of whom I have heard who have died at the hands of an underfunded IHS this year. The callousness of the wealthy and their servants in Congress sickens me. The most vulnerable have no voice. They simply suffer or die without a whimper.

The Pine Ridge Indian Reservation, also known as The Pine Ridge Agency, or *Wazí Aháŋhaŋ Oyáŋke* in Lakota, was established in 1889 in the southwest corner of South Dakota for the Oglala Sioux after Washington broke up the Great Sioux Reservation. The federal government gave nine million acres of Sioux land to the newly formed states of North Dakota and South Dakota. Pine Ridge, one of six reservations left within the old boundaries of the Great Sioux Reservation, is the eighth largest reservation in the United States, larger than the states of Delaware and Rhode Island combined. Population estimates on the reservation run from twenty-eight thousand to forty thousand. In addition to the high unemployment, forty-nine percent of those on the reservation live below the poverty level, a figure that rises to sixty-one percent for all those under the age of eighteen. The infant mortality rate is five times the national average. The teen suicide average is 159 percent of the national average. At any given moment more than sixty percent of the dwellings, including sod huts that can hold as many as a dozen people, lack electricity or running water.[18]

We stand one afternoon with Ivis Long Visitor, Jr., outside his sod hut a few miles southeast of Oglala. The hut is on a dirt track, marked by puddles, ruts, and craters about a mile from Highway 18. He is wearing a red baseball cap that reads "Native Pride" and a 2009 South Dakota State Cross-Country T-shirt. His daughter ran briefly for the team. He lives on the property of his grandparents, Harry and Cecelia Jumping Bull, who are now deceased. It was here that a 1975 shoot-out between Indian activists in AIM and two FBI agents left the agents and one Indian activist dead. One of the agents, Ronald A. Williams, appeared

Ivis Long Visitor, Jr., in front of his hut, on the property where two FBI agents were killed in a shootout with AIM members in 1975.

to have been killed in the shoot-out itself. The other, Jack R. Coler, incapacitated from earlier bullet wounds, appeared to have been shot twice in the head execution-style. Three AIM members were indicted for their deaths. Two were acquitted. The third, Leonard Peltier, who fled to Canada and was deported to stand trial, was convicted despite glaring irregularities and inconsistencies in the federal case against him.[19] He is still in prison.

Long Visitor, like many who live on the rez, has no running water. He uses a pump and outhouse. He recently lost his job with a moving company and is out of work.

"The other guys I worked with were white," he says. "We used to move people who lived up in the hills. They always watched me touch their stuff, all these doctors and people like that. They wanted to make sure I didn't damage anything."

Long Visitor survives on food stamps and welfare. He does not own a car. Outside his shack are piles of old beer cans.

"The electricity is in my dad's name," he says, "and since he has $25 credit a

month, they haven't turned if off yet. We used to have a lot of cows. Now there are only ten left."

Pine Ridge has vast tracts of open land, although only eighty-four thousand acres are suitable for agriculture, so much of the reservation's prairie is leased out to white or mixed-blood cattle ranchers. The reservation includes Shannon County (where the per capita income is $7,880, making it the second poorest county in the United States), the southern half of Jackson County, and the northwest portion of Bennet County.[20] There are 3,143 counties in the United States. The three on Pine Ridge are consistently ranked among the most impoverished in the nation.

Darrin Merrival, forty-five, a Marine Corps veteran and high-school teacher, takes us in his truck one afternoon out to his small herd of buffalo. The buffalo herds once ranged into Canada's northwest and as far south as the Mexican states of Durango and Nuevo León. By the end of the nineteenth century, the American buffalo was close to extinction. Merrival said his father started the

The Merrival buffalo farm.

herd to make money, but after two white buffalo calves were born, an animal sacred in the Lakota religion, "he began to think of wealth in a different way."

"It was like seeing Jesus in the manger for Europeans," he says of the calves.

The rolling prairie includes within it the stark and majestic rock formations of the Badlands, one of the most fossil-rich areas in the United States.[21] The land mass in South Dakota was once covered by an ancient sea. Outlines of fish and other aquatic creatures lie encased in the layers of rock. Lone trailers, sod huts, and crude shacks sit isolated amid the severe landscape, linked to the main road by winding dirt tracks.

Joe, Thomas, and I are traveling this morning into Pine Ridge from Rapid City with Michael Red Cloud, thirty-three, who works at Charlie Abourezk's law firm. He is not long out of prison on drug charges and is finishing his degree in social work at one of the tribal colleges. As we head down a long, desolate road cutting through the heart of the Badlands, Red Cloud suggests we turn off the asphalt road and onto a rugged dirt track that winds its way up to the top of Sheep Mountain.

"It's a great view," he says.

We turn right and soon kick up clouds of dust. The Toyota Highlander rocks back and forth on the uneven surface. We slow down to a crawl and climb from the valley floor to the 3,106-foot summit of Sheep Mountain. We park at the top. The four of us, under the sweltering sun, sit on boulders on the flat surface of the peak. The 360-degree vista is dramatic. Stunted yucca and juniper trees surround us. A few feet away, the sheer rock face falls abruptly a couple of hundred feet. Flat-topped plateaus, including islands of faint green prairie grass, and arid gorges twist and undulate outward into canyons, peaked by these narrow spires and sharply eroded buttes. The rock formations and razorback pinnacles, once part of the ancient seabed, date from the late Cretaceous, Eocene, and Oligocene epochs. It was into the Badlands, following the 1890 massacre at Wounded Knee, where at least one hundred and fifty men, women, and children of the Lakota Sioux were killed and fifty-one wounded, that the last bands of Sioux warriors fled before finally surrendering, at the urging of Mike's ancestor Chief Red Cloud, to the U.S. Army. The Sioux gave the vast rock formations their name *mako,* which means "land," and *sica,* which means "bad."

It is here, according to Lakota mythology, that the world will end. Somewhere in the Badlands, the myth goes, is a secret cave, not far from where the prairie and the Badlands meet. This cave is home to an ancient seamstress who for hundreds of years has been working on a blanket strip of dyed porcupine quills for her buffalo robe. Beside her is her huge, black dog, Shunka Sapa. The woman and the giant dog sit next to a roaring fire lit more than a thousand years ago. The fire warms an earthen pot of *wojapi*, or berry soup. When the woman gets up to stir the soup, Shunka Sapa surreptitiously pulls the porcupine quills out of the blanket strip. Her work, like Penelope's nocturnal unweaving of the burial shroud in Homer's *Odyssey*, remains forever uncompleted. If the seamstress is ever permitted to finish her work, according to the legend, the world will vanish.[22]

Michael Red Cloud is five feet, eleven inches and two hundred and eighty pounds, with the thick, muscular arms of a weight lifter. We sit and speak quietly. A tiny brown field mouse darts in and out of the rocks, sometimes pausing on a boulder, its face twitching. Michael, who is related through his biological mother to Chief Red Cloud, was born in Rapid City. His father, whom he has never met, is Mexican. His blood ties to Red Cloud, whom he defends as a great and misunderstood chief, give his perspective on Lakota history an interesting edge. Red Cloud, one of the principle chiefs of the Oglala Teton Sioux, successfully fought back the prospectors and settlers who carved out a wagon route known as the Bozeman Trail, which ran through the heart of Lakota territory in Wyoming to the Montana gold fields from Colorado's South Platte River. Red Cloud's campaign, known as Red Cloud's War, which lasted from 1866 to 1868, closed the trail and destroyed the forts that guarded it. He was the only Indian chief to win a war with the United States. His victory resulted in the 1868 Treaty of Fort Laramie. The treaty ceded to the Indians the western half of South Dakota, including the Black Hills, along with much of Montana and Wyoming. But, like most treaties Washington signed, it would soon be violated.

After Custer's 1874 discovery of gold in the Black Hills, the government set out to seize the land promised to the Indians. Custer's defeat a year later gave the government the opening it was looking for and, threatening to cut off the rations of Indians living on the Indian agencies, it forced a compliant group of Sioux leaders to sell the Black Hills. Federal law required three-quarters of the adult males of the tribe to approve any new treaty. It proved impossible to collect this number of signatures, but Congress ratified the agreement anyway. Red Cloud, who signed the new treaty, later said he did not understand what was in the documents, which historians suspect is true.[23] But his compliance, as well as his decision to remain at peace while Crazy Horse and Sitting Bull continued to resist westward expansion, tarnished his reputation among many Lakotas. Crazy Horse and Sitting Bull bitterly denounced him.[24]

The four of us sit in the harsh sunlight on the top of Sheep Mountain and listen as Mike narrates over the next couple of hours the story of his life.

As for his biological mother, who had him when she was a teenager and was "kind of caught up in the drug culture... "I never had no contact with [her] again until I was eight or nine years old... and [then] she tried to come in and be a part of my life...

"I didn't want nothing to do with her."

Growing up in Rapid City, in a development called Lakota Homes," we lived in this like terrible housing and stuff.

"My mom [Florence] was actively drinking back then.

"[She] used to always have these big crazy parties... and there'd be fist fights and like all kinds of craziness going on in our house."

Mike was being raised with five step brothers, who tormented him and each other.

Their dad, who didn't live with them, "was abusive and irresponsible... He was just a big, miserable drunk."

Mike was closest to Gene.

"He was the only one of the brothers that wasn't mean. He was real caring, compassionate, raised a lot of animals."

"Mike began selling small amounts of weed at school and in parking lots."

"He smoked a little himself, but —"

"BECAUSE ALL THE STUFF MY BROTHERS PUT MY MOM THROUGH... I WAS ALWAYS AFRAID TO BECOME LIKE AN ALCOHOLIC ...OR DRUG ADDICT."

RUSHMORE MALL

When Mike was 15, he was formally initiated at a TBZ house party by being "jumped in" — beaten up by gang members.

"There were six guys that circled me,

"and then they were supposed to jump me in for 30 seconds.

"They couldn't beat me up."

The initiation culminated in ritualistic scarring with a red-hot knife.

"They stick it on your arm and then just burn it.

"Four times...

"It was like a [Native] thing: four directions...

"[TBZ] had this saying. It was a credo to who we were.

"It was: 'Don't walk in front of me and be my leader;

" 'or don't walk behind me and be my follower;

" 'walk beside me and be my brother.' "

J. SACCO 2-12

One of Mike's only supports during this period was a man in California, who his biological mother had named as his possible father. Over several visits "he kinda gave me the motivation to keep going in sports and excel..."

But a paternity test proved he wasn't Mike's dad.

I HAD ALL THESE HOPES AND EXPECTATIONS AND STUFF THAT MY LIFE WAS GONNA TURN AROUND.

IT JUST WENT DOWN THE DRAIN.

Mike began smoking meth, staying up for days at a time. He was selling drugs provided by a relative and her friends.

He was making about $2,000 a week.

He dropped out of high school, spent time in jail for a weapons charge, had a short relationship that produced a child — given up for adoption — and spent more time in jail for domestic violence.

THERE WERE TIMES WHEN I GOT OUT OF JAIL WHERE I HAD THESE LITTLE MOMENTS OF CLARITY WHERE I WANTED TO GO TO A.A. AND SOBER UP.

BUT I LOVED THE GLAMOUR OF IT, YOU KNOW.

I LOVED GOING TO BARS AND SLEEPING WITH ALL THESE DIFFERENT WOMEN AND JUST BEING ON TOP OF THE FOOD CHAIN.

Mike had proved that he could move large quantities of dope, and he was now working directly for a dealer coming and going from Mexico.

Eventually Mike had 14 or 15 dealers under him in Rapid City and on the reservations.

"I'd drop off at those places...and they had dealers working under them and stuff, and I would go and collect my money."

Mike was now making up to $180,000 a month.

"When I first started off I didn't want to be like some big drug dealer. I just wanted, you know, to sell enough to just stay high. But it got to the point where I was making so much money I didn't know what to do with it.

"I couldn't stash it nowhere so I had to spend it."

He lived in motel rooms and sometimes took a suite at the Radisson in downtown Rapid City.

"I would change addresses all the time. You got crackheads and stuff, and they'd find you wherever you're at when you didn't want to be found.

"I would rent people's cars out ...so people didn't know what I was driving.

J. SACCO 2.12

After 17 months in county jail Mike was transferred to Pekin Federal Correction Institution in Illinois.

A cousin was there too —

AND I WASN'T EVEN ON THE COMPOUND FOR TEN HOURS AND [HE] STABBED THIS GUY 37 TIMES.

His cousin had killed the dominant Native-American prisoner, a so-called "shot caller."

Mike was put in isolation for his own protection, and two and a half months later he was sent to Engelwood Federal Prison in Colorado.

On his first day there he opened a door to look for cleaning supplies and found "this big black guy ...fucking this little white guy.

"That was my first incident of rape.

"And, you know, within a week I saw my first murder.

"Every time someone gets killed, you can hear the drop of a pin... and everyone knows someone's going to die.

"So you got all your people together... Native Americans... You gotta keep your shit together so that they are accused of nothing...

"You gotta stay away from that spot."

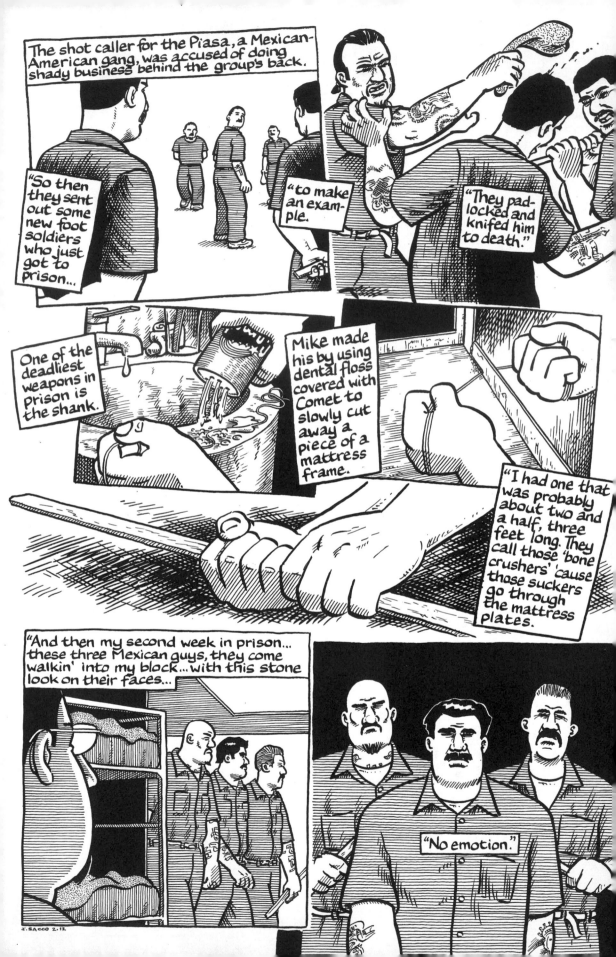

The shot caller for the Piasa, a Mexican-American gang, was accused of doing shady business behind the group's back.

"So then they sent out some new foot soldiers who just got to prison...

"to make an example.

"They pad-locked and knifed him to death."

One of the deadliest weapons in prison is the shank.

Mike made his by using dental floss covered with Comet to slowly cut away a piece of a mattress frame.

"I had one that was probably about two and a half, three feet long. They call those 'bone crushers' 'cause those suckers go through the mattress plates.

"And then my second week in prison... these three Mexican guys, they come walkin' into my block...with this stone look on their faces...

"No emotion."

J. SACCO 2.12

A few seconds later Mike heard "banging on metal...and then...this gurgling and blood and stuff.

They had killed a snitch, Mike says. "They stuck that shank in him so hard that when the guards tried to pull it out...it was stuck in that metal."

"And they walk by and one of them says," YOU DIDN'T SEE NOTHING.

Mike adjusted to prison life and even began to thrive.

He built up a little commissary, ran a betting operation on football games, and sold "wine" made out of tomato paste, sugar, and moldy oranges.

Other inmates believed he'd been involved in the murder of the shot caller in Pekin, and so Mike had come with a ready-made if unearned reputation.

"So right away they thought I was a hit man or big shot...

"Everyone wanted to invite me into their crew and...I had all these Native Americans bringing me tribute."

I MOVED UP THE RANKS UP THERE IN THE PRISON LIKE REAL FAST.

MICH
WOLVERINE

At first Mike resisted getting dragged into inmate politics, but he began to notice how young Native Americans were being preyed on by older Indian prisoners.

"These little kids would come in fresh off the bus, and the predator— they were drug fiends and stuff— they would come in and they would cook a good meal for the kids and make them feel they were involved."

At first the predator would freely share home-made alcohol and smuggled-in drugs, including heroin. But then he would begin charging the new arrival, who would soon run up a ruinous debt.

[THEN] THEY WOULD SAY,

YOU KNOW, SINCE YOU CAN'T PAY ME AND I CAN'T KILL YOU, YOU BETTER SUCK MY DICK OR YOU BETTER LET ME FUCK YOU.

SO THEN I HAD THESE KIDS THAT WERE GETTING RAPED IN THERE.

AND I JUST THOUGHT THAT WAS THE LOWEST OF THE LOW.

Mike took on a leadership role, and as such he sanctioned a couple of beatings of sexual predators, which "let everybody know that we was handlin' our business."

The tacit understanding was that each prison community policed itself. "We only fought our own unless it came down to a whole race war," Mike says.

Michael Red Cloud takes us later that afternoon to visit his cousin, Will Andrews, who is a gang leader. Recently released from prison, where he was serving time for armed robbery, he now is hiding out on the reservation after Rapid City police put out a warrant for his arrest for a fight that violated his parole. We find him with his girlfriend and small daughter, in a small house built by Habitat for Humanity. Twenty-five and heavyset, he sits shirtless in his living room. The word *FOLKS* is tattooed across his chest. His face is bruised and bloodied from the gang fight. He was hit in the head with a brick and a chair during the brawl, which took out one of his front teeth and left a gash on his forehead. On his arms are gang tattoos from the Gangster Disciples. The words *RIP Manuel* are tattooed on his right forearm along with praying hands. He says he never had a job and made money "husslin'."

He describes in detail the brawl, the bricks thrown, the broken chair legs used as weapons, and the squad cars that arrived and forced them to run. But he offers no more than a few vague words about the workings of the gang.

"Gangs function like your family," Andrews says. "The gang has been my family since I was twelve."

Robert E. Gamer's book *The Developing Nations* includes a chapter called "Why Men Do Not Revolt." In it Gamer notes that although the oppressed often do revolt, "the object of their hostility is usually a particular incumbent in an office, an individual they attack in a fight, or another racial group." There is a deliberate set-up of people of the same race as targets for this hostility. Tribal leaders willing to do the dirty work for the railroads, Indian agents, missionaries, white ranchers, and federal programs are effective masks for what Gamer calls the "patron-client" networks responsible for oppression. This plays out at the highest and lowest levels of the power structure. Gangs of Native Americans, such as the one led by Andrews, vent their fury on rival Native American gangs.

"The fact that alienated people can be counted on to vent their spleen in ineffectual directions—by fighting among themselves—relieves the government of the need to deal fundamentally with the conditions which cause their frustrations," Gamer writes. "It even relieves authorities (except following moments of shrill violence) of the need to minimally affect environment and attitudes to reduce alienation. The government merely does the minimum necessary to prevent those few who are prone toward political action from organizing into politically effective groups."[25]

The Indian Reorganization Act of 1934 was the last blow to the traditional leadership structure. It replaced traditional tribal elders with elected tribal governments that were easily controlled and manipulated by the federal authorities. This form of colonialism—one perfected by the British, French, and much earlier, by the Roman Empire—permitted the colonialist to rule behind a local, indigenous hierarchy, obscuring the real beneficiaries of colonialism. These collaborators sought to instill the rules and beliefs of the oppressor's culture.

Will Andrews, Pine Ridge Reservation.

This attempt at forced integration, however, can backfire. The Indian children shipped to boarding schools became at times the most potent rebels. They could, like their educated counterparts in the Occupy movements, communicate with the dominant culture as well as the oppressed. They spoke, in essence, two languages. Those who were on track to be assimilated, but who were endowed with a conscience, were acutely aware of the suffering of their people as well as the duplicity and mendacity of the colonialist. They understood power and oppression. They returned to the rez as bicultural and bilingual residents to battle the oppressor. Ho Chi Minh, Mohandas Gandhi, Patrice Lumumba, and the Indians who led the 1973 uprising at Wounded Knee were products of the colonialists' attempts at assimilation.

The last act of government assimilation directed toward Indians came in the 1950s, when the federal government created the Relocation Program, an effort to detach Indian people from their land and send them to urban areas where the government would subsidize them while they received job training. Desperate Indian families moved to Minneapolis, Los Angeles, the San Francisco Bay Area, Cleveland, Chicago. Once there, they found that the government provided no assistance if they wanted to go home.[26]

"It was the children of these relocated parents who became the American Indian Movement," said Abourezk:

Young people who were turned on by the civil-rights movement, who were still connected by family, funerals, summer trips back home, and who were searching for an identity, came back to the reservations in the early 1970s. They were a perfect marriage with the traditional people who had been disempowered and largely ignored on the reservation. These traditional people, who had held off the dominant culture, needed allies against the mixed-bloods, called *iyeskas* in Lakota language. It was the *iyeskas* who dominated tribal governments and who soaked up most of the resources and power within the tribe.

⚜

The internal contradictions between Native history and American history are evident the morning Joe, Thomas, and I drive to Crawford, Nebraska, where about one hundred Native Americans on horseback wait a few yards from the spot where Crazy Horse was murdered at Fort Robinson. They are about to begin the fourteenth annual Crazy Horse Ride, a week-long horseback journey to Pine Ridge. American flags, which were once detested strips of cloth to Crazy Horse, are carried by the lead riders. Amid the American flags are the red Lakota flag and a black MIA-POW flag. Many Native Americans insist they fly the American flag as a trophy, since it was captured by their ancestors at Little Big Horn, but the explanation is not entirely convincing. Native Americans, like many minorities and the poor, serve in disproportionately high numbers in the military. The ride this year coincides with the naming of a portion of Highway 20, from Fort Robinson to Hay Springs, as the Crazy Horse Memorial Highway. Nebraska governor Dave Heineman speaks at the event, along with John Yellow Bird Steele, chairman of the Oglala Sioux Tribe. Near the speakers is a small marker that reads: "On this spot Crazy Horse, Oglala Chief, was killed September 5, 1877." A riderless paint horse serves as Crazy Horse's honorary mount.

There are few resistance figures in American history as noble as Crazy Horse. He led, long after he knew that ultimate defeat was inevitable, the most effective resistance on the plains, wiping out Custer on the Little Big Horn and two other large cavalry units. "Even the most basic outline of his life shows how great he was," Ian Frazier writes in his book *Great Plains*, "because he remained himself from the moment of his birth to the moment he died; because he knew exactly where he wanted to live, and never left; because he may have surrendered, but he was never defeated in battle; because, although he was killed, even the Army admitted he was never captured; because he was so free that he didn't know what a jail looked like." His "dislike of the oncoming civilization was prophetic," Frazier writes. "He never met the President" and "never rode on a train, slept in a boarding house, ate at a table." And "unlike many people all over the world, when he met white men he was not diminished by the encounter."[27] He was bayoneted to death after being tricked into walking toward the jail at Fort Robinson. The moment he understood the trap he pulled out a knife and fought back. General Phil Sheridan had intended to ship Crazy Horse to the Dry Tortugas, a small atoll in the Gulf of Mexico, where a U.S. Army garrison ran a prison with cells dug out of the coral, covered with metal bars. Crazy Horse, even dying, would not conform. He refused to lie on the white man's cot. He insisted on being placed on the floor. He was guarded until he died by armed soldiers. And when he breathed his last, Touch the Clouds, Crazy Horse's seven-foot Miniconjou friend, pointed to the blanket that covered the

The Crazy Horse Ride.

chief's body and said, "This is the lodge of Crazy Horse." His grieving parents buried Crazy Horse in an undisclosed location. The legend says that his bones turned to rocks and his joints to flint. His ferocity of spirit remains, a guiding light for all who seek lives of defiance.

Heineman helps unveil the green road sign, covered by a traditional Indian star quilt that reads "Crazy Horse Ride." He thanks the Crazy Horse Ride organizers for their commitment to the warrior's legacy.

"This is a special day as we honor an iconic leader and warrior," says Heineman, dressed in gray slacks, a blue blazer with an American flag lapel pin, a white dress shirt, and a red tie. "This marks a very important moment in our collective past.

"Nebraskans have a tremendous admiration and respect for those who have defended freedom," Heineman says, adding that he is also a veteran. "We are honored to be part of this important tribute today."

Before the riders set off on the trip to Pine Ridge, drummers and singers perform traditional Lakota songs. An Indian leader in a war bonnet drapes a brown and white Indian quilt over the governor's shoulders. Heineman holds it around himself uncomfortably in the sweltering heat. The tension between service to the nation and service to the ancestors which that nation sought to exterminate plays out at the spot where Crazy Horse had his arms pinned behind him and was bayoneted to death by a white soldier. It imparts to Indian existence a peculiar schizophrenia.

"Poverty has a lot to do with it," Jake Little, an Army veteran, tells me as we speak one night in Rapid City, "along with the concept of the *akicita*, the Lakota protector and provider concept, the male concept":

This has been true since the boarding schools from the late 1800s on, although it stopped in 1990. Students were regimented in military fashion, and during the process of being stripped down psychologically, losing their ancestors, their cultural understanding. This concept of being a provider and a protector was directed toward the military. It became honorable to fight in wars on behalf of the U.S. That's the way it stands. It's an overwhelming majority of the people on Pine Ridge who honor that U.S. military participation. The strange thing about it, I guess, maybe it's expected, maybe it's the whole Stockholm syndrome idea. I don't think the *akicita* principle would transfer to any other military around the world. You wouldn't say, "Well, I'll fight for Venezuela." I disagree that there is a valid comparison between our ancient *akicita* principle, where the *akicita* were protectors and providers, and the modern use of *akicita* to enlist in the U.S. military and do as you are told.

"You see someone standing there saying, in a meeting like, they'll be talking, 'The United States violates treaties, they don't respect international law, they don't even uphold their own Constitution,' they go on and on like that but turn around and be proud of how they served in Vietnam for freedom, you know? It drives you nuts when you sit there and you try to . . . I guess, reason in a conversation, try and point some things out, but it all doesn't fit."

"Poverty causes people to enlist," he goes on. "They do not see beyond the recruiting posters, video games, and Pentagon sponsored movies. All they know is that they are going to make their lot in life. But the biggest recruiting machine, bigger than the movies, is the Pow Wow, *Teca Wacipi Okolakiciye*, especially school-sponsored Pow Wows, held for students in K through 12 about twice a month from about October to the end of April. Veterans march in front of the dancers, behind the Lakota staff but holding an American flag. They dress in military garb and sometimes hold dummy rifles. Some are on leave status for recruiting. Hundreds of children every other week witness this. And keep in mind this is a cultural event. Pow Wows are supposed to be about cooperation and life. Now they are a major recruiting tool. I am an Army veteran, but I have never been proud of it. In fact, I am ashamed of it."

The United States, unlike the European powers, colonized its own country before extending its empire overseas. It is through the process of colonialism, especially when Indians went to fight in Vietnam, that many came to recognize their own status as colonial subjects.

"I had a revelation when I was in Vietnam," said AIM leader and U.S. Army veteran Bill Means, whom we meet one afternoon at a Pizza Hut in the town of Pine Ridge. "Whenever we took over a village, first thing they brought in was these MACV pacification teams," Means says:

One of the first things they would do is have an election. The only ones that would vote was the ones that hung around us Army guys gettin' the handouts. The ones that stood in the background, they didn't know who we were. They didn't vote. They didn't even participate. So here you get a leader elected who's basically a lowlife of society. They actually were sellouts, the ones takin' handouts. Now he's runnin' things. He doesn't work. He's a dependent person and kinda like an alcoholic. He depends on the United States government. That was kind of a revelation. I saw the method of colonization and an election that totally ignores the traditional leadership. So when they made decisions like . . . they're gonna use Agent Orange on these rice paddies 'cause they're sympathizers with the Vietcong . . . they never asked traditional leadership. They never asked them if they wanted to move to the strategic hamlets. And so a lot of the traditional leadership was forced into backing the Vietcong. That's why the movement was so overwhelming when the United States left. Many just wanted to be left alone, but they had no choice. Either go live in a strategic hamlet or join the movement, fight for your land, which Ho Chi Minh had been teaching them a long time.

The first public protest by the emergent Indian radicals occurred when some two hundred Indians, led by a Mohawk activist, Richard Oakes, who would be shot and killed in a dispute not long afterward, occupied Alcatraz Island in 1969. They demanded that it be turned over to Native Americans.[28] In 1972 Indian leaders, including Means, occupied the Bureau of Indian Affairs in Washington during Richard Nixon's Inauguration. The activists called for the restoration of the 1868 treaty.[29]

But the most dramatic standoff came when some two hundred armed activists, protesting the killing of Raymond Yellow Thunder in Gordon, Nebraska, and the series of beatings, drive-by shootings and assassinations of Indian activists on Pine Ridge, occupied Wounded Knee on February 27, 1973. The activists took over the 1890 massacre site and demanded tribal chief Dick Wilson's removal. They called on the federal government to fulfill the promises of broken treaties. The activists were swiftly encircled.

The U.S. Marshalls, FBI agents, BIA police, and a collection of local and state law enforcement surrounding the activists were issued fifteen armored personnel carriers mounted with .50 caliber machine guns, automatic rifles, sniper rifles, grenade launchers, night flares, and 133,000 rounds of ammunition. Helicopters and planes carried out aerial photography. The siege would last seventy-one days. By the end, an FBI agent had been paralyzed from a gunshot wound, and Frank Clearwater, a Cherokee, and Oglala Lakota activist Lawrence "Buddy" Lamont were killed.[30] It was after Lamont was shot dead by a government sniper on April 26 that the tribal elders called for an end to the occupation. The activists agreed to disarm on May 5.

Perry Ray Robinson, a black civil-rights activist who joined the AIM militants at Wounded Knee, disappeared on April 25, 1975, apparently after a dispute with AIM security guards. His widow, Cheryl Buswell-Robinson, insists he was murdered by AIM. Robinson, who refused to pick up a weapon and apparently criticized AIM leaders for using violence, may also have been suspected of being a government informant.

Robinson ran headlong into the radically different culture, history, and aspirations of Native Americans, who were acutely aware that African American soldiers, nicknamed Buffalo Soldiers, played an active part in the Indian Wars of extermination. The civil-rights movement, to activists such as Robinson, was about integration into white society. It was about becoming a full and equal partner in the American nation. The Native American activists were demanding something very different. They called for complete independence, a return of their sovereignty, and the removal of all federal and state power from their land. They declared the territory of Wounded Knee to be the independent Oglala Nation during the siege and demanded to negotiate directly with the U.S. Secretary of State. Robinson's body was never found.

Charlie Abourezk takes us to the Rosebud Indian Reservation, next to Pine Ridge, to meet Leonard Crow Dog, a medicine man. We find him at his plot of land, which he calls "Crow Dog's Paradise." Crow Dog, although he did not carry a weapon, joined the AIM militants who occupied Wounded Knee. He oversaw the religious ceremonies and sweat lodges and streaked combatants' faces with war paint. Many of the Indian activists were born and raised in urban settings

Leonard Crow Dog.

away from the reservations, and they turned to Crow Dog to recover their traditions, religious practices, and language. It was under Crow Dog's influence that Indian activists began to wear their hair long and in braids, along with bead or bone chokers and ribbon shirts. Eagle feathers were tied to their hair or placed in their hatbands. And in 1971 Crow Dog brought Dennis Banks, Russell Means, and Clyde Bellecourt to a Sun Dance in Pine Ridge.[31]

Crow Dog was a victim of the witch-hunts following the murder of the two FBI agents and the manhunt for Peltier. Crow Dog spent twenty-seven months in prison, most of that time in solitary confinement. His home burned down while he was incarcerated. He was paroled in 1977 after a nationwide campaign on his behalf by the National Council of Churches.

Crow Dog never went to school. His father, he says, chased away the truant officer with a gun so he could raise his boy to be a Lakota medicine man and protect him from teachers who would make his son white. Crow Dog's first language is Lakota. He accuses the white missionaries and teachers in the tribal schools of carrying out a campaign of religious and linguistic "genocide." He is a stocky man, with long braids. His arms are pocked with scars from numerous sacrificial offerings of skin and piercings from numerous Sun Dances. He has little time for the U.S. government or the mythology of the American West, heaping scorn on both. He refers to Mount Rushmore as the carved faces of "George Washington and the rest of his goons."

The violence on the reservation took the life of one of his teenage sons. Seven years after his son's murder he met the killers.

"My son was really good," he says. "Real good, real nice. He was murdered. Goons. I met them at the post office. I walked in post office door and all of them standing right there. They asked for forgiveness. It's hard . . . your son . . . you want to do something . . . but I put creator first, grandfather first."

Personal animosities, which see Indian murder Indian, have a way of dissolving in Lakota culture that is rarely replicated elsewhere.

Duane Brewer, a Vietnam veteran, sits in a wooden rocking chair. He holds a black and white kitten. Brewer, who stands a little over six feet, is wearing shorts, a black and white striped polo shirt, and plastic brown Crocs. He has a brown moustache that droops down either side of his mouth, and tinted wire-

Mount Rushmore, in the Black Hills of South Dakota.

frame glasses. Outside his small house in Pine Ridge, several grandchildren are playing in a small plastic pool on the front lawn.

Brewer, in the 1970s, was a BIA police officer and a zealous opponent of AIM. He was in the tribal police force during the 1973 occupation of Wounded Knee by AIM, and he also worked closely with reactionary tribal president Wilson. Brewer had a reputation as one of Wilson's prized enforcers.[32]

Wilson, who sported a crew cut and denounced his opponents as communists, pilfered tribal funds to enrich himself, his family, and his supporters. He used fear and violence to silence opponents, and allegedly engaged in voter fraud to stay in office. He was cavalier with tribal lands, leasing huge swaths to white ranchers at bargain prices and handing over nearly one-eighth of the reservation's mineral-rich lands to private companies for exploitation. AIM militants insist their own turn toward violence was a legitimate act of self-defense. They point out that at least sixty opponents of Wilson met violent deaths while he was in power, including Pedro Bissonette, executive director of the Oglala Sioux Civil Rights Organization.[33] Wilson was beloved, however, by state and federal officials.

Brewer was in the Fourth Infantry Division, stationed in Pleiku in the central highlands, in 1968 and 1969.

"I was a lieutenant during the 1973 occupation of Wounded Knee," Brewer says:

My duties were to cover the outside perimeter of Wounded Knee, let's say, the west side of it. I would go in whenever they had prisoners, the roadblocks, where the FBI and Marshals caught people sneakin' in and sneakin' out. I would go pick them up and bring them in. Then we did a long interview process with them to get all the information we could. I did that plus I answered calls, you know, your normal police duties, drunks and whatever. So there was a time, a number of times I went out there, like seven in the evening, to pick up prisoners, and there was a firefight going on, and there was automatic weapon fire comin' from the inside, there was automatic weapons from the outside, so this . . . reminded me of Vietnam.

"Russell Means and Dennis Banks and the Bellecourt boys, they had a way of communicating to people . . . " he says. "They could come in to a rally. People would go just to listen. By the end of the meeting, shit, these guys would say, 'I'm

AIM, man.' They had this thing about them, charisma and whatever. Russell Means was a hell of a speaker. But, yeah, they could influence people. We found out since the trials that . . . that they could order death."

He mentions Robinson.

"They say they killed him and that he's buried around the crick out there," he says of Robinson.

Brewer had left the tribal police force when FBI agents Williams and Coler were killed on June 26, 1975, in an exchange of fire with activists a few yards from the sod hut where Ivis Long Visitor, Jr., lives. He was in charge of the tribal Highway Safety Program, which sent the ambulance to pick up the bodies of the slain agents.

"The driver's door [on the agents' car] was open," he says. "Both were kneeling there, and both were executed. One of them had his co-worker's shirt wrapped around his wounded arm. The other one, this spot right here"—he taps his temple—"was blowed away":

> There was a whole bunch of bullet holes in their backs. Lot of them holes weren't bleeding, so they really had to be dead when they shot them. Their heads looked like they were, you know, they weren't blown about them . . . they weren't all missing and stuff. It was a real hard thing to go up and look at their bodies. I had an ambulance worker tell me, "Hell, I quit, I don't ever wanna do this again." Apparently, one of the guys got wounded right away, so they went to the trunk to get the AR-15, and then they both got wounded. Apparently, they surrendered to 'em. You know, there was a lot of bullets fired at them before they surrendered. It looked like the ground was plowed up in front of that car, full of bullet holes, holy smokes, man, there was a lot of rounds fired at them guys. So when they surrendered, apparently they had them knelt and executed them.

He insists Peltier carried out the executions, although the government case brought against Peltier included what later appeared to be falsification of evidence.

"He came walkin' down, and shot 'em," Brewer says, "Then there were these young guys there. Apparently he made these guys shoot into 'em. That's why you see the bullet holes in the back."

But when I ask Brewer, a lifelong enemy of AIM, about the legacy of the radical Indian movement, I get a surprising answer.

"I guess people started looking more at, you know, who they were as an Indian, you know, Indian nation," he says. "Kinda opened their eyes to that and a lot of the history."

"I started working for Xerox in '79," he went on. "I was repair. Some of the things people said were real funny, like, 'Where'd you come from?' 'Pine Ridge.' 'You mean they make you live with them people?' I'd go, 'No, I'm one of them people. I've lived there my whole life.' Here you are, suit and tie, you know . . . off the reservation, they were wantin' to know about Indian things, and on the reservation, people thought you were an FBI agent or you were a Mormon.

"I started wanting to learn about it," he says of traditional Indian ceremonies. "I started sweatin' in '70. I went to a medicine man and said, 'Hey, I wanna learn about this.' So, I started sweatin'."

I ask him about Leonard Crow Dog.

"Yeah, he was their spiritual leader," he says. "You know, Leonard is a pretty good guy. He got involved with AIM and he stood by 'em."

His son comes in the room and asks for the car keys.

"Get out, kiddo," Brewer tells him. "We're almost done."

"I had a job to do, I liked my job, a family to support, and since I was back from Vietnam, I wasn't afraid of death," he says. "And I always thought, 'I'm a federal police officer. If guys try to gang me, then, a .357 revolver with six rounds, then six guys are gonna be down with me,' you know? 'Cause I wasn't afraid, and that's what AIM said. 'Duane Brewer patrols by himself so there's no witnesses when he beats them up.' But I didn't do that. I didn't beat people up. But I wasn't very flexible when I did my job. And that's probably why I was the youngest BIA officer ever to be a lieutenant, twenty-five years old."

All that, he says, is over.

"The sweats teach you that you can't carry grudges, you can't carry hatred in your heart. It'll make you sick, so you have to learn to forgive," he says:

That took a long time when this medicine-man knew everything about me. He said, "You've been involved in a situation, you have a lot of enemies, and so when you get into this, your enemies are gonna be there. But if they're true Lakotas, they'll forgive you." So I talked to him about—I have a list from here to that wall over there of all the guys I'm still gonna kick their asses—and he said, "You're gonna have to put that list away." I was able to find peace because I went to a lot of my enemies and I said, you know, "I am sorry, man, I did these things . . . " They said, "You have to go and get forgiveness from your relatives, you know, from the creator, you have to ask him for forgiveness."

"When you first went to the sweat lodge, what did you ask forgiveness for?" I ask.

"It's a long process," he says. "You don't just go in there and ask for that right away. You work your way to it. When you're in a sweat, you think about all these things that bother you, and you pray that the Great Spirit will give you the strength to forgive them, and for them to forgive you."

"What did you ask forgiveness for?" I ask again.

"For all of my weakness," he says.

"And what were your weaknesses?" I ask.

"It would've taken a day and a half to start talking about them," he says.

"Was there any particular thing that you wanted to be forgiven for?" I ask.

"A lot of them," he answers softly. "You're not a priest, and can't do a confession, but that's kind of a personal thing and you deal with that. You always feel good when you come out of there because you don't only pray for your weaknesses, you pray for all of the people that are in there and their families, all the sick, people who have lost loved ones, you know, they're dealing with some real deep issues. Lot of things to pray for."

His son comes in again and asks for the keys. Brewer hands them to him with the admonition: "Don't go south."

South is Whiteclay. His son, who has a drinking problem, goes there frequently to buy alcohol.

Brewer rummages through a small desk before we leave and hands me a few pieces of paper. On one is a poem he wrote in 1989 titled "A Warrior Waits for Death":

O Grandfather, it has been twenty years since I returned from the war in Vietnam, yet the memories are so clear it seems like yesterday.

Sitting in a bunker, rockets, mortars, bullets exploding all around. You can see the fear on the other faces, as the explosions continue, shaking the ground around you. Waiting for death.

O Grandfather, why can't I forget these times?

The other is a story he wrote in 1991 called "Release Their Spirits," about an Indian grandfather and his two grandsons who are drafted and sent to Vietnam. One grandson is killed by a land mine during a firefight. The second grandson returns to Pine Ridge severely crippled and psychologically broken. He drinks himself to death. At the end of the story the grandfather, Little Thunder, takes the medals and awards of his two grandsons, lays them in a pile on a hillside, lights them on fire, and in his prayer to the Great Spirit says that they "have no meaning to me without my grandsons."

The old conflict between Indians and Euro-Americans, between colonizers and colonized, between masters and serfs, is the template for the last act of the corporate state. The tyranny we imposed on others is now being imposed upon us. We too are wage slaves. We, too, no longer know how to sustain ourselves. We, too, do not grow our own food or make our own clothes. We are as dependent on the state as the Indians who were herded into the agencies and stripped of their self-sufficiency. Once trapped on reservations, once the buffalo herds no longer existed, once Indians could no longer move in bands to gather wild potatoes, wild turnips, berries, medicines, and cottonwood bark for their horses in the middle of winter, once they could no longer hunt in different places to prevent exhausting the game supply, they became what most of us have become—prisoners.

⚜

I stand next to Michael Red Cloud on a July afternoon at the edge of a Sun Dance on the property of Richard Moves Camp. The dance ground, open to the sky, is ringed by a large circular arbor made of wooden posts draped with military camouflage netting. Inside the circle, more than a hundred men and about a dozen women move slowly to the music of drummers who chant traditional Lakota songs around a sacred cottonwood tree covered with colored ribbons. Many of the men are overweight and have crude prison tattoos. They hold eagle-bone whistles and eagle-wing fans, and they wear long skirts down to their bare feet. On the last day of the Sun Dance, ropes are run from the top of the tree in the center of the dance circle to small pegs that pierce their chests. At the end of the ceremony they step back from the tree and pull until the peg is dislodged and rips away a small portion of flesh. The families of the dancers sit on blankets and folding chairs in the shade of the arbor. Michael softly sings some of the songs in Lakota. He leans toward me and whispers a brief translation: "Grandfather, take pity on us."

The dancers fast for four days, only drinking sage tea. They appeal to Wakan Tanka, the Great Mystery, and make their offerings of flesh, some by hooking a train of buffalo skulls to ropes fixed onto their backs for relatives, friends, and the community. The dance is a ritual that demands sacrifice and purification.

The dancers move off the field for a rest. One of the medicine men speaks to the families in a mixture of Lakota and English.

"Mahatma Gandhi was one of the most powerful men in this world, but he was one of the most humble men that we ever met," he says. "And that's the way we teach here in the Lakota belief. It is sad that some people see that as a weakness. But in reality that's a strength, and that's what these Sun Dancers learn here. When they leave, when they are out there in the world, it is hard for them at times. They have to turn around and show that forgiveness and show that humility to *wasushala*, other people, even though they treat them bad. The Sun Dancers have to learn to keep focused on their belief and their prayers, no matter what. This is a good time for them. It's kind of a time to rejuvenate. Then they leave. A lot of them are gonna be by themselves this next three hundred and seven days till they come back here again to rejuvenate. A lot of them come here almost depleted of energy, depleted of spirit, so they come here to energize themselves."

Bill Means, seated on a folding chair next to his brother Ted, who is gaunt and hooked up to an oxygen tank, watches as his son moves among the dancers. Means did his first dance four years after he returned from Vietnam, when the Sun Dance was still banned.

"Through sacrifice and prayer, you begin to understand that sometimes . . . you're involved in things you don't want to be involved in, but if you survive and live to tell about it, you could make it a life experience to better yourself," Means says. "I thought that since I did what I did over there, my role in life was to help people, either through education or organizing, projects, anything I could. I would dedicate my life to doing that instead of trying to accumulate wealth. That's why I dedicated my life to try to help people for the treaty rights.

"For the first time you're not saying prayers that come out of Christianity," he says:

I went to mission school. I knew what prayer was like on Lent. We went to church about three or four times a day. I knew all about that side. I never knew our prayers and our language. I never knew the sacred ceremony of songs. So it was like a whole cultural, Indian Bible opened up. We always taught parts of that through the oral history of our grandfathers, but it was like, we can't practice it. It's against the law. "If you go to this family over here they'll tell you about it. They'll maybe let you in one of the secret ceremonies." The Sun Dance I first danced was 1973. It was one of the first Sun Dances since the 1890s. It was outlawed. It was at Crow Dog's. Crow Dog's family was like . . . how would you say, spiritual leaders of the American Indian Movement. They taught many of us where we came from. We have our cultural peers and our family, like Steven Young Bear, who was a singer, and my Uncle Henry, who taught me and my brother the songs of our ceremonies, the Sun Dance songs. I read *Black Elk Speaks*. I knew we had seven sacred ceremonies, but I never participated till 1973. Well, a few, like sweat lodge, stuff like that, probably started in about '69, '70. The Sun Dance, fasting, all that came later.

There is a brief memorial ceremony, held with an empty chair covered by a black star quilt, for the recently deceased Webster Poor Bear, a Vietnam veteran wounded in the 1973 occupation of Wounded Knee. A crowd that includes most of those in his large family, including two sons, five daughters, seven brothers, and four sisters, clusters around the chair. The family administers the traditional "giveaway," a Lakota tradition in which gifts are given to the deceased's closest friends in a public forum. It is an old ritual, which, like the Sun Dance, had been outlawed for nearly a century. Family members call out the names of Poor Bear's closest friends, several of whom were with him in the Wounded Knee siege, and, as the friends come up, give them a star quilt. One, Bill, is a white veteran who served with Webster in Vietnam. He is a stocky man with a white beard and a baseball hat that reads "Purple Heart." He walks up and silently takes a blanket. He and Charlie Abourezk are the only white friends honored by the family.

Poor Bear's daughter reads from a letter he wrote to her shortly before his death:

The white male hurries because of money. Do not allow that influence of the male inside your heart because they have already influenced your mind. The male-influenced world is based on money. Our world is not. We come from the other side. That world is not based on money. There are two senses. One is in this dimension. That one is your flesh. The one in our dimension is our heart. It gives life in a different way. That is the real strength. The absolute gift is the warming of the heart not of the flesh. I give you that gift. That is the way, my girl, we are going to live as a people—not as individuals, but as a people, the people of earth. We all come from our great mother and she is the earth, a child of Tunkasila [Our Grandfather]."

2

DAYS OF SIEGE

Camden, New Jersey

I sit and look out upon all the sorrows of the world, and upon all oppression and shame;

I hear secret convulsive sobs from young men, at anguish with themselves, remorseful after deeds done;

I see, in low life, the mother misused by her children, dying, neglected, gaunt, desperate;

I see the wife misused by her husband—I see the treacherous seducer of young women;

I mark the ranklings of jealousy and unrequited love, attempted to be hid—I see these sights on the earth;

I see the workings of battle, pestilence, tyranny—I see martyrs and prisoners;

I observe a famine at sea—I observe the sailors casting lots who shall be kill'd, to preserve the lives of the rest;

I observe the slights and degradations cast by arrogant persons upon laborers, the poor, and upon negroes, and the like;

All these—All the meanness and agony without end, I sitting, look out upon,

See, hear, and am silent.

—WALT WHITMAN, "I SIT AND LOOK OUT"

For twelve years I, and others like me, held out radiant promises of progress. I had preached to them about my dream. I had lectured to them about the not too distant day when they would have freedom, "all here and now." I had urged them to have faith in America and in white society. Their hopes had soared. They were now booing because they felt we were unable to deliver on our promises. They were booing because we had urged them to have faith in people who had too often proved to be unfaithful. They were now hostile because they were watching the dream that they had so readily accepted turn into a frustrating nightmare.

—DR. MARTIN LUTHER KING,
"WHERE DO WE GO FROM HERE: CHAOS OR COMMUNITY?"

Again I say that each and every Negro, during the last 300 years, possesses from that heritage a greater burden of hate for America than they themselves know. Perhaps it is well that Negroes try to be as unintellectual as possible, for if they ever started really thinking about what happened to them they'd go wild. And perhaps that is the secret of whites who want to believe that Negros really have no memory; for if they thought that Negroes remembered, they would start out to shoot them all in sheer self-defense.

—RICHARD WRIGHT, *JOURNALS, 1945–47*

Silvia Ramos watched a teenage girl open the door and enter her bakery. The girl nervously scanned the room with its colored figurines of saints and papier-mâché piñatas hanging from the ceiling.

"I want a piece of that cake," the girl told Ramos's husband, Oscar Medina Hernandez, pointing into a refrigerated glass case of cakes and Mexican pastries.

Hernandez, in broken English, told her the *tres leches* cake, with glazed strawberries and white frosting, was not sold by the slice. The peach and pineapple cakes were sold by the slice.

"I don't want that," the girl answered. She left the store, disappearing into the darkness, past the faint red neon rays of the "OPEN" sign over the door and the two picnic tables in front of the bakery.

It was 8:40 P.M. and the store was closing in twenty minutes. Ramos and her husband discussed which of them would leave early to be with their two children, ages six and four, who were being cared for by Ramos's sister. Hernandez said he would stay and watch the Mexican soccer match and close the store.

The girl was soon back. She again went up to the case. She again asked for a slice of the *tres leches*. Hernandez again told her he did not sell it by the slice. He showed her other cakes.

"I don't like that," she said.

As she walked out, two men, one brandishing a pistol, burst through the door.

Hernandez, when he saw the pistol, turned to open the wooden swing door to the kitchen. His wife pushed a silent alarm, calling the police.

"Where do you think you're going?" the man with the gun shouted.

He shot Hernandez in the back. The bullet went through his heart. He crumpled in a heap behind the counter, his body a tangle of twisted limbs and blood. His breathing became raspy and labored.

"I couldn't move," Ramos says. "I was in shock."

The gunman stepped over Oscar Hernandez's body and tried to push his way into the kitchen, but Oscar's body blocked the door.

"He told me to walk over to where he was," Ramos said in Spanish. "I started walking towards him but I collapsed when I saw my husband's body. I fell on top of Oscar and started weeping. The gunman screamed, 'Come on! Come on!' I ignored him. The other man, who was by the door, grabbed two women customers who were in the store and held them. The gunmen tried to open the cash register. He couldn't do it. He yelled at the man holding the two customers to help him. And then a man, who was outside in the street, opened the door. He shouted that the police were coming. The three men and the girl, who had been waiting by the trash cans, ran down the street. Oscar died before we could get him to the hospital."

The three men, two from Camden, New Jersey, and one from over the river in Philadelphia, were later arrested and sentenced. [1] It was over in about fifteen minutes. Hernandez was twenty-nine. His wife was thirty.

The undocumented Mexican immigrants, who worked for several years as restaurant workers to buy Alex's Bakery and Food Store, with its blue exterior and large painting of a wedding cake on the front wall, became another unheralded casualty in Camden, a city that, like most postindustrial landscapes in America, dooms its inhabitants to grinding poverty, violence, and despair. Lives and dreams, whether here, or in Pine Ridge, or in other expanding sacrifice zones, are broken and shattered.

A few weeks after Joe and I interviewed Ramos in the bakery, gang members from the Bloods in Camden murdered a young couple inside a dilapidated row house. Michael "Doc Money" Hawkins, twenty-three, was seized on the street by gang members from the Lueders Park Piru Bloods, named after the gang's Los Angeles chapter. Hawkins was hustled into the abandoned building,

Abandoned houses, Camden, New Jersey.

bound, gagged, and savagely beaten until all the bones in his face were broken. He was pushed into a closet and finally shot. The process took several hours. Hawkins's girlfriend, Muriah Ashley Huff, eighteen, was at the same time taken to the basement and beaten and choked to death by another group, including a fourteen-year-old girl.[2]

Hawkins was killed because the Bloods suspected him of being a member of the rival Crips gang. His girlfriend, a cosmetology student at Burlington County Institute of Technology, had no gang affiliation. A dozen gang members watched passively. They stood by as gang leader Kuasheim "Presto" Powell tortured Hawkins and then shot him five or six times. Powell then went to the basement to help beat and strangle Huff, who, witnesses said, "begged for her life." Shatara "Feisty" Carter, fourteen, told police how after the killings, gang members scrubbed the blood off the walls, ripped out the blood-soaked carpet, and buried the two mutilated bodies in a shallow grave in a backyard on Berkeley Street.

Violence begets violence. It is as old as the Bible. The violence of the state—brute force, internal colonies from which the poor can rarely escape, and massive incarceration—is countered with the street violence of the enraged. These internal colonies funnel the dispossessed into prisons and out again in a circular system that ensures they never escape from the visible and invisible walls that hem them in like sheep. Brutalized on the street, sometimes brutalized at home and brutalized in prison, they strike out with a self-destructive fury. Since most lack education and a huge proportion are branded by the state as convicted felons, there is no place for them to go other than where they came from.

Slavery. Segregation. Sharecropping. Convict leasing. Jim Crow. Lynching. Urban squalor. Poverty. Racism. Prison. It is a continuum.

"You got to fight to make it [freedom] mean something," Solly Two Kings says in August Wilson's play *Gem of the Ocean*. "All it mean is you got a long row to hoe and ain't got no plow. Ain't got no seed. Ain't got no mule. What good is freedom if you can't do nothing with it?"[3]

The United States is home to twenty-five percent of the world's prison inmates.[4] One out of every three African American males go to prison. More African Americans today are subject to the coercive forces of correctional control through prisons, probation, or parole than were enslaved a decade before the Civil War.[5]

The days of segregated buses and lunch counters may be over, but integration never became a reality except for a few middle class blacks. Integration would mean new taxes to lift African-Americans out of their internal colonies, new schools to educate the poor and give them a chance, and making sure there were jobs available with living wages. The civil rights movement was a legal victory, not an economic one. And the economic barriers remain rigid and impenetrable for the bottom two-thirds of African-Americans whose lives today are worse than when King marched in Selma. The violence of overt segregation ended. The violence of poverty remains. Wealth was never redistributed. And when cities were deserted by whites, who took with them the jobs and tax base to keep those cities alive, who made it plain by their departure that they would not live with or allow their children to be educated with blacks, city halls were turned over to compliant black elites whose loyalty rarely extended beyond their own corrupt inner circle. White power hid, as in any colony, behind black faces.

"And what we got here in this town?" Amiri Baraka's fictional black mayor in *Tales of the Out and Gone* says. "Niggers in high places, black faces in high places, but the same rats and roaches, the same slums and garbage, the same police whippin' your heads, the same unemployment and junkies in the hallways muggin' your old lady."[6]

⚜

Camden sits on the edge of the Delaware River facing the Philadelphia skyline. A multilane highway, a savage concrete laceration, slices through the heart of the city. It allows commuters to pass overhead, in and out of Philadelphia, without seeing the human misery below. We keep those trapped in our internal colonies, our national sacrifice zones, invisible.

Joe and I walk one morning into the homeless encampment in Camden. It is a collection of blue and gray tents, protected by tarps, set up next to the highway ramp behind the city's police department and has a population of about sixty, ranging in age from eighteen to seventy-six. The tent city, or "Transitional Park," is overseen by Lorenzo "Jamaica" Banks, fifty-seven, who buys damaged tents from Walmart and Kmart at reduced prices, repairs them, and provides them—police say for a $10 rental charge—to other homeless people. There are about fifty tents in Transitional Park, and Banks owns forty of them.

When we enter the tent encampment, Banks, with receding black hair and a beard, is chopping firewood. He wears carpenter's jeans and a red and blue plaid shirt over a gray, hooded sweatshirt. Banks speaks in the drumbeat staccato of a man who seems at any moment about to snap. He claims to have been a Vietnam veteran, to have been a heroin addict now "clean for thirty-seven years," to have ended up after the war in a mental institution, to have jumped in a suicide attempt off the Ben Franklin Bridge because of "a lot of flashbacks," and to have spent "twenty-two years, six months, three hours and thirty-three seconds" in prison for shooting to death his best friend because he was "killing his baby in front of me." He insists he provides his tents to fellow homeless people at no cost.

"I'm better now," he assures me as the PATCO high-speed commuter train

into Philadelphia rumbles along the tracks nearby. "I'm on medication. I live here because it reminds me of the jungle."

Banks, who calls himself "the mayor," runs Transitional Park with an iron fist. He has a second-in-command, his "CEO," who takes over when Banks has to leave to buy supplies. There are weekly tent inspections on Saturday, weekly meetings every Tuesday night, and a list of sixteen rules written on plywood tacked to a tree. These include restrictions on fighting and arguing, admonishments to clean up the trash, an order not to sell food stamps, and several other

Lorenzo "Jamaica" Banks at the "Transitional Park" tent camp.

blunt prohibitions, including: "Don't Bring Your Tricks Here" and "No Borrowing Money or Sex from Anyone." Residents receive two warnings for infractions before they are evicted. Drugs are banned. Alcohol is not. Banks has even set up a bank account for the enclave. At night there are shifts where someone—Banks says he prefers a vet—stands guard. There is a Dumpster filled with trash at the edge of the encampment, white plastic folding tables and chairs, as well as five-gallon plastic containers with water outside many tents. Firewood lies scattered about the site for fuel.

Camden officially has seven hundred and thirty-three homeless,[7] but there are only two hundred and twenty beds for homeless in the county, so city officials tolerate Transitional Park despite its illegality. Those released from jail without a Camden address are often deposited here by corrections officers. Church groups bring food donations and blankets. The residents are allowed to shower and receive mail at the homeless shelter on 523 Stevenson Street. The tent city would be replicated, this time with the fire of political revolt, when Joe and I reached the Occupy Wall Street encampment. And like Banks, the organizers of the Occupy encampment would have to struggle to prevent those with addictions and mental illness, from bringing everyone down with them.

"Take a look at the American dream," Banks says as he guides me through the tents, stepping among old bicycles and shopping carts. "In today's society no one is exempt from Transitional Park. Everybody is one paycheck away from being here."

"We have all nationalities, but nobody is a fugitive," he says. "We don't house fugitives, and we don't tolerate rapists or child molesters."

Banks shows me an E.T. plush toy with a rope around its neck hanging by a wire from a tree branch. "This is what will happen if you get hooked on heroin," he says. "It will kill you. It will make you green." He shows me another stuffed toy, an upside-down Tweety Bird, also suspended from a wire. "This one did crack and it turned his family upside down." He walks with me to the entrance of the camp, where a soiled Cookie Monster, hanging over a boardwalk leading to the tents, looks as if it was put through a trash compactor. "This represents what will happen to you if you are not a man from this camp and someone from this camp comes here and their clothes are torn and they are crying. If you get caught here doing a woman wrong, you will be hung by the neck. We will seek justice."

A small collection of homeless are gathered this morning around a Weber grill warming their hands. Smoke rises from the grill. A man next to them rakes up leaves and trash on the dirt patch in front of his tent.

I ask a forty-six-year-old woman, who does not want to give her name, what the security is like.

"It's all right," she says. "It's too all right."

She says she has lived here a year after being evicted from her apartment. She is wearing a pair of blue corduroy pants and sneakers.

"I go to my brother's house to eat," she says. "I give him my food stamps. And I go to the Cathedral [Kitchen] dinner at four every day. My goal is to get my diploma and be a nurse's aid."

The decline of America is a story of gross injustices, declining standards of living, stagnant or falling wages, long-term unemployment and underemployment, and the curtailment of basic liberties, especially as we militarize our police. It is a story of the weakest forever being crushed by the strong. It is the story of unchecked and unfettered corporate power, which has taken our government hostage, overseen the dismantling of our manufacturing base, bankrupted the nation, and plundered and contaminated our natural resources. Once communities break down physically, they break down morally.

The corporations and industries that packed up and left Camden and cities across the United States seeking cheap and unprotected labor overseas are never coming back. And in moments of candor our corporate overlords admit this truth. When Barack Obama had dinner in February 2011 with business leaders in Silicon Valley, each guest was asked to come with a question for the president, according to a story in the *New York Times*. As Steve Jobs of Apple Inc. spoke, President Obama interrupted, the paper reported, with an inquiry of his own: what would it take to make iPhones in the United States? Almost all of the seventy million iPhones, thirty million iPads, and fifty-nine million other products Apple sold in 2011 were manufactured overseas.

"Those jobs aren't coming back," Jobs responded, according to another dinner guest.

In 2011, Apple earned more than $400,000 in profit per employee, more than Goldman Sachs, ExxonMobil, or Google, the *Times* pointed out. It has more cash in its vault than the U.S. Treasury.[8] It employs forty-three thousand people in the

---

Overleaf: On the street in Camden.

United States and twenty thousand overseas, "a small fraction of the over 400,000 American workers at General Motors in the 1950s, or the hundreds of thousands at General Electric in the 1980s."[9] But these numbers do not include the seven hundred thousand people who work for Apple contractors to engineer, build, and assemble iPads, iPhones, and Apple's other products. Almost none of them work in the United States. Working conditions for these Apple workers typify the misery endured by the corporate global labor force—low wages; excessive overtime, in some cases seven days a week and up to twelve hours a day; squalor and overcrowding in worker dormitories; swelling in the legs and difficulty walking because of so many hours on their feet; underage workers; improperly disposed-of hazardous waste; falsified records; a callous disregard for workers' health; lax or unenforced labor and safety laws; and union busting.[10]

Whole sections of U.S. cities, because of the ability to export manufacturing overseas, are industrial ghost towns. The human cost of this relentless search for greater profit is never factored into the balance sheets of corporations. If prison labor or subsistence labor in China or India or Vietnam makes them more money, if it is possible to hire workers in Bangladesh sweatshops for 22 cents an hour, corporations follow the awful logic to its conclusion. The requiem for Camden is the requiem for us all.

Camden is a dead city. It makes and produces nothing. It is the poorest city in the United States and is usually ranked as one of the most, and often the most, dangerous.[11] In early 2011 nearly half of the city's police force, one hundred and sixty-eight officers, were laid off because of a $26 million budget shortfall. By the end of 2011, although more than one hundred officers had been rehired, homicides had climbed by thirty percent and burglaries by more than forty percent from the previous year. Mayor Dana Redd, an African American, responded to the upsurge in crime in December 2011 by calling for a county takeover of the city's police force, a call the police union said was designed primarily to break the union to hire cheaper, nonunionized officers. Camden City Council President Frank Moran proposed that the state send in the National Guard or increase the numbers of state troopers assigned to the city.[12]

Camden is beset with the corruption and brutal police repression reminiscent of the despotic regimes I covered in Africa, the Middle East, and Latin America. The per capita income in the city is $11,967. Nearly forty percent of the city lives below the poverty line.[13] Large swaths of the city are abandoned. There are more than fifteen hundred derelict, gutted row houses. The empty shells of windowless brick factories, warehouses, and abandoned gas stations surround the city. There are overgrown vacant lots filled with garbage and old tires and rusted appliances. There are neglected, weed-filled cemeteries, and boarded-up storefronts. There are perhaps a hundred open-air drug markets, most run by gangs such as the Bloods, the Latin Kings, Los Nietos, MS-13, or Mara Salvatrucha. Knots of young Hispanic or African American men in black leather jackets, occasionally flipping through wads of cash, sell weed, dope, and crack to clients, many of whom drive in from the suburbs, in brazen defiance of the law. The drug trade is the city's only thriving business. A weapon is never more than a few feet away from the drug dealers, usually stashed behind a trash can, in the grass, or on a porch. Camden is awash in guns, which are easily purchased across the river in Philadelphia, where Pennsylvania gun laws are notoriously lax.[14] Guns are kept for protection from rival gangs that send out groups to prey on drug dealers, stealing their drugs and cash. Nonviolence is a luxury few on the streets can afford.

While Joe and I are in the city, a federal grand jury charges a Camden police officer whose nickname is "Fat Face," along with some of his colleagues, with planting drugs on suspects, bribing prostitutes with drugs for information, lying on police reports, beating up suspects, and conducting searches without warrants. Three of the city's mayors have gone to prison for corruption in the last couple decades. The school system and the police department have been taken over by the state.[15] The deeper the descent, the more the criminal class and the city authorities become indistinguishable, in a microcosm of corporate infiltration of the national power structure.

Camden was once as full of industrial promise as the nation itself. It began as a modest riverfront town in 1828 in the shadow of Philadelphia. The arrival of the railroad to Perth Amboy made Camden. The ferries out of Camden transferred goods across the Delaware to Philadelphia or north to New York City. Because of its strategic location, Camden swiftly became a manufacturing giant. New York Shipbuilding Corporation, which opened its first yard in Camden in 1900, was one of the largest shipbuilding companies in the United States. The Campbell Soup Company was born in Camden in 1869 with a small canning operation by Joseph Campbell, a fruit merchant, and Abraham Anderson, an icebox manufacturer. They produced canned tomatoes, vegetables, jellies, soups, condiments, and minced meats. The Victor Talking Machine Company—which later became RCA—built recording studios and production

Abandoned factory, Camden, New Jersey.

facilities in Camden.[16] The greatest tenors in the world, from the Italian Enrico Caruso to the Irish John Count McCormack, traveled to Camden to record.[17] Camden employed some thirty-six thousand workers in its shipyards during World War II and built some of the nation's largest warships, including the USS *Kitty Hawk* and the USS *Savannah*.[18] The city was for several decades a destination for Italian, German, Polish, and Irish immigrants, as well as African Americans from the South, who could find, in the middle of the last century, decent-paying factory jobs that required little English or education.

And then, little by little, the city, like the nation, was strangled and slain. Manufacturers left to find cheaper labor in the South and then overseas. Hurley's Department Store, the Stanley Theater, the Towers Theater, and the *Camden Courier-Post* closed or moved by the 1960s. Neighborhoods began to decay. Community cohesion broke down. White flight from Camden became a stampede following riots that erupted in August 1971 after city police beat a Puerto Rican motorist to death.[19] Swaths of the city were looted and burned. Less than five percent of the city today is Caucasian, and the city's population has declined by thirty-six percent since 1950.[20,21] Camden, which once had eighteen movie theaters, numerous churches and synagogues, and the grand, eight-story Walt Whitman Hotel with its two hundred guest rooms, ballroom, and banquet halls, fell into a death spiral. The hotel, the crown jewel of the city, named for the poet, who spent the last nineteen years of his life in Camden and is buried here, was demolished in the 1980s. It was replaced by a parking lot. The movie theaters are boarded up or gone. There are no longer any hotels or motels. There are no more factories. There are used car lots, but no new vehicle dealerships. The only supermarket is on the outskirts of the city, isolated from the street crime. Camden, like many poor pockets in the United States, is a food desert. Camden is dominated by Church's Chicken—where nearly everything on the menu, from Jalapeño Cheese Bombers to the Double Chicken N Cheese, is fried—and doughnut shops. Grease and sugar. Decay and crime. Despair and poverty. Cities and manufacturing hubs across the country suffered similar assaults, but in Camden the breakdown was total, and the city, at least as a self-sustaining community, was obliterated.

⚜

"When I came to Camden forty-one years ago, the parish St. Josephs, where I was in East Camden, that year was 1968, there were twenty-five families a month leaving," remembers Father Michael Doyle, who is the priest at Camden's Sacred Heart Church:

> And African American people were moving north, and white people were in flight. There's nothing unusual about that. It's the same story in a lot of cities. And they start moving out to suburbia. The New Jersey Turnpike changed a lot of things. Exit 4 was opened. Mount Laurel was there. It was where poor African Americans for two hundred years had their chicken farms. They were driven out. If you go to Chicago or Philadelphia or any of these places, you're going to find areas that are poor and dilapidated and areas that are deteriorated and housing and all of that, but Camden, the whole thing went. It all went. There's no saying, 'This area survived and that didn't.' None of it survived.

The development of Mount Laurel was part of a classic two-pronged attack against the working class and poor African Americans. Many freedmen or escaped slaves had lived on farms in places like Mount Laurel since the seventeenth century. They now were pushed off their properties by developers. Mount Laurel Township, using the weapon of code enforcement, began in the 1960s to remove black residents, claiming they resided in substandard, dilapidated housing, including converted chicken coops. Properties of black farmers were condemned. The township ordered the occupants to leave. The black community, led by Ethel R. Lawrence, a day-care teacher, wife, mother of nine, and church leader, organized in 1969 to fight back. Through her efforts, Lawrence obtained some affordable housing,[22] but the damage was done. Economic segregation is the new, acceptable form of segregation. And it turned New Jersey into one of the most segregated states in the nation. Mount Laurel, seized by developers, became a haven for whites fleeing urban decay. Its original inhabitants could no longer afford to live there. The blacks were driven from their land, forced into squalid internal colonies such as Camden.

"Camden, I would say, is a casualty of capitalism," Father Doyle said as we sat one afternoon in his rectory. "It's what falls off the truck, and can't get back on the truck."

There is a fifty-four percent high-school graduation rate in Camden. Less than twelve percent of Camden High's students manage to pass the state's proficiency exams in math and barely thirty-seven percent in language arts.[23] The city spends seventy-five percent of its budget on the police and fire departments,[24] a harbinger of the corporate state where only the security apparatus is maintained. The main branch of the city's library has been shut down due to lack of funds.

And once Camden died, its carcass became a dumping ground. The county took over forty acres of land on the city's waterfront and built a sewage treatment plant that receives fifty-eight million gallons of wastewater a day.[25] The stench of sewage wafts through the city streets. There is a huge trash-burning plant on the waterfront, which releases noxious clouds. There is also a prison, a massive cement plant, mountains of scrap metal, a giant shredder, and a planned methadone clinic. Camden is the poster child for postindustrial America. It is a window into the dead end that will come to more and more Americans as corporations "harvest" what is left of the nation for short-term profit and leave behind wreckage and environmental disaster.

❧

In Camden the world is divided between the prey and the predators. And the weaker you are, the less money and legal status you have, the more the predators hover like vultures. "Home invasions," where armed gunmen climb or crash through windows into dilapidated row houses, are rife, especially in the Latino neighborhoods, where most undocumented workers, who do not have bank accounts, hide their cash at home.

Miguel Benito runs a small photo store and videotapes weddings and *quinceañeras*, or fifteenth birthday celebrations, an important milestone for teenage girls in Mexico. He drove home one night after closing his store, Universal Foto Estudio on 2411 Federal Street. His three brothers, wife, and three children gathered in the living room at about 11:00 P.M. to watch the movie *Transformers* that his five-year-old son wanted to see.

Benito's small house has five rooms. Two of the rooms are rented out, one to a couple and the other to the couple's father. Benito heard noises on the stairs after the movie started but assumed it was one of his renters. It turned out to be an African American man in a black ski mask. The robber walked up to him with a pistol, put the barrel to his head and said, "Give me all your fucking money." The intruder had climbed through an upper-story window that had no lock. Benito and his brothers handed over their wallets and cell phones. The gunman, who let in two accomplices from the street, then went back upstairs to search the bedrooms and rob the renters.

"He came down again and had filled his pockets," Benito says in Spanish. "I told him to take the computer. He put the pistol to my head and said, 'Shut up!' He asked for the car keys. I gave him the keys to my 2002 Impala. Then he and the others left. None of us moved. We did not know if there were other gunmen upstairs. We sat there until one of the renters came down. They had been robbed and the rooms had been ransacked. Then we called the police.

"But a lot of the Mexicans who get robbed never call the police," he says. "They don't speak English and they don't have documents."

He stops and seems lost in his thoughts.

"I think the people who robbed my house were the same people who robbed me on December on the street in front of Crown Fried Chicken," he adds.

We go to the port to see Joe Balzano, seventy-six, one of the handful of white residents who never left the city. And it is with him as a guide that we try to recreate the Camden that was lost.

HE TALKED IN BROKEN ENGLISH BUT WOULD DO SO WELL IN ANY CONVERSATION.

AND ALMOST—

AND I THINK I HAVE THE SAME TRAIT

—HE DEPENDED ON BODY LANGUAGE, AND HE KNEW WHAT HE COULD DO AND HE COULDN'T DO.

"He was a longshoreman in New York harbor, and for some reason, and it's only hearsay, he mighta had a problem with some of the people up there."

"And he had to leave New York, and he came to Camden."

Joe's dad found a job at the bustling port.

"He was noted for being able to load cargo ships and knowing exactly how much space it would take for cargo."

"But his big reputation was the fact that he always wanted people to work."

And when the stevedores were idle, "when the cargo wasn't moving, he would yell,

THE HOOK SHE HANGS!

THE HOOK SHE HANGS!

"My mother was born in this country, a very soft-spoken woman. Had tuberculosis more times than we could think about...

"From the age of about 12, I worried about my mother dying every day."

Joe grew up poor with his brothers and a sister in the Italian-American community around the Our Lady of Mt. Carmel church.

His eldest brother Anthony, "a beautiful-looking kid," had epilepsy and died when Joe was four.

"And in those days, because the houses were built in such a way you couldn't get the coffin through the parlor, so you had to take the window route ...And it was like a procession of some kind with some musical instruments... I can remember that so well."

Joe used to tune in to hear Kate Smith singing 'God Bless America' every Sunday at noon and recalls a Camden where at the end of the workweek "you could walk up and down the street and everyone had the Friday Night Fights on...

THERE'S JERSEY JOE WITH A LEFT!

JERSEY JOE WITH A RIGHT!

"We would go to the movies on Saturday at 10 o'clock in the morning and probably not get out until 5 o'clock at night. We would look at the double-features..."

"We would come home. Mom would have a stew, which was delicious."

MY BROTHER JOHNNY, THE SECOND BORN, WAS A SPECIAL CHILD, OKAY.

AND THE THIRD CHILD, WHO WAS MYSELF, WAS SIMPLY PERFECT— UNTIL I GOT SCREWED UP WHEN I WAS ABOUT TEN YEARS OLD.

Joe had kept the shoes belonging to his dead brother Anthony.

"And they were beautiful shoes, and we were playing...soccer or what[ever]...and the shoe had such a point. I loved it. But evidently the shoe...had a nail in it [and] I got an infection in the right foot."

Joe developed blood poisoning, which traveled to one of his fingers and into his hip, impairing his ability to walk.

Watched over by his mother, he spent two months in the hospital.

Despite the adversity,

"somehow I won an award in 1945: Camden's outstanding young citizen."

This brought Joe to the notice of New Jersey state Supreme Court Judge Ralph W. Donges.

[HE] MUST HAVE TAKEN A LIKING TO ME...

I THINK HE SEES A POOR KID, AND HE WANTED TO REACH OUT...

AND HE MADE CERTAIN THAT I HAD AN OPERATION AT THE COOPER HOSPITAL, WHERE THEY STRAIGHTENED MY LEG OUT AND CUT MY [DISEASED] FINGER OFF.

"He had an apartment in the Walt Whitman Hotel, and he would occasionally have me go to dinner with him and his wife... It was probably like going to a big hotel today — elevators, and people would come in, and they had the table.

"It was beautiful..."

With the money he was making, Joe bought his first car, and he could now cruise Broadway, Camden's main drag.

He likens those days to the movie 'American Graffiti.'

"When [I] watch that movie, it plays in my mind... I can tell you it was a fun time."

He would start at the Star movie theater— "then you'd go up to the Walt Whitman Hotel, make a U-turn, and you'd go again."

Still self-conscious of his limp, Joe found he never really had to leave his car.

"You know, you would say, YO! JANE!

MY NAME'S NOT JANE. IT'S ALICE.

OH, I THOUGHT...

"and they'd come over to the car, and you're talking.

J. SACCO 6-11

"I would literally meet girls... go to a drive-in movie, go to a drive-in luncheonette, go to a drive-in park, and never get out of the car."

YOU KNOW SOMETHING, LOOKING BACK, I DON'T KNOW WHAT I WAS THINKING.

BUT IT WAS A COVER UP.

RUTGERS

Despite his handicap, Joe rose through the ranks to become general manager of the South Jersey Port Commission.

Meanwhile, the neighboring shipyard facility, which had once employed tens of thousands, was winding down its operations and closed for good in the mid 1960s.

"A hell of a blow," Joe recalls. "Everybody at one time or another worked at the shipyard. My two brothers worked at the shipyard at different times."

Joe's company was tasked by the state with converting the abandoned shipyard into part of the port facilities.

J. SACCO 6.11

Industry was leaving Camden, and the city began its decline.

Eventually the landmark Walt Whitman Hotel, where young Joe had sometimes dined with a state justice, was replaced by a parking lot.

Theaters where he and his brothers had sat for hours were boarded up or put to other uses.

MIRACLE CENTER CHURCH
1117 BROADWAY
CAMDEN NJ

The library building, from where he had once watched President Roosevelt on his way to inspect the wartime ship-yard, was abandoned.

DANGER
DO NOT ENTER

J. SACCO 6·11

The city, bankrupt and plagued by mismanagement and corruption, was turned over to the state in 2002 in the biggest municipal takeover in American history and given $175 million in bonds and loans to stay afloat. Under the Municipal Rehabilitation and Economic Recovery Act, the state appointed a chief operating officer to run the government and gave the governor control of the school board. The takeover was promoted as a way to create jobs, improve the quality of life, and reduce crime. The state promised to tear down thousands of abandoned buildings, bring in new businesses, and repair the city's infrastructure, including sewers that leak raw sewage into home basements, requiring a truck to pump it out.[26]

When the act was signed, then-Mayor Gwendolyn Faison burst into song at the ceremony with the words "Good things are happening," reported Dwight Ott of the *Philadelphia Inquirer*.[27] Camden clergy on hand shouted, "Amen." State Senator Wayne R. Bryant, who helped formulate the recovery, and who was later sent to prison for corruption, called the act a "liberation."

But the infusion of money did nothing to alleviate the poverty in Camden. Its residents remained just as poor, just as unemployed, just as likely to be victims of assault and homicides, and just as poorly served by city institutions, from schools to the police, as they had been before. The money was simply a vehicle for other predators, this time white predators who did not live in Camden, to swell their bank accounts.

❧

Poverty is a business. And those who profit most from Camden's poverty are the state's Democratic Party leaders, and New Jersey's most powerful political boss, George E. Norcross III, although he holds no elective office and does not live in Camden. The majority of the state bailout funds appropriated to Camden—nearly $100 million of the $170 million spent—were funneled to firms and construction companies that are invariably large contributors to the Democratic Party, Matt Katz of the *Philadelphia Inquirer* reported.[28] Norcross runs Conner Strong & Buckelew, one of the country's largest insurance brokerages. He has collected tens, perhaps hundreds of millions of dollars in governmental work across the state for his insurance firms. His insurance division serves more than half the state's municipalities.[29]

Norcross, nicknamed "King George," lives in the upscale suburban community of Cherry Hill. He is a college dropout. He decides, according to several

Camden politicians, who runs for office and who does not, who gets contracts and what projects receive state funds. Norcross influences the language of every state budget and can block or pass legislation. Little is done in South Jersey without his approval. And when the money came into Camden, nearly all of it went to his pet construction projects.

Norcross's methods of control were captured on tape. John Gural, a town councilman from Palmyra, N.J., a municipality with 7,091 people, went to authorities in 2001 with allegations that his employer, JCA Associates of Moorestown, threatened to fire him unless he voted against the rehiring of Palmyra Borough Solicitor Ted Rosenberg. Rosenberg was on Norcross's black list for opposing his leadership. Gural was wired during a series of conversations with Norcross by then-Attorney General John Farmer, a Republican. The investigation, however, went nowhere. Three hundred hours of tape remained locked in an evidence vault in the state Division of Criminal Justice's office in Cherry Hill.[30] Three tapes made their way into the hands of Lou Gallagher, the former chairman of the Burlington County Democratic Party. One was acquired by Alice Furia, the party's vice chair.[31] The recordings, although representing only ninety minutes of the many hours of conversations, capture the internal political mechanisms of New Jersey and much of national politics. It sounds like the recordings released from Enron's trading floor.

Norcross is heard on the tape, which surfaced in 2005, telling Gural to fire Rosenberg, who had criticized Norcross's stranglehold over South Jersey politics: "I want you to fire that fuck. [Y]ou need to get this fuck Rosenberg for me and teach this jerk-off a lesson. He has to be punished."

"A lot of people don't like John Harrington," Norcross is heard saying of an attorney then being considered for a judgeship. "The best thing you do . . . Make him a fucking judge and get rid of him . . . Harrington disappears . . . whatever the case. We move on."

Norcross later explains how he handled a member of the New Jersey legislature: "I sat him [the legislator] down and said . . . 'Don't fuck with me on this one . . . Don't make nice with Joe Doria [a Norcross enemy and Assemblyman] . . . if you ever do that and I catch you one more time doing it, you're gonna get your fucking balls cut off.' He got the message."

Norcross brags on the tapes that his political enemies will always respect him because "they know we put up the gun and we pulled the trigger and we blew their brains out. . . . " Norcross may be a Democrat, but he has become a political ally of Republican governor and rumored presidential hopeful Chris Christie.

The brief taped conversations are perhaps the only window the public has into the tactics that make Norcross and those with his economic clout a formidable force within the state and the nation. Norcross, like most who wield corporate power, is able to operate from the shadows, entering the State House through a private entrance, or working through lieutenants. His penchant for brutality surfaced publicly only one other time in 2002, when he demanded that State Senate co-president John Bennett hand over $25 million in state funds for a proposed civic arena in the town of Pennsauken. Bennett says Norcross began to shove him around, something Norcross denies, but it is not disputed that when Norcross stormed out of the office he shouted to Bennett: "I will fucking destroy you." Bennett, not surprisingly, was defeated the next year in a vicious and ugly campaign.

"That was the worst time of my life," Bennett told Richard Rys of *Philadelphia Magazine*. "He has those who stand in his way defeated or removed. I will never seek public office again."[32]

Norcross is the prototype of the new political boss, the one who wears tailored suits, serves on bank boards, and runs insurance companies. Power arises from their vast wealth and the legalized bribery that permits the rich to buy the candidates and judges who serve corporate interests, while using their money to intimidate and destroy those who stand in the way. The old tactics of thugs and physical intimidation are no match for the sums available to oil the political system. Politicians in statehouses or Washington must assiduously placate these corporate interests or endure the wrath of corporate masters.

On the tapes, Norcross says that in the end, "the McGreeveys, the Corzines"—two of the state's former governors—"they're all going to be with me. Because not that they like me, but because they have no choice."[33]

"This is no petty corruption," lawyer Carl Mayer says. "It is systemic, its tentacles radiate from top to bottom, it reaches across all three branches of government, and it is bipartisan. Graft is destroying democracy in New Jersey."[34]

The result of the political and corporate graft is a state and federal government controlled by the corporate elite. The taping never led to any charges by the Attorney General's office against Norcross. Gural and Rosenberg filed a federal racketeering suit against him. This, too, went nowhere. It was dismissed. And the remainder of the taped conversations are locked away.

I spent two hours with Norcross on December 15, 2009, in his expansive penthouse office. He refused to let me tape the interview and prohibited me from using much of the conversation, although I took notes, on the record. He studiously shuns publicity. During the conversation he maintained that he was a force for good. It was hard to tell whether he believed all of his own rhetoric, but he clearly believed some of it. He spent most of his time talking about Cooper University Hospital, which exists like a separate city within Camden, with its own 65-member security service. When I talked with him, he was planning to put in a charter school. He is chairman of the board of trustees of Cooper, and the hospital has been lavished with state money. A law, sponsored in part by Norcross's political allies, earmarked $12.35 million—the second-biggest recovery check to the city—to Cooper's $220 million expansion. An additional $3 million was provided for its neonatal unit.[35] The hospital received $9 million toward the construction of the $140 million Cooper Medical School, which will open in the summer of 2012. Cooper, according to the *Philadelphia Inquirer*, received $52 million in state funding in 2012, more than any other hospital in South Jersey. The hospital, with $775 million in annual revenue, is a major employer and, the *Inquirer* reported, during the last decade firms involved with Cooper have given more then $ 1.5 million to oil Norcross's Camden County Democratic machine.

Trim—he is an avid golfer—and with a full head of silver hair, Norcross insisted that his state contracts amounted to only five percent of his total business. But there is little dispute about Norcross's personal wealth. It is great. He admitted that at one point his goal was to be a billionaire. Norcross earned $121 million alone from the sale of his shares of Commerce Bank to Toronto-Dominion Bank. He was able to buy back the insurance division. Norcross is part of a small group of investors that in April 2012 bought the Philadelphia Media Network, which owns *The Philadelphia Inquirer, Daily News*, and the Philly.com website.Parks, bridges, roads, and municipal construction projects in South Jersey usually go through Norcross's hands. Hundreds of state and municipal employees owe their jobs to Norcross.

"Chances are the streets in your town have been reviewed or designed by engineers who've donated millions to Norcross's political machine," the *Courier-Post* newspaper wrote of Norcross, who would later be invited to sit on the newspaper's board of directors. "Look at the men unloading the food at the grocery store, the hospital workers caring for your sick mother or father, the government workers spending your tax dollars. With few exceptions, they're members of unions with direct ties to the Norcrosses."[36]

And if you want a job on any of the dozens of state and municipal projects controlled by Norcross, you spend your time on Election Day getting out the vote for Norcross candidates.

The one recurring thread in our conversation was Norcross's father. At one point he moved from behind his large desk to show me a wall of photos on which there was a black and white picture of him as a small boy with the Three Stooges and his father, George Edwin Norcross, Jr. His father, a New Jersey union boss, made sure his son was integrated into the South Jersey power structure. And Norcross is grateful. He is a frequent visitor to his father's grave in the Colestown Cemetery in Cherry Hill. A large stone, with the letters *NORCROSS*, is held fifteen feet up in the air by four heavy Greek columns. It is one of the largest tombs in the cemetery.

Norcross's father began as a television antenna installer, but he rose through the ranks of the union and became the head of the South Jersey AFL-CIO and one of the most important union bosses in the state. George tagged along to meetings with his father, who schooled him in the art of political patronage. George, not much of a student by his own admission, dropped out of Rutgers-Camden. His father advised him to get insurance and real estate licenses. He rented a tiny office in Camden and began to build his empire of Keystone National Insurance Companies with a chair, a single phone, and the lucrative connections provided by his father. It became a multimillion-dollar corporation. Municipalities that needed to insure everything from buildings to employees were steered to the young Norcross. He keeps a tight rein on the two institutions that made him very, very rich: labor, and his huge investment and insurance company. He was running the Camden County Democratic Party by 1989 and began targeting politicians who he saw as impediments to his own advancement. One of the first politicians he took down was State Senator Lee Laskin, who had the misjudgment to block the appointment of Norcross's father, who loved the racetrack, to the New Jersey Racing Commission.

"Norcross devised a plan of attack that focused on both the big picture and his backyard: Laskin's State Senate seat, and the Camden County freeholder board, which today oversees a $289 million operating budget and influences the appointment of countless jobs," Rys of *Philadelphia Magazine* wrote. "Control the freeholders, and you control the county. String a few counties together, and you overcome their weakness in the legislature with sheer fund-raising might. Combine that financial strength with influence in the Assembly and the Senate, and you've built hotels on every square from Mediterranean Avenue to Boardwalk."[37]

When he travels, Norcross, who does business in some twenty-five states, carries an eight-by-ten photo of his dad and his young self, smiling and sitting on his dad's knee, his dad's arm around him.

Norcross's brother, Donald Norcross, once president of the Southern New Jersey AFL-CIO Central Labor Council, representing eighty-five thousand workers, was elected with Norcross's backing to replace Assembly Speaker Joseph J. Roberts, Jr., a former Norcross business partner, in the State Assembly. Don Norcross is also the business manager of International Brotherhood of Electrical Workers Local 351, which, the *Philadelphia Inquirer* reported, wrote checks totaling more than $125,000 to Camden County Democratic Party and its candidates between 2001 and 2008.[38]

The party, the *Inquirer* reported, does not send out explicit demands for donations to business owners, construction companies, or law firms. A packet of invitations to fund-raising events arrives in the mail. The number of invitations indicates how much the machine expects businesses to contribute. Ten $1,000 invitations are not uncommon. Donors can mail in money without ever attending the event. Those who receive contracts are also apparently expected to fund political action committees. One committee controlled by Camden County Democratic operatives, the Leaders Fund, began in 2002 with a vague eight-word mission to support Democrats. It had collected six figures by year's end, according to the *Inquirer*.

"Thousands of dollars in Leaders Fund money have come from companies that received Camden recovery money, and those dollars have in turn gone to politicians around the state, winning South Jersey statewide influence over the selection of politicians, the creation of laws, and the hiring of government workers," reporter Matt Katz wrote.[39]

Tens of millions in state funds have been devoted to infrastructure projects to make Norcross and his associates wealthy. Millions have been donated by these hired firms and contractors to the machine's bank accounts. Less than five percent of the $175 million recovery package was spent addressing the most pressing concerns in the city—crime, schools, job training, and municipal services.[40]

Not that much of this is new. White supremacy, wielded by those of privilege, has remained one of the uninterrupted constants in American life. The poor and the working class were excluded, along with women, slaves, indentured servants, and Native Americans, by the white male elites at the Constitutional Conventions. The white upper class viewed Europe's poor, fleeing to America from squalid slums and workhouses, as commodities, fodder for the armies carrying out the genocidal campaigns against Native Americans in the West or cheap labor in the squalid workhouses and mills. Blacks, first imported as slaves, later became part of a disenfranchised underclass. American history, as Howard Zinn illustrated in *The People's History of the United States*, has been one long fight by the marginalized and disenfranchised for dignity and freedom. There have been moments when radical movements, especially on the eve of World War I or during the Great Depression, have pushed back to expand opportunities. But corporate capitalism has over the last few decades reversed most of these gains.

⚔︎

On Election Day, November 3, 2009, Angel Cordero, who is running for mayor against the Norcross-backed candidate Dana Redd, sits in his headquarters. It is a dilapidated house missing whole sections of the floor on the upper level. He has handwritten slogans on yellow poster board, including, "First They Ignore You! Then They Laugh at You! Then They Fight You! Then You Win!" and "Stop Violent Crime and Corruption," along with "Let's Rebuild Camden Together." All are tacked on the walls downstairs.

When I ask him about Norcross and his allies, he calls them "the pimps of poverty."

"When the state took over Camden, they told the people the money would go to them," says Cordero, dressed in a dark business suit, a pink shirt, and a pink tie. "Instead it went to Rowan University, Rutgers University, Cooper Hospital. They gave $30 million to the fish of Camden," he adds, referring to Adventure Aquarium on the waterfront. "All this happens while we drink water contaminated with lead, while our pipes burst and raw sewage leaks into our houses. Kids get locked up for selling drugs even when they don't have any drugs or sell any drugs. The community has lost the will to fight. People are so repressed and have been abused for so long they think abuse is normal."

Cordero stops to answer his cell phone.

"Pedro, the only way to help is if you vote for me," he says to the caller. "If you are homeless, why would you vote for the people in power?

"You never voted?" Cordero says into the phone.

"The only thing I can tell you is that I am for the people," he continues. "All the homeless that are here and are not from the city will be sent back to where they came from. You live in Camden and you don't even have a home."

He hangs up. When we see him next morning, he is just another devastated former candidate who got caught in the ugly maw of the Norcross machine.

When we arrive at her office, Mayor Gwendolyn Faison, eighty-four, is serving out her last days as Camden's lame-duck mayor. She was a council-woman when she was voted into office in 2000 to replace Milton Milan, the third Camden mayor in two decades to be convicted and sent to prison for corruption. Her first task, she tells us, was to clean up an office ransacked by the FBI. She sits behind her desk wearing an orange leather jacket and matching skirt. Her walls are decorated with gleaming shovels that represent ground-breaking ceremonies for construction projects. Faison, who is active, lively, and at times coquettish, has no real power. No mayor in Camden does. The city's budget is controlled by a state-appointed official, and the priorities for the city are set by a shady bureaucracy that even she, as the mayor, is not permitted to penetrate. She is blunt about her distaste for the arrangement, saying the city's "constitutional rights are being violated." During her tenure, she says, she was never invited to city planning meetings, and when new development projects were approved, she usually found out about it afterward, often, she says, by "reading about it in the newspaper."

I ask her why Norcross, a white multimillionaire who does not live in the city or hold elective office, is Camden's overlord. She answers slowly and carefully, aware she is stepping into a minefield.

"I wish I knew," she says. "It is something about his cleverness and his money. There are no jobs, and probably it is due in part to the education system. People need help. He has been successful overpowering people who have needs and controlling them.

"There is something about him," she goes on. "He seems to have that kind of control. He is a humanitarian in one sense and a dictator in another. If you are hungry he will bring you food, but you don't know what the payback will be. He seems to have a way of raising money. I heard him say, 'I take politics as a blood sport.' Politically he is funny. Norcross always has two horses in a race. When he found out I would be the winner in the election, rather than the other girl, he put money in my campaign, although I didn't know that. He makes offers you can't refuse."

She tells us that when she called mayor-elect Redd and offered to meet with her, Redd told her she would have to ask permission from Norcross first.

"People who have stood up to him were destroyed," she says quietly.

On the corner of Mt. Ephraim Avenue and Jackson Street, Ali Sloan El, a vocal critic of Norcross, is leaning against his blue 1990 Cadillac, which he purchased off a lot for $550. He wears a black hat, jeans, and a black leather jacket. He has a beard and speaks with the studied eloquence of a preacher.

"Camden is the poorest, richest city in America," he says. "It is like a third world country. You have the rulers and the rich. They control everything while the people die and perish. It's a slow-moving Katrina. Poverty hits. It gets worse and worse and worse. It deteriorates until it becomes an emergency."

Sloan El was a community organizer before he was elected to city council, where he swiftly ran afoul of the Norcross machine. He found himself investigated in 2007 and sentenced to twenty months in federal prison for accepting $36,000 in bribes from a contractor working undercover in a sting operation for the FBI. Sloan El had promised to steer Camden redevelopment work to the informant.[41] He insists he was set up.

Sloan El is chatting with some men in the street, several of whom, like Sloan El, are Muslim. They all have shaved heads and long black beards. The men had witnessed a botched robbery at a barbershop a few minutes earlier. A young gunman, nervous and unsure of himself, had pulled a pistol and tried to rob the barbers inside. He was chased out of the shop and tackled on the sidewalk. One of the barbers is at the police station giving a deposition.

The mood inside the barbershop is hostile and reflects the insular, distrustful, and closed world of Camden's streets.

"How did you know about the stick up?" asks a barber who says his name is Sam.

"We were told about it on the street," I say.

He arches his eyebrows in disbelief.

"No one would talk to you on the street," he says coldly. "No one would tell you nothin'."

"A mother with a two-year-old in a stroller told us," I tell him.

"Yeah," he admits reluctantly, "maybe that's right, maybe a mother would talk."

The rumor on the street, Sloan El tells us, is that the robber, like the stickup men at Oscar Hernandez and Sylvia Ramos's bakery, was high on a narcotic called "wet." Wet is the preferred drug of Camden's criminal class. It is produced by soaking marijuana in phencyclidine or PCP, known on the street as angel dust. Wet is smoked dry, but the leaves, which glisten with the dried chemical, give the drug its liquid name. Wet numbs its users and endows them with what seems to them like superhuman strength. Their body temperatures rise, their blood pressure is lowered, and they frequently hallucinate. The high can last for several hours. Two Camden police officers told us they most feared confronting suspects on wet.

"You shoot them and they just keep coming," one says warily.

Darnell Monroe, thirty-three, wearing a new pair of brown Timberland boots, a black leather jacket, jeans, and a black-and-white checkered *kafiyeh* as a scarf, sits with us in the barbershop. One of the barbers immediately turns up the radio. It blasts through the shop with deafening thumps, a not-so-subtle invitation for us to leave. Monroe, also a Muslim, is a tall man with a shaved head and a black beard. He spent four years in prison for dealing drugs. He became a father when he was thirteen. The girl was sixteen. He steers clear, he says, of the street violence. Those that do not belong to a gang live without protection. They must dart like minnows through the city streets to avoid the predators.

"I'm sociable," he says when I ask him about surviving in Camden, "but I keep moving. I don't want to draw the wrong kind of attention. I don't want no conflict."

Monroe was shot three times in the stomach in 1998 when he was coming out of a bar and tried to break up a fight. "To this day I don't know who shot me," he says. He awoke in the hospital twelve weeks later. His kidney, liver, and upper and lower intestines had been severed or badly damaged. He lifts his shirt and exposes a massive scar—it looks like a tiny mountain range with jagged edges—crawling up his stomach. "It was a .380 automatic," he says. He worked as a forklift operator in the scrap yards by the port but was laid off. He is unemployed and barely hanging on. On the back of his right hand is a tattoo of a padlock with his current wife's initials—*EGK*—and under his left eye is a tattooed teardrop he got in jail in 1993, when his sister died.

The only other business besides drug dealing that flourishes in Camden is the sale of scrap metal. Colossal scrap piles rise along the banks of the Delaware River on the waterfront. The piles, filled with discarded appliances, rusted filing cabinets, twisted pipes, old turbines, and corrugated sheet metal, are as high as a three- or four-story house. At their base are large pools of brackish brown water. A crane, outfitted with a large round magnet, sways over the pile and swings scrap over to a shredding machine. A pickup truck and a U-Haul filled with old refrigerators, gates, screen doors, and pipes are unloading in front of a small booth.

There are about twenty scrap merchants in the city. They have created a market for the metal guts of apartments and houses. As soon as a house is empty, even if only for a few days between renters, a battalion of hustlers break in and strip every pipe, radiator, screen door, and window screen. Without pipes, the basements swiftly flood with water. Thousands of owners over the past three or four decades, faced with the instant destruction, have walked away. It is often difficult to determine who owns the abandoned properties in the city.

A Camden metal scrap yard.

The collection of metal is weighed at the booth. This morning four men wait to see how much they will collect for the day's haul. Camden produces one million tons of scrap a year. Its huge shredding machines in the port can chop up automobiles and stoves into chunks the size of a baseball. Ships from Turkey, China, and India pull into the port, fill their holds with the scrap, and take it back to smelters. The scrap industry literally cannibalizes the city.

I stand one chilly afternoon on a corner of Ferry Street, trying to talk to two gaunt streetwalkers while Joe, in the car, discreetly takes pictures. One of the prostitutes is white. The other is black. Their eyes are ringed with dark circles. They are chain-smoking thin brown cigarettes.

I ask the African American woman if she is from Camden. She says she is from Philadelphia.

"You ask too many questions," the white woman abruptly says and turns to walk up the street with her companion.

Being homeless is not the bottom rung in Camden. That spot is reserved for the hookers. Most of the city's hookers are white. They can be seen standing near the highway ramps into and out of Camden. They are usually heroin addicts infected with AIDS, hepatitis C, and other sexually transmitted diseases. The women often sleep in abandoned apartments without running water, heat, or electricity.

If arresting someone on wet is the least pleasant duty for a Camden police officer, arresting a hooker is the second. Most come from outside Camden—the

Prostitutes on Ferry Street.

police say some are deposited in Camden by neighboring police departments—to be near their drug suppliers.

"Ninety-nine percent of them are heroin addicts," a police sergeant who did not want to be named says. "They take the money they get and immediately get high. I try not to deal with them. They have diseases. You pat them down and you find needles. You can get stuck with a needle. And they have MRSA, a skin disease with open sores. We have to get our cars disinfected afterwards. Ninety-five percent have outstanding warrants, although they usually give us a wrong name."

The hookers, police officers say, usually begin the day with an injection of heroin before looking for clients. As soon as they make enough, they return to the dealers for another hit. The services they provide are usually performed in the front seat of a car or the cab of a truck. A few have pimps, but most work on their own.

We make another attempt to interview a hooker by inviting a white woman with dyed blonde hair and heavy blue eyeliner, in a short denim skirt and knee socks, along with a man escorting her, to the McDonald's near City Hall. They devour three cheeseburgers, a large coffee, and a diet Coke.

"I'm Erika," says the woman, slurring her words. She smells heavily of alcohol. "This is my fiancé, Michael."

"This is me," she says, explaining herself to us. "I grew up on the beach. I came to Camden. People think I am a prostitute dressed like this, but I'm not. I'm unique."

"I don't do drugs," she says, hastily pulling down her sleeve to hide what look like needle tracks.

"I drink," she adds.

Michael, wearing a hooded sweatshirt under a black leather jacket, sits in front of a large coffee and two cheeseburgers on his tray. He has arranged ten sugar packets in a neat row in front of him. He rips each packet open and pours the sugar methodically into his coffee.

Erika, warming to the idea of being interviewed, is now chattering incoherently. She says she is a college graduate. She then tells us she is attending college to get her degree. She announces a few minutes later that she works in a preschool and is in charge of story time for the children. She says that today is her day off. She informs us as she rambles on that she is a drug counselor and "works to help kids get off drugs." She is finally cut off by Michael, who gives her a sour look. He launches into a long history of the city, including the riots and how they destroyed Camden.

"Tell him about the methadone clinic being closed, being moved to the port," Erika whispers, lurching in her seat toward him.

"Shut up," he says. "Eat your cheeseburger."

Two women we had seen in Transitional Park watch us at the next table. A mother in the booth next to us, unable to control an unruly small boy, chases him down an aisle and then smacks him on the side of his head. The boy wails as she hauls him by his collar back to the seat.

And yet, even here hope refuses to die. It flickers and wavers, a tiny flame in a sea of neglect, violence, and despair. It never comes with the great recovery plans or hospital expansions or the building of an aquarium. It never comes from those with the schemes to restore a city that cannot be restored. It never comes from the hollow promises of politicians. It comes with the decision made by one who is wounded to reach out to another who is wounded.

In a room across the street from Sacred Heart Catholic Church, where meals are provided for the homeless on Saturdays, a group of African American women bow their heads over a table and hold hands. They are led by Lallois Davis, sixty-seven, known as Lolly, a heavyset woman who radiates an indomitable spirit.

"The poor have to help the poor," Davis says, "because the ones who make the money are helping the people with money."

Davis raised four children, and then when a neighbor died and left behind her two small grandsons, Davis took them in and raised them as well. She wears a large cross around her neck. Most in the neighborhood call her "Aunt Lallois."

"My heart is heavy," says a sixty-nine-year-old woman named Brenda Hayes, her head bowed and her eyes shut. "There is so much heaviness. It is wounding me. How can I not worry?"

"Yes, Jesus, yes, Jesus," the other women respond.

"I know you didn't carry us this far to drop us now," Hayes says. "I know there is no burden so heavy that we can't carry it with your help. I thank you, Lord, for friends who have carried me through the roughest times."

"Yes, Jesus, nothing is impossible with you, Jesus," the women say in unison.

"Bodies," Hayes says to me after the prayer. "Bodies out back. Bodies upstairs. People stabbed. I don't go out at night. The last one was twenty feet away from me on my floor. There was one kid, he lived in the back of the projects, eighteen years old. They buried him two months ago. Gunshot. There were four kids I knew murdered, one in the parking lot who was killed last year. He was twelve or thirteen. He was sleeping, some say he was living, in a car.

"There are parents who are addicts who send their children out to sell drugs," Hayes says. "I know a mother who is a prostitute. Her oldest daughter sells weed to go to school, and then the mother stole the weed and sold it to buy crack."

Black Christianity, while it uses the same iconography and language as white Christianity, is very different. It clings ferociously to the cross. "The cross is a paradoxical religious symbol because it *inverts* the world's value system with the news that hope comes by way of defeat, that suffering and death do not have the last word, that the last shall be first and the first last,"[42] writes the theologian James Cone in *The Cross and the Lynching Tree.* And this belief is absurd to the intellect, yet, as Cone points out, "profoundly real in the souls of black folk." The crucified Christ, Cone writes, for those who are also crucified, manifests "God's loving and liberating presence *in* the contradictions of black life—that transcendent presence in the lives of black Christians that empowered them to believe that ultimately, in God's eschatological future, they would not be defeated by the 'troubles of the world,' no matter how great and painful their suffering."[43]

Cone elucidates this paradox, what he calls "this absurd claim of faith," by pointing out that to cling to this absurdity was possible only when one was shorn of power, when one was unable to be proud and mighty, when one understood that he or she was not called by God to rule over others. "The cross was God's critique of power—white power—with powerless love, snatching victory out of defeat."[44]

Lolly Davis lives in one of the brick row houses on Emerald Street, some of which have been refurbished through Father Doyle's Heart of Camden project. Other brick and wooden row houses on her street, a block from Sacred Heart, bear the scars of decay and long abandonment. There is a pungent smell of garbage. Davis, whose blood pressure had recently shot up and whose kidneys shut down, is home from the hospital. Her twenty-one-year-old adopted grandson, nicknamed Boom Boom, or Boomer, answers the door and says his grandmother will be right down. The white blinds are closed on the front window. The living room, with its two beige couches, matching armchair, and a large flat-screen television, is dim. There is a stone fireplace with a mantle crowned with family photos. Rain lashes the window. Boomer finished a special education program last year. He is a heavy young man and wears an orange T-shirt and blue shorts. He is making a peanut butter and jelly sandwich in the kitchen.

Lolly gingerly makes her way down the stairs. She settles into an armchair and begins her story.

Lolly can't quite keep track of all the people who've lived under her roof.

FOUR, FIVE, SIX, SEVEN, EIGHT KIDS, NINE KIDS, BUT I ALWAYS HAD KIDS STAYING AT MY HOUSE, EVEN THE KIDS IN THE NEIGHBORHOOD.

WHEN THEY HAD PROBLEMS WITH THEIR PARENTS, THEY COME TO MY HOUSE.

"I had straight everything ou

Lolly also kept two white children for a while.

"Their mother and father lived on our street, and she started messing with this black guy, and she left. [Their father] had to work. He had nobody to take care of the kids.

"I told him bring on the kids. I'll take care of the kids.

"So the they starte stayir at my place.

Referring to Boomer, whom she would later adopt, she says,

"My neighbor was talking about having an abortion, and I told her,

ARE YOU READY TO STAND BEFORE GOD AND TELL HIM THE REASON THAT YOU GOT RID OF THAT BABY?

NO.

GIVE THAT CHILD TO ME.

Lolly began babysitting Boomer when he was three days old and watched his brother too.

J SACCO 1-12

When their legal guardian was dying of cancer, "I would go by [her] house, get the kids, I would feed her dinner.

Nobody was there to help her. I would wash her clothes, do the dishes, all that.

"I'd take the boys, bring them home, help with their homework, wash their clothes at my house, hang the clothes.

IT DON'T HAVE TO BE BLOOD ALL THE TIME FOR SOMEONE TO BE IN YOUR FAMILY.

AND THAT'S WHAT I TELL MY CHILDREN.

Of her siblings, only a sister and two brothers remain. All the boys served in the military, and mostly they came home embittered.

One of them, who did a couple of tours in Vietnam, "drunk himself to death I guess."

Another died because of problems with his liver.

"Mostly all my brothers were drunk," she says.

Lolly, too, watched Camden's decline, which she dates to the riots of the late '60s and early '70s.

She remembers her brother coming to warn her that white people's houses were being burned.

He told her to put something red in the window so that her home would be passed over.

She immediately went across the street to warn a white neighbor.

Y'ALL GOTTA PUT SOME RED IN THE WINDOW.

Y'ALL CAN'T TELL NOBODY WHERE YOU HEARD FROM BECAUSE THEY GONNA KILL ME, YOU KNOW.

"So they put [up a] red Christmas sock.

"I put my brother's red underwear...

"I go ta[p] [it] in my window."

Lolly knows the mayhem was sparked by anger at the police, but she has little patience for those who "broke into stores and all that and took furniture."

After the riots, she says, "Camden went downhill," but like Joe Balzano, Lolly retains great affection for the city—

I LOVE CAMDEN. IT'S SOME GOOD PEOPLE HERE.

—and a personally optimistic outlook.

I ALWAYS BELIEVE THAT THE NEXT DAY MIGHT BE A BETTER DAY.

AND I BELIEVE THAT SOMETIMES THINGS HAPPEN IN YOUR LIFE — I DON'T QUESTION WHY...

I ASK THE LORD TO GIVE M[E] STRENGTH T[O] GO THROUG[H] IT.

It is morning and the children from Sacred Heart School, located next to the church, are seated in the pews. They have been let out of class to wish Father Michael Doyle a happy seventy-fifth birthday. Doyle was a member of the Camden 28, a group of left-wing Catholics and anti-Vietnam War activists who in 1971 planned and executed a raid to steal and destroy all A-1 status draft registrations at the local draft board in Camden. The defendants were arrested but acquitted when it was found that the FBI, which had an informant in the group, had provided tools for the break-in and facilitated much of the logistics for the act of civil disobedience. Doyle, however, lost his teaching job and was transferred to Sacred Heart in 1974, a poor parish in one of the blighted corners of Camden.

Wearing a black suit with a clerical collar, Father Doyle sits in a front-row pew. His ruddy cheeks are capped by snow-white hair. The first grade class walks up the aisle with their teacher to the front of the church. "Take your hands out of your pockets," the teacher whispers to several boys.

"I would fly, fly away and be at rest if I had the wings of an eagle," the children sing. "I would fly away and be at rest. Since I have no wings, oh, since I have no wings, I'm going to sing, sing, sing."

The priest taps his foot to the music. His eyes glisten slightly. He sits thinking, he tells me later, "Let them be saved, let them get through this, give them the strength to get through."

Students read passages from the priest's monthly letters to his parishioners. Father Doyle then speaks to the children about arriving in Camden thirty-five years ago. "You are my great joy," he says to the children, "and in the summer I miss the sound of your laughter and conversation, and I thank God when you return in the fall."

The murals on the walls of the church, built at the end of the nineteenth century, show the Ascension, the baptism of Jesus by John, the marriage of Mary and Joseph, and the return of the Prodigal Son. The school, which the archdiocese tried to close twenty-five years ago because few of the students were Catholics, was kept open when Father Doyle solicited donations from outside sponsors for the children. He has organized twenty-seven hundred sponsors who each pay $300 a year to keep the school functioning. The families cover the rest by paying a tuition fee of $1,000 per child. Doyle founded an organization named the Heart of Camden in 1984, which has renovated more than one hundred and seventy derelict homes. His parish oversees a second-hand clothing store, a local greenhouse, and community gardens. It has a medical clinic and an after-school program, and it runs a food bank.

"The best four-letter word in the English language is *hope*," he says afterward. "It is my job, my vocation, to promote and celebrate hope, to hold it up. When I look at these children, I can cry. I am afraid at some point they will make a turn.

"Today's a very hard time to be poor," Father Doyle says as I sit with him later:

Because you know that you're poor. You hear people my age get up and say, 'We were poor. We put cardboard in our shoes.' We talk like that. But we didn't know we were poor. Today you do. And how do you know you're poor? Your television shows you that you're poor. So it's very easy to build up anger in a, say, a high-voltage kid of seventeen, and, he knows he's poor, he looks at the TV, and 'All these people have everything and I have nothing.' And so he's very angry. And so that's, I think I see a violence—I'm not talking about violence on TV, which might be a violent show—but I'm talking about the violence that rises out of the marketing that shows the kid what he could have, creates a huge anger that explodes, easily. That I discovered very quickly when I came to Camden. I discovered the anger was so near the surface, you just rub it and it explodes. And there's no respect for you if you have no money. I think that the constant assault of the marketers, never-ending, it's building up an anger that's—you can understand it, but it's so violent.

Children of the Sacred Heart School singing to Father Michael Doyle.

I ask him why the rage is invariably self-destructive.

"They can't get at it," he says:

I grew up in Ireland and we had the songs of our struggle, and it was clear against whom we were struggling. The enemy was very clear. I was saying about Ireland, that it's nosediving now at an enormous rate. And I was saying before it was nosediving, that we have an enemy and we don't know it's an enemy. It's the money crowd. It's an enemy. But people don't see it as an enemy. And you can't challenge it because you don't see it. And I think it's the same way for the young people here. You have an enemy, and that enemy is greed and prejudice and injustice and all that type of thing, but you can't get at it. There's no head, there's no clarity, so you take it out on your neighbor, it's just horrendous what people do.

"Women have some dignity in a poor ghetto because they bear children and raise them," Father Doyle went on:

Men are adding nothing and feeding from the trough. Like the welfare was huge destruction, as you know very well, of the men of this country, the poor men of this country, it was aid for women, with dependent children. I'd ask young girls, "When you get married . . . " "I'm not going to get married! I'm going to have children, but I'm not going to get married." So, there's a lot of destruction there. At present times, over the last thirty years, a lot of destruction of the man, the male person, a lot of destruction. And so the women have a better chance, they do. Because they have dignity. A woman walks down the street pushing a little cart, and a child on it, she's somebody. But the man standing watching her is nobody, and so, it's very hard.

"We do a mass here on a Sunday in November every year, we invite families of murder victims to come, a small number will come who don't know us, maybe fifteen families will come, and we call out the names of those who were, you know—'John Smith, twenty-two, gunshot,'" he says:

Like that. And then somebody stands up wearing that name. And then you have fifty people standing. And we have a service acknowledging the reality of the destruction and to connect it with something decent or something affirming or something prayerful. But it is awful, you know. A murder in Camden could get seventy-five words. A murder in Cherry Hill could go on for months. It's so common. The crime is connected to the poverty. They're not killing each other in Cherry Hill. It's connected. Connected to the anger, and then of course, the other thing about Camden, is, there's a devastating dropout in high school. I mean fifty-two percent never make it, never get past sophomore year. So they're on the street, can hardly read or write. Can't get a job, can't even work in a gas station if you can't write. So they're there with no future, no opportunity. The immigrants who came with a shovel on their shoulder, could dig a canal. You could walk till you turn blue with a shovel on your shoulder, and there's no job [now]. So there was a job for the poor uneducated Irish men, there was, or the Italian or the Polish or whatever they were that didn't have much education, but there were jobs that they could do, and make that little bit of a living and have the dignity of a job. So, these poor kids, there's nothing within their reach that they can live on. There's a big place up here, it's now called the Susquehanna [Bank] Center, here on the river, which has big concerts. So there'll be a bunch of kids up there parking cars, and I said, "How much are you making?" "Six dollars," you know. You can't live on six dollars. So you get little jobs that are no real value in terms of living. So it's very hard to solve the problem, it is, it's very difficult. There are hardly any job training centers in Camden, they're not funded. That's what would be good. Well, if you paid people, like they do in the military, pay them to do something, it'd be a better investment than to pay them to learn how to shoot a gun. You'd make a better investment in the future if you did that. And the people are like, "Oh, my God, we can't do that." Well, of course you can, why not, then, why couldn't you? You wouldn't pay them a lot, but they would come and learn, if there was something in it for them, indeed they would. I notice that poor people at a meeting have a lot to say if they're coming from work. Work is like the great sign of success and dignity and all of that. No matter what the job is.

⚜

It is a bleak, rainy afternoon when we visit Harleigh Cemetery. Walt Whitman's tomb, based on a design by William Blake, is here. It has a heavy stone front, peaked roof, and iron gates. The poet's name in imposing stone letters is above the gates. The grave of another Camden poet, Nicholas Virgilio, who, as

Father Doyle says, "mined beauty out of the gutters of Camden" is also here. Virgilio died of a heart attack in 1989. The Irish priest, a close friend of the poet, designed Virgilio's grave in the shape of a podium. One of the poet's haiku verses is engraved on the stone:

lily:
out of the water . . .
out of itself.

Virgilio, who wrote his poems in his basement under a naked lightbulb next to his washing machine, chronicles the slow strangulation of his city: the hookers knitting baby booties on a bus, sitting alone as he orders eggs and toast in an undertone on Thanksgiving, latch-key children "exploring the wild on public television," the frozen body of a drunk found on a winter morning in a cardboard box labeled: "Fragile: Do Not Crush," as well as lamenting his brother Larry who was killed in Vietnam.

I open Virgilio's thin book, *Selected Haiku,* and place it on the marble top of his grave. Droplets of rain splatter the book.

the sack of kittens
sinking in the icy creek
increases the cold

3

DAYS OF DEVASTATION

Welch, West Virginia

꙳

I first began to understand what I have learned since, that there are forces in this world, principalities and powers, that wrench away the things that are loved, people and land, and return only exile.

—DENISE GIARDINA, *STORMING HEAVEN*

The notion that a radical is one who hates his country is naïve and usually idiotic. He is, more likely, one who likes his country more than the rest of us, and is thus more disturbed than the rest of us when he sees it debauched. He is not a bad citizen turning to crime; he is a good citizen driven to despair.

—H. L. MENCKEN

J OE AND I ARE WALKING ALONG THE RIDGE OF KAYFORD MOUNTAIN IN southern West Virginia with Larry Gibson. Small wooden shacks and campers, including Gibson's simple wood cabin, dot the line of ridge where he and his extended family have lived for more than two hundred and thirty years. Coal companies are blasting hundreds of thousands of acres of the Appalachians into mounds of debris and rubble to unearth seams of coal. Gibson has preserved fifty acres from the destruction. His forested ribbon of land is surrounded by a sea of gray rock, pale patches of thin grass, and barren plateaus where mountain peaks and towering pines once stood. Valleys and creeks, including the old swimming hole Gibson used as a boy, are buried under mining waste. The wells, including his own, are dry and the aquifers below the mountain poisoned. The fine grit of coal dust in the air settles on our lips and leaves a metallic taste in our mouths. Gibson's thin strip of trees and undergrowth is a reminder of what has been destroyed and will never be reclaimed.

Gibson, sixty-five, stands five feet tall. He is wearing a straw hat and overalls, has a moustache, and usually walks his property with a loaded Glock .45 pistol. He left his pistol today in his tiny cabin, where he gets his electricity from solar panels and a generator. We are headed down a dirt road with his lumbering, twelve-year-old black dog whose name, Gibson tells us, is "very complex. His name is Dog." Loss of habitat has driven the remaining wildlife, including bears and wild boars, onto his property: "When I was a boy you didn't see bears. You might see a paw print, but the coal companies done drove the bears in on us."

Larry Gibson was born on the mountain and spent his boyhood there. There were once sixty families clustered around the mountain, along with a small general store and a church. Gibson's father was a coal miner who had his leg shattered in 1956 in a mine collapse. The coal company did not pay any benefits. The bills piled up. The family sold its furniture. The house was seized, and for a few months Larry and his parents camped out under a willow tree. Gibson remembers that as a young boy he came upon his father during this time, a man who always seemed to him a tower of strength, sobbing.

The Gibsons—like the families of thousands of other coal miners, who in the 1950s could no longer find work as the mines were mechanized and diesel and oil replaced coal—were forced out of the mountains. They went to Cleveland, where Larry's father found work in a barrel factory. He later worked for Ford. Gibson moved back to the mountain after he retired from General Motors on disability.

"Livin' here as a boy I wasn't any different than anybody else," he says:

First time I knew I was poor was when I went to Cleveland and went to school. They taught me I was poor. I traded all this for a strip of green I saw when I was walkin' the street. An' *I* was poor? How ya gonna get a piece of green grass between the sidewalk and the street, and they gonna tell me *I'm* poor. I thought I was the luckiest kid in the world, with nature. I could walk through the forest. I could hear the animals. I could hear the woods talk to me. Everywhere I looked there was life. I could pick my own apples or cucumbers. I could eat the berries and pawpaws. I loved pawpaws. And the gooseberries. Now there is no life there. Only dust. I had a pigeon and when I'd come out of the house, no matter where I went he flew over my head or sat on my shoulder. I had a hawk I named Fred. I had a bobcat and a three-legged fox that got caught in a trap. I wouldn't trade that childhood for all the fancy fire trucks and toys the other kids had. I didn't see a TV till I was thirteen. Didn't talk on a phone till I was fourteen. There was crawdads in the streams down at the bottom of the mountain. I could pick them out with my toes. Now nothing lives in the water. It stinks. Nothing lives on the land. And it's irreversible. You can't bring it back.

By the time he returned as a middle-aged man, the land of his boyhood was barely recognizable. His family's five hundred acres had shrunk to fifty. Old claims to mineral rights underground, many of them deeded by ancestors who could not read or write, gave coal companies the ability to seize the land. The spine of the Appalachian Mountains is being obliterated to gouge out the seams of black coal. The constant, daily explosions at the edge of his property—which in one typical week in West Virginia equals the cumulative power of the blast over Hiroshima—rains showers of rocks down on his property. We walk among the graves of his family cemetery on the crest of the hill. Coal operatives in the late 1980s stole more than one hundred and twenty headstones in an effort to erase the face of the cemetery and open it up for mining. These vandalized grave sites are now marked by simple wooden crosses. We stop at the grave for Larry's brother Billie, who died in 2004. His stone reads: "Back to the Mountains for which you loved and eternal peace that had eluded you."

"Buddy, when they was blastin' out here, for instance, when they was this close to me, they was blowin' rocks as big as basketballs," Gibson says. "Me and my uncle got caught in a dynamite blast four different times on this place, not on their place, on *our* place. It was fly rock. It was like *Star Wars,* where you see all them rocks comin' at ya in the movie. Well, this wasn't a movie."

He was able to save the cemetery near his house but watched helplessly in 2007 as bulldozers demolished an adjacent cemetery that also held family remains.

"They pushed one hundred and thirty-nine graves over a high wall," he says:

They left us eleven graves. It was Massey Coal. The graves are now surrounded by their property. It didn't belong to them. It belonged to my uncle, his grand-father, my great-great-grandfather. The cemetery was three hundred years old, but there was coal underneath. I always tell people, "Ya got to stay cool, ya got to stay calm, got to be responsible, reliable, credible." I was givin' a tour and lookin' across this valley when I seen this 'dozer goin' through my cemetery. I was jus' 'bout on my way back home to git one of my guns. An' I'm a very good shot. This is what they do in the coalfields. They do what they want, and then they go fight it in court because they got the money and the attorneys and the time to do it.

He laments that in many of the grave sites there are probably no longer any caskets or bodies. The underground mining, begun more than a century ago, has created vast honeycombs beneath the earth that open huge fissures in the land, causing many of the graves to sink into the deep depressions. The wide cracks and gaping holes that dot the landscape mark the earth collapsing in on itself. Some of the cracks, three or four feet wide, run through the graves in family cemeteries. You look into the pit and see a deep, empty hole.

But Gibson refused to yield. He formed a nonprofit foundation in 1992 to protect the property. He has steadfastly refused to sell it to coal companies, although there are probably, he estimates, hundreds of thousands of dollars worth of coal beneath his feet. The relentless stripping of the forests, the vast impoundments filled with billions of gallons of toxic coal waste known as slurry, and the steady flight by residents whose nerves and health are shattered, has left Gibson one of the few survivors.

"There was one thing I was taught as a boy livin' in the coalfields," he says, "and that was bein' organized. We didn't know who the United States president was, but we knew the United Mine Workers president. We had learned to always fight back."

His defiance has come with a cost. Coal companies are the only employers left in southern West Virginia, one of the worst pockets of poverty in the nation, and the desperate scramble for the few remaining jobs has allowed the companies to portray rebels such as Gibson as enemies of not only Big Coal but also the jobs it provides. Gibson's cabin has been burned down. Two of his dogs have been shot and Dog was hung, although he was saved before he choked to death. Trucks have tried to run him off the road. He has endured drive-by shootings, and a couple of weeks before we visited, his Porta-Johns were overturned. A camper he once lived in was shot up. He lost his water in 2001 when the blasting dropped the water table. He has reinforced his cabin door with six inches of wood to keep it from being kicked in by intruders. The door weighs five hundred pounds and has wheels at the base to open and close it. A black bullet-proof vest hangs near the entrance on the wall, although he admits he has never put it on. He keeps stacks of dead birds in his freezer that choked to death on the foul air, hoping that someday someone might investigate why birds in this part of the state routinely fall out of the sky. Roughly a hundred bird species have disappeared.

"By the way," he says, arching his eyebrows:

y'all bin talkin' to me fer an hour now, and y'all ain't never asked me my opinion on coal. I'm against coal. I think coal should be abolished, 'cause the science is in. Ther' been test after test after test 'bout the coal an' related disease that kills people. Coal-related disease that kills people who never worked in the mines. We lose forty-five hundred people every year who never worked in a mine except they live in the coalfields. Mostly a lot of them is women, a high percentage of them is women, because women's tolerance against coal dust is lower than men's. Now, you have this here black lung, which affects fifteen hundred men a year. And then we have the emissions code. You heard about the World Trade Center terrorists? You heard about them? Bombing, three thousand people dying, but have you heard that with the emissions of coal we lose twenty-four thousand people a year in this country? You know, eight times bigger than the World Trade Center. Nobody say anything about that. Then you have the something like six hundred and forty thousand premature births and birth defects, newborns, every year, *every* year, and nobody's doin' anything about that. Coal kills, everybody knows coal kills. But, you know, profit.

"They passed laws that ya can't go down in Charleston in certain places and smoke in public," he says:

Think 'bout it. I'm allowed to breathe this air here. The people within the coalfields are allowed to breathe the same air I'm breathin' because the profit margin is higher than the price of a man's life. So long as we can make a profit, we can step over the bodies, and the man can breathe the poisoned air. Why do they pass all these health and safety laws 'bout smokin' cigarettes in public places an' they let the kids go to school beneath a 2.5 billion-gallon dam filled with mine waste two hundred and fifty feet away from a preparation plant? As long as they're makin' a profit. But how do the people make a livin' here? The people have become submissive jus' like a woman who is abused and beaten. An' they have a high degree of respect fer the people who are doin' it to 'em.

"I expect to lose my life to it, I guess," he says about his defiance. "I expect, somebody scared, you know, somebody who normally wouldn't do anything wrong, seeing me up here by myself. Because of my belief and my stand. And the fact that they may lose a job. And they got a baby on the way and one at home. They may lose their job, and they had a couple beers that day maybe. You know. And they see me. I'm hit, I'm hit, you know. Scared people make dangerous people. They act without thinkin'. An' the industry uses people like that.

"But if I stop fightin' for it, they'll take it," he says. "Do you know what it's like to hear a mountain get blowed up? A mountain is a live vessel, man; it's life itself. You walk through the woods here and you're gonna hear the critters moving, scampering around, that's what a mountain is. Try to imagine what it would be like for a mountain when it's getting blowed up, fifteen times a day, blowed up, every day, what that mountain must feel like as far as pain, as life.

"I'm not a highly-brained guy here," he continues, "don't have a lot of education. I just point at the common denominator of things: You screw up one thing, another is gonna fall, and if that falls something else is gonna fall, and how much more do we have to fall before we start saying, 'Whoa, there's something wrong here somewhere,' you know?"

"See that red pole up there?" he says, as we move toward the far end of the ridge. "It's a marker. From this corner across there, OK? What gets me about this is, my family owned this. And when I go up through here, I look at it as if I was walkin' on what was my family's before. *They* say it belongs to *them* now. An' 'member I told you how they took it? I look at it as if it still belongs to me and my family. But now you are on coal company property. You can be subject to arrest. You like peanut butter and pork and beans? That's what they serve ya in jail now. I'm pretty regular."

We climb up an incline at the edge of Gibson's property. At the top we see vast pits and rocky outcroppings where there once were mountains. Seams of coal run like black ribbons through sheer rock face. The wind whips across the barren slate flatlands. Idle earthmovers, diggers, and bulldozers lie scattered on the rock face before us. A few patches, sprayed with fertilizer and grass seed, are a faint green. In most spots the thin topsoil and grass, sprayed on by the coal companies as part of their reclamation of the land, have washed away, exposing the stone beneath. White drill marks dot the top of the rock. The company will soon drill down and blast away another eighty feet of stone on the ravaged peak before us to get to more coal seams. About a dozen men with heavy machinery can carry out this kind of mining. When coal companies had to dig underground, they would employ hundreds, and at times thousands, of miners to extract the same amount of coal.

Gibson points to a huge impoundment of toxic coal waste that lies behind a dam in the distance:

They are dynamiting within two hundred feet of the face of that dam. It's over a one-thousand-feet dam. They say when the dam breaks, seventeen miles away the sludge will be forty feet high comin' at you. Ya must understand, now, mine waste per gallon weighs four times more than a gallon water. Ye'r' lookin' at a lot of waste over there, and a lot of heavy waste. It's sittin' at thirty-five feet above an abandoned mine shaft, too. So it's gonna come out. One way or another it gonna come out. An' them dynamitin' within two hundred feet of the face and vibratin' the waste down below. In

Larry Gibson surveys mountains shaved for their coal near his property.

this part of the country we call it blowout—when the mouth opens up in the middle of a hill and shoots stuff out like a rifle. At the rate they're talkin' 'bout, it will kill people here.

"An' what chance are these people gonna have?" he says, looking down to a cluster of houses in the "holler" below. The mountains lie so close together that houses and communities scratch out space tucked in hollows, long rows between them known locally as *hollers*: "Ya see how narrow these hollers are? We're gonna lose a lot of people.

"When it comes right down to it, I been callin' fer a revolution across this country fer a long time now," Gibson says. "I think it was Thomas Jefferson said, I think it was 'im, who said we should have a revolution every twenty years to keep the country in check. We' bin way overdue."

"What would it look like?" I ask.

"It would be holdin' the government in contempt," he says. "It would be holdin' the government to credibility and accountability. It would be holdin' people accountable fer their actions. That's all I'm askin' fer. They come in here and tell me, 'Larry, you have to be reliable, accountable, responsible, credible,' all the things they tell me, everything they jus' taught me, I jus' told you now, they ain't bin doin'. That's all I'm askin'.

"They're gonna destroy my state, and the government's gonna give them the incentives to do it," he says. "My grandchildren and great-grandchildren won't have any heritage here. They won't have any mountain culture here, 'cause they're wipin' it out. I had the best of time of my life not knowin' I wasn't rich or comfortable or wealthy. How could I enjoy myself outdoors if I wasn't wealthy? Who measures wealth? How do you do it? All the energy we have, all the people they destroyed, all the fatalities on these mine sites, and they keep makin' reference to this as cheap energy."

"What keeps you going?" I ask.

"I'm right," he says. "That's all."

The next morning Joe and I are at Yeager Airport in Charleston, West Virginia, to fly over the coalfields with Vivian Stockman, the project coordinator for the Ohio Valley Environmental Coalition, and Susan Lapis, a pilot and chemistry professor. The flight was arranged through SouthWings, a nonprofit group that flies observers across the Southeast to promote conservation. Stockman, who gets airsick when buffeted by the winds, has pressure-point wristbands and a patch on her neck to combat the nausea. We settle into the worn, black leather seats of Lapis's 1977 Cessna 182 Skylane, which she calls the "station wagons of the air," and put on earphones. We are parked next to a gray Air Force C-130 cargo plane. The Cessna rocks slightly in the gusts as we lift off from the concrete runway. We head south.

Lapis, as if she is patiently speaking to first-year chemistry students, explains what happens when heavy metals are blasted into the air. Enzymes, she says, depend on heavy metals. She tells us what happens when the balance is ripped apart by the release of calcium and magnesium into the atmosphere.

"When I was an organic chemistry student working in the lab, the way we would get a relatively insoluble substance to dissolve in a solvent was to grind it up with a mortar and pestle into a powder or little pieces. This increases the surface area of the substance to be dissolved, and thus makes it more readily soluble," Lapis tells us through the headphones. "To harvest the coal in MTR [mountaintop removal], the layers of mountain in between the layers of coal are blasted to smithereens and dumped into valley fills. When rainwater trickles through this pulverized rock—more surface area—it can more easily dissolve minerals from the rock, some of which are heavy metals that are toxic in high concentrations. The metal ion-rich runoff from the valley fills then goes into streams, rivers, and groundwater of West Virginia in unnatural concentrations, sometimes toxic.

"From the air you can see weirdly-colored pools of water on the mine sites," she says as we fly over an impoundment of coal slurry streaked with swirls of bright green, gray, and black, "colored by these metals in unnatural concentrations. Some people up in the hollows get foul-smelling, discolored water coming out of their wells or their kitchen spigots, and the coal companies are providing them with safe drinking water in huge containers. Some folks have to carry these giant jugs down the hill into the house for water to bathe the baby!"

Lapis explains that she could once move south by identifying landmarks from the air such as Williams Mountain, whose long, rocky outcrop resembled a battleship. But when we reach the mountain, we see only a denuded plateau of looping ring roads and gray rubble. She banks the plane so we can see down into another massive impoundment, filled with circles of bright green. "Heavy metal pollution," she says as we fly over the dam. The coal ash in the slurry ponds, often the size of small lakes, contains high levels of arsenic, lead, cadmium, selenium, and mercury.[1] Many of these waste ponds are perched perilously in mountainous crags above towns and even schools. When the dirt walls of the ponds burst, the damage is catastrophic.

We fly over hundreds of trees, which along with the topsoil and sandstone, are being bulldozed over the side of a mountain by seventy-five-ton Caterpillar D10 bulldozers. Many of the trees lying like matchsticks on the sides of the peak are on fire. The gray smoke drifts upward.

"When we come back next month all the trees there will be gone," Lapis says.

We see the thin layers of green that cling to the remaining rock face and the streaks where the sprayed-on grass seed has washed away.

"What are we thinking?" Lapis says softly.

As the plane dips over Clear Fork, we see, snaking through the trees, the old

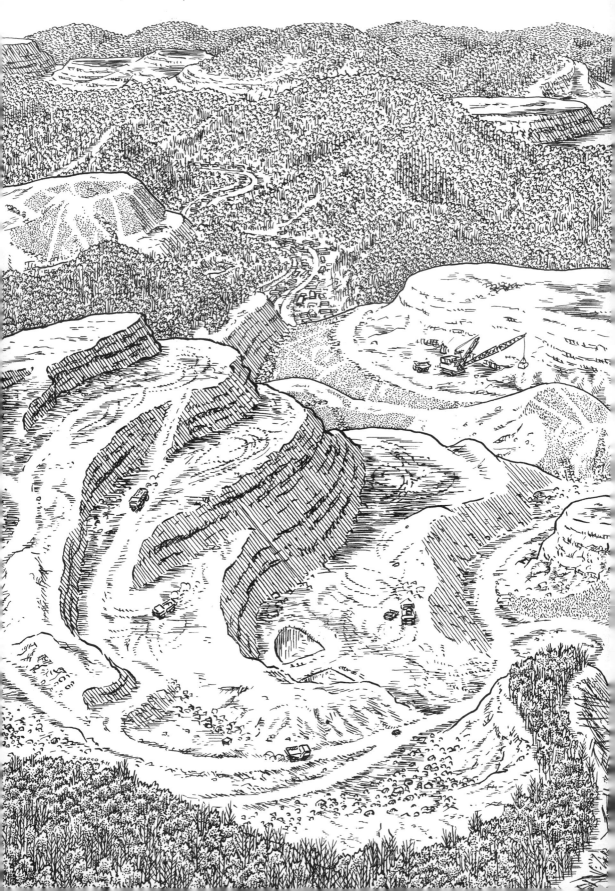

The effects of mountaintop removal as seen from the air.

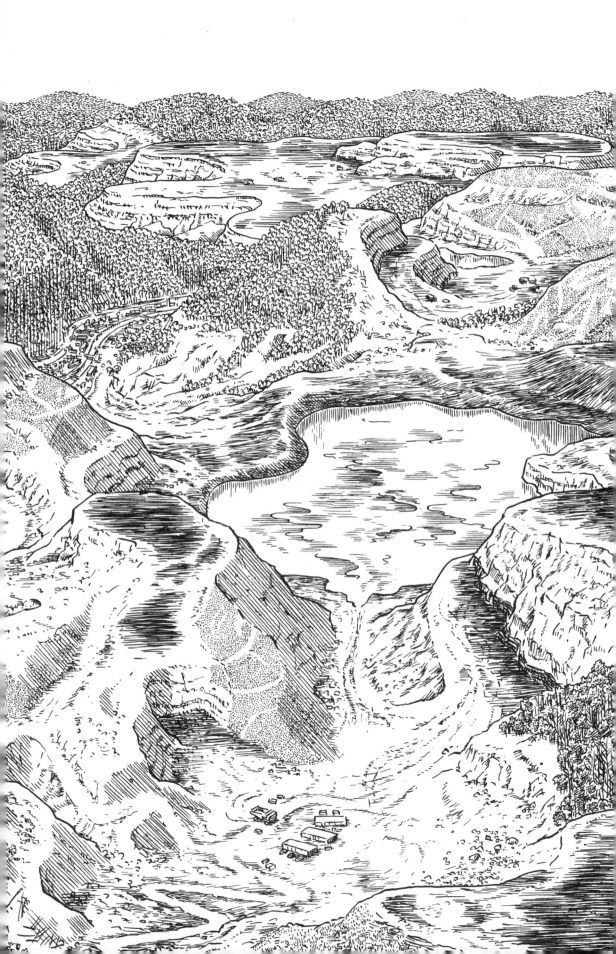

logging roads from the 1920s, when companies stripped southern West Virginia of its virgin forests. We fly over Brushy Fork Slurry Impoundment, the largest earthen dam in the Western Hemisphere, which was built above the Marsh Fork Elementary School, now closed because of the threat of a dam burst. Yellow construction vehicles crawl across the blasted moonscape.

"Your eye tricks you from up here," Lapis says. "Those are some of the largest machines on earth. They have twelve-foot tires."

She noses the plane toward a dragline excavator. Draglines, which cost upward of $100 million dollars and can be twenty stories tall, are among the largest pieces of mobile equipment built on land. Bulldozers, container trucks, and backhoes, even the oversized versions we see below us, look like children's toys next to the draglines. The draglines do the work of hundreds of miners. Half a century ago it took a miner a day to dig and haul sixteen tons of coal out of the ground. A dragline, once a few hundred feet are blasted off the top of a mountain, can fill the back of a truck with sixty tons of bituminous coal rock in a few minutes. Jobs in the mining industry have fallen from a high of about one hundred and thirty thousand a few decades ago to about fourteen thousand workers. Once the unions were broken and the mines were mechanized, the coal companies began to strip-mine and then blast off the tops of mountains. Most "miners" are, in fact, heavy machine operators.[2]

The coal companies write the laws. They control local and state politicians.[3] They destroy the water tables, suck billions of dollars' worth of coal out of the state, and render hundreds of acres uninhabitable. And ninety-five percent of the coal companies are not even based in West Virginia. The rights and health of those who live on the land are meaningless. The fossil-fuel industry's dirty game of corporate politics was on display following the arrests in the fall of 2011 of 1,253 activists from the environmental group 350.org outside the White House. The protestors opposed the proposal to build the Keystone XL pipeline, which would have brought some of the dirtiest energy on the planet from the tar sands in Canada through the United States to the Gulf Coast. James Hansen, NASA's leading climate scientist, has said that the building of the pipeline would mean "game over for the climate." President Barack Obama, ducking the issue, said he would review the proposal and make a decision after the November 2012 presidential election.

The U.S. House of Representatives, urged on by lobbyists, however, voted a few days later 234 to 194 to force a quicker review of the pipeline. The House attached its demand to a bill proposing a popular payroll tax cut. Oil Change International calculated that the 234 Congressional representatives who voted in favor of the measure received $42 million in campaign contributions from the fossil-fuel industry. The 194 representatives who opposed it received $8 million. Speaker of the House John Boehner, a champion of the pipeline, has received a total of $1,111,080 in campaign contributions from the fossil-fuel industry. His counterpart in the Senate, Mitch McConnell, who pushed it through the Senate, has received $1,277,208. Obama, saying the Republican deadline left no time to approve the project, did not sign off on the pipeline. But his administration did not reject it, either. The president invited the company building the pipeline, TransCanada Corporation, to reapply, which it has done. Obama, who approved the southern section of the oil pipeline, pushed a final decision on the full pipeline into 2013, beyond the presidential elections.

Elected officials at the state and federal level are paid employees of the corporate state. The U.S. Chamber of Commerce, the front group for the major corporations in the country, including Bank of America, Goldman Sachs, Chevron, and News Corp, spent more money on the 2010 elections than the Republican and Democratic National Committees combined. A staggering ninety-four percent of the Chamber's contributions went to politicians who deny the existence of climate change.[4]

Disease in the coalfields is rampant. The coal ash deposits have heavy concentrations of hexavalent chromium, a carcinogen. Cancer, like black lung disease, is an epidemic. Kidney stones are so common that in some communities nearly all the residents have had their gallbladders removed. More than half a million acres, or eight hundred square miles, of the Appalachians have been destroyed. More than five hundred mountain peaks are gone, along with an estimated one thousand miles of streams, which provide most of the headstreams for the eastern United States.

The spine of the Appalachian Mountains, a range older than the Himalayas, winds its way through Kentucky, Virginia, and West Virginia. Isolated, lonely patches of verdant hills and forests now lie in the midst of huge gray plateaus, massive, dark-eyed craters, and sprawling, earthen-banked dams filled with billions of gallons of coal slurry. Gigantic slag heaps, the residue of decades of mining operations, lie idle, periodically catching fire and belching oily plumes of smoke and an acrid stench. The coal companies have turned perhaps half a million acres in West Virginia and another half million in Kentucky, once some of the most beautiful and fertile land in the country, along with hundreds of towering peaks, into stunted mounds of rubble. It was impossible to grasp the level of destruction in the war in Bosnia until you got in a helicopter and flew over the landscape, seeing village after village dynamited by advancing Serb forces into ruins. The same scale of destruction, and the same problem in realizing its true extent, holds true for West Virginia and Kentucky.

That destruction, like the pillaging of natural resources in the ancient Mesopotamian, Roman, and Mayan empires, is one of willful if not always conscious self-annihilation. The dependence on coal, which supplies the energy for half the nation's electricity, means that its extraction, as supplies diminish, becomes ever more extreme. The Appalachian region provides most of the country's coal, its production dwarfed only by that of Wyoming's Powder River Basin.[5] We extract one hundred tons of coal from the earth every two seconds in the United States, and about seventy percent of that coal comes from strip mines and mountaintop removal, which began in 1970.[6]

Those who carry out this pillage probably believe they can outrun their own destructiveness. They think that their wealth, privilege, and gated communities will save them. Or maybe they do not think about the future at all. But the death they have unleashed, the relentless contamination of air, soil, and water, the physical collapse of communities, and the eventual exhaustion of coal and fossil fuels themselves, will not spare them. They, too, will succumb to the poisoning of nature; the climate dislocations and freak weather caused by global warming; the spread of new, deadly viruses; and the food riots and huge migrations that will begin as the desperate flee from flooded or drought-stricken pockets of the earth. The steady plundering of the natural world, the failure to heed the warning signs of the planet, will teach us a lesson about the danger of hubris. The health of the land and the purity of water is the final measurement of whether any society is sustainable. "A culture," the poet W. H. Auden observed, "is no better than its woods."

Joe and I drive from one decrepit coal camp to another, our four-wheel-drive vehicle splattered with mud and coal dust. We pull over and unwind wads of paper towels periodically to wipe away the soot that coats the rear window.

At the small bridge leading into the town of Gary, two young women in dark parkas are sitting listlessly on the concrete base of the crossing sign. A few feet away is a road that leads down a small slope into a more isolated stretch known

---

The remnants of the Alpheus Preparation Plant, once the largest coal-cleaning facility in the world.

as "the Pines." Cars come in and out of the Pines until late into the night to buy or sell drugs. It is, in this old coal-mining town, one of the few signs of activity.

Gary is located in a big bend of the Tug Fork of the Big Sandy River. It was built in the early twentieth century by U.S. Steel, the country's first billion-dollar corporation. The company operated one of the largest coal preparation plants in the world. But when U.S. Steel closed the plant in Gary in 1986, twelve hundred workers instantly lost their jobs. Personal income in McDowell County plunged that year by two-thirds. Huge numbers of families packed up and left. The community fell into terminal decay. There are today 861 people in Gary.[7] There were 98,887 in McDowell County in 1950.[8] Today there are fewer than 23,000. The countywide per capita average income is $12,585. The median home value is $30,500.[9]

Gary's rutted streets are lined by empty clapboard houses with sagging roofs. Porches fall away from the buildings. Wooden steps are rotted. Rusted appliances, the frames of old cars, tires, and heaps of garbage lie scattered in front of rows of deserted dwellings or clog the brackish water in the creeks, where low-lying branches are tangled with plastic bags and bottles. Boarded-up storefronts, neglected churches, the bleak brick remains of Gary High School, and the shuttered, flat-roofed stone bank building give the landscape the feel of a ravaged war zone. The spindly remains of chimneys jut up out of the charred timbers of burned houses. The guts of most buildings, as in Camden, have been stripped of piping and copper for sale in the scrap yards. The gold dome of the empty Orthodox church disappeared one night when a thief somehow commandeered a crane. The train station, the restaurant, and the old company stores, meticulously planned by Judge Albert Gary, the architect of J. P. Morgan's U.S. Steel empire and the man for whom the town was named, are skeletal remains. Mobile homes stand empty along the side of the road, their siding and torn insulation flapping in the wind in tattered strips. There is no supermarket. Canned or packaged food, high in sodium, sugar, preservatives, and fat, along with cheap bottles of liquor, are sold at the local convenience store and gas station, located across the road from the drug market.

There are rarely mayors in these towns. Basic services such as water, electricity, and fuel are often no longer available. When Joe and I visit the water treatment plant outside of Gary, the two cement collecting pools for wastewater are empty. The gate is padlocked shut. The closed plant is ringed by cyclone fencing topped by three rows of barbed wire. The stench of sewage rises from a pipe where the town's untreated sewer water pours directly into Tug Fork. It has been like this for more than two years. The feces discharged directly into the creek are nicknamed, by the locals, the "brown trout."

One morning Amanda Reed, the minister at the Welch Methodist church in nearby Welch, takes us to see Destry Daniels, the minister of the small Methodist church in Gary. The four of us head over to a small house where Rudy Kelly and his wife, who are members of Destry's congregation, live. Rudy, even at ninety, is a large, robust man who worked as a miner for forty years and has spend the last couple of decades fighting off black lung disease.

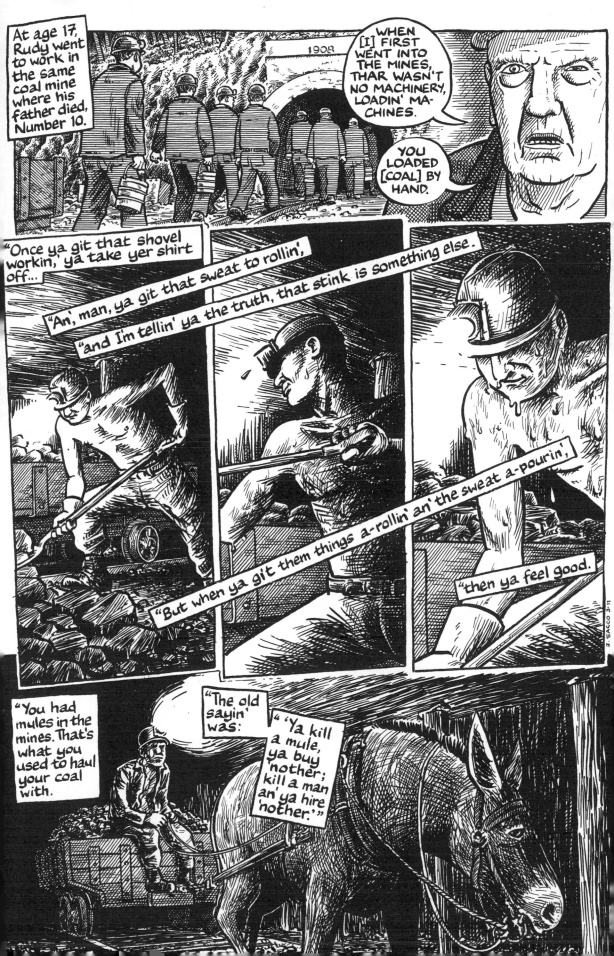

Mines have always been dangerous places, and what worried Rudy most were kettle bottoms, exposed, flat-bottomed rocks—petrified tree stumps—in the roof of the mine.

YA CAN'T TELL NOTHIN' 'BOUT A KETTLE BOTTOM.

'CAUSE IT SITS SMOOTH UP THERE...

THE LEAST BIT OF ERROR AND THAT THING'LL DROP—

JUST LIKE THAT!

A LOT OF PEOPLE GOT HURT BY KETTLE BOTTOMS.

As for his employer, U.S. Coal & Coke Company,

"[they] do anything they want to do...

"You had to make a livin', and they knowed it.

"They knowed you'd do anything to try to feed yer people.

"And they was hard on ya.

"You [find] water... in yer place and they'd tell ya, well, carry it out,

"or drink it,

"or do what you want with it,

"or get your tools and go home."

J. SACCO 3-11

"Everybody was drinkin'... Ya had a whole lot of 'em git twisted on the weekend.

"But nine times out of ten they would be at work Monday."

Besides European immigrants, Rudy worked alongside African-Americans, who were segregated in their own communities.

"We always got along. We never had no trouble...

"Yeah, we played ball...

"But there's still coloreds that live over thar in [Gary] Bottom, over thar where they lived."

Rudy had never traveled far, only to neighboring Virginia.

THAT'S THE FURTHEST I'VE BEEN 'CAUSE MY ROPE WOULDN'T REACH MUCH FURTHER.

World War II changed that.

"I was in the military for three years... I went to Europe. I went into Omaha [Beach]... It was St. Lo, or somewhere up in thar.

"I got hit in the leg...

"They fixed me up and I went right back to the same outfit...

With the war over, Rudy returned to the mines, which were now mechanized.

"I run the cutting machine for I dunno how many years...

"Well, I couldn't understand how that thing was gonna do it, but it done it."

The mines had changed in other significant ways. The United Mine Workers of America had triumphed in its struggle to unionize the miners at the Gary operations by the early 1940s.

According to Rudy, the advent of the union—

WAS THE BEST THING THAT HELPED IN THE COAL MINES.

J. SACCO 4·11

For one thing, miners were no longer expected to clear out standing water themselves.

"See, when the union come, the union says, 'You can't put that man in that water.

"You pump it out and then he'll load yer coal...'"

For another, company officials could no longer arbitrarily refuse to pay a worker for the coal he'd loaded.

"The union come an' they made 'em put scales in. And it all changed."

Under the leadership of union president John L. Lewis, the miners began to reap some of the benefits of their labor. They became among the best paid workers in West Virginia. They exercised their power to strike when they had a grievance.

"When John L. said everyone was coming out, everyone come out.

"Yeah, they followed him real good."

J. SACCO 4.11

In the 1980s, U.S. Steel ended its operations in Gary Hollow.

"Well, the mines quit. They shut down. An' I was 62 years old...

"I had to take Social Security at a cut."

Like so many West Virginia miners, Rudy was diagnosed with black lung. He underwent a number of operations.

MY DOCTOR TOLD ME I WAS SUPPOSED TO BE DEAD 20 YEARS AGO.

I DON'T KNOW WHAT'S KEEPING ME ALIVE.

Rudy's minister is present and mentions that Rudy still attends service every Sunday.

THAT'S MY BIG DEAL: THE GOOD LORD'LL LET ME GO TO CHURCH.

As our conversation wraps up, Rudy has a request.

He asks for the minister to pray with him.

Those who want fresh produce or meat, or those who need a doctor, have to find a ride into the county seat of Welch, which has seen its boom population in the 1950s of one hundred thousand reduced to 2,180. Welch, like Gary, is little more than a ghost town.[10] But at least it still has a hospital and a supermarket.

Nearly thirty percent of those in Welch live on less than $10,000 a year. Joe and I stay at a small motel outside of Welch called the Count Gilu. One night a woman, disoriented and high, asks us for a bowl so she can eat in her room. On another night a belligerent drunk bangs on Joe's door in the early hours of the morning. Forty percent of families with children in the city live below the poverty line, a proportion that skyrockets to seventy-five percent of families with children under the age of five. The high-school dropout rate is twenty-eight percent, compared with about eight percent nationwide. The city has had no new construction in nearly twenty years, and seventy percent of the buildings were put up before 1960. The remaining thirty percent were built before 1940. Little is done to keep these structures maintained even if they are inhabited. Whole streets in Welch, like Gary, are deserted, the empty storefronts remnants of another era when shoppers in the county converged on G. C. Murphy's Department Store, J. C. Penney, the Flat Iron Drug Store, King Cut Rate, Franklin's Dairy Bar, the Model Furniture Company, or the Carter Hotel, now hollow shells with vacant windows and faded signs over their chained and padlocked doors. One of the few places to eat is the Sterling Drive-In Restaurant on Stewart Street. It opened in 1945. A low roof over the car park allows drivers to have their food delivered to their cars. The sign in front of the drive-in, partially buried by snow the day we are there, reads: "Happy New Year. Today's Specials. Chicken Livers. Chicken Club Platter." Nearly everything on the menu is fried, including the chicken livers. The Sterling Drive-In is one of the faded reminders of what life used to be, of a time when the American working class, after the long and bloody battle to form unions, had basic rights, decent salaries, pensions, and medical coverage, a life in which dignity was attainable. The time when the Powhatan Arrow train, which came with a dining car equipped with tablecloths, silverware, and waiters, stopped at the Welch station—a time when Welch was worth stopping at—seems as distant and unreal as an old black-and-white movie.

The southern part of West Virginia is cursed by its resources. The Appalachian Mountain chain, which may be the oldest mountain range in the world, is made up of hundreds of steep razorback mountains. The glaciers during the Ice Age never reached this far south, and the topsoil is some of the oldest and richest in the world. The soil produces ramps, ginseng, and "molly moochers," or morels, among other ten-thousand-year-old species, that are gone forever once the soil is removed.[11] Billions of dollars of timber and coal have been plundered for more than a century by outside interests, while those living here have become among the poorest in the nation. But even with mountaintop removal, coal production in 2009 fell by thirteen percent—one of the biggest declines in fifty years.

The scale of the assault is visible across the landscape. In December 2008 the coal ash spill at the Tennessee Valley Authority's Kingston Fossil Plant in Roane County, Tennessee, released 1.1 billion gallons of waste across three hundred acres and into nearby rivers. The ash-filled sludge had accumulated for decades from the Kingston coal-fired plant. The spill was a hundred times larger than the *Exxon Valdez* oil spill. The 1972 Buffalo Creek disaster, caused

by the bursting of a slurry impoundment dam at the Pittston Coal Company in Logan County, West Virginia, sent more than 132 million gallons of swirling poison into the valley towns below. The flooding left one hundred and twenty-five people dead and more than twelve hundred injured. Some four thousand people were left homeless.[12] Lives and whole communities vanish after such dam bursts. And as we drive the back roads of southern West Virginia, Joe and I see long rows of deserted and desolate structures in the twilight and long mudflats where buildings once stood. The depletion of soil and trees has resulted in frequent flash floods. In 2001 and 2002 rains dumped some ten inches in twelve hours. Torrents of water poured down the denuded slopes and ripped through communities, leaving forty dead. Those whose homes are destroyed usually take what money they can get from the government's disaster relief program and move. Those who remain live amid the ruins.

We drive from Gary to Jenkinjones. It was once a bustling coal town built and operated by the Pocahontas Fuel Company. The road into the holler that

Jenkinjones, West Virginia.

shelters Jenkinjones—named for the coal baron who was one of the founders of the company—is bordered on either side by a desolate row of chimneys that stand over charred wrecks of clapboard houses. The brick and concrete structures that were the anchor of the company town, including the old payroll office downtown and the company store with carved letters reading *Pocahontas Fuel Company 1917* over the entrance, are hollow shells. Piles of rubble line the floor inside the three arched doorways of the company store. We kick our way through the debris. A mangy gray dog slinks past us, tail tucked between its legs, head lowered, teeth bared. The wind whistles forlornly through the trees.

The only building with any sign of life is the small post office. But with the planned cuts proposed by the U.S. Postal Service, it is scheduled to be shut in

May 2012. At that point civic life will be extinguished. Post offices in the surrounding towns of Cass, Elkhorn, and Eckman were closed at the end of 2011. Postmistress Kathy Miller has lived in Jenkinjones for forty-seven years. She sits alone behind the counter. She says she has about seventy regular visitors. Nearly all are disabled or retired.

"I will go from working forty hours a week to three hours a week in the post office on Saturdays," Miller says of the anticipated closing. "Everyone here is hoping Congress will do something."

"The decline was gradual at first," she says, "then we had those two major floods in 2000 and 2001. The main street was four or five feet under water. Twenty-four houses washed away."

Eighteen-wheeler coal trucks rumble down the back roads. They spew clouds of coal dust into the air. Black grit covers the sides of the roads, the trees and the ground. It coats lawns and the fronts of houses. It blankets cars and lawn furniture. It leaves a film of grime on windows and seeps inside houses. Mercury, lead, cadmium, arsenic, manganese, beryllium, chromium, and other carcinogenic substances from coal saturate the landscape. You eat it. You drink it. You breathe it. In the elementary schools there are lines of inhalers in the nurse's office for the boys and girls.

Maria Gunnoe lives with her husband and three children in Bob White on Route 85 in Boone County. Five acres of her land have washed away from repeated flooding. She has been flooded out of her home seven times. The massive mounds of rubble from blown-off mountaintops have triggered thirteen landslides that, with each rainfall, creep closer and closer to her home. If the rain is heavy, these landslides can move forward as much as five feet in a day. If they are not stopped, she will be buried.

"All the water I consume, including tea and coffee, is bottled," she says:

I spend about $250 a month on bottled water. The West Virginia Water Company wants $46,000 to put water in to me, even though it is only five hundred feet of water line. I can't afford that. My garden, which we have had for thirty-seven years, is covered with coal slurry. We can't grow food in that. My front yard was washed out. My fruit trees are gone. My nut trees are gone. I was left with a massive trench in my front yard. That was in 2003 and I am still mad. My well is contaminated. And those who do drink the water get very sick, usually pancreatic cancer, liver disease, gallstones, or digestive tract problems. Our newest building in town is a kidney dialysis unit. The DEP [West Virginia Department of Environmental Protection] doesn't allow citizens to submit samples of their water. The DEP doesn't work for the citizens. It works for the coal companies. I have seen them lie to citizens so the coal companies can continue mountaintop removal. And people are being smothered to death from breathing all this coal dust. We thought about leavin', but my property has been devalued so much I can't get nothin' for it.

"The coal companies control everything, including what my kids learn in school," Gunnoe says. "My son's school textbook says that surface mining leaves the land in better condition once the mining is over. The coal companies and the government depend on us to be uneducated and moldable. I recently adopted my six-year-old nephew. Mountaintop removal scares him. We drive through the twilight and literally see mountains being pushed into the valleys. This is terrifying to a child. The disassembling of mountains—what does that message send to our kids?"

She adopted her nephew because her brother, after he broke his back working in a sawmill, became addicted to painkillers.

"He has been on OxyContin for the last eleven or twelve years," she says. "And once these people become addicted, they are like zombies. They will steal anything they can get their hands on. I bought my nephew a bicycle, but he never even saw it. It got sold for drugs.

"When I pick up my yearbook from high school, I can see on almost every page someone who has died of a drug overdose, and I am only forty-two," she says. "It kinda takes away from your class reunions.

"The best experts say we got about twenty-two years of coal left," she says. "But no one is thinking ahead. We should be figuring something out, and we should be doin' it quick, otherwise our kids will be left with no energy, no water, and no plans for what to do."

Gunnoe is a thin woman with curly black hair. She is part Cherokee. Her vocal opposition to the coal companies, like Larry Gibson's, has engendered the fury of many of her neighbors, who fear the loss of the coal industry will mean an end to any viable employment. One of her dogs was shot dead and left in the parking lot where her children catch the school bus. Another dog was shot and killed while tied up in the back of her house. The gas tank to her truck was filled with sand, requiring $1,200 in repairs. Her children have been taunted at school as "tree huggers." She has erected a six-foot protective fence around her house that she calls "my cage." But she says that even for the miners who blast away the mountains, the destruction can be overwhelming.

"I know men who work on these operations, and they are emotionally impacted," she says. "Not all of them want to be doin' what they are doin'. They don't have a choice. They fish and hunt in these mountains so they know what is happenin'. They are physically ripping out the backbone of this country, and they know it will never be the same. There is emotional stress in this."

As societies become more complex they inevitably become more precarious and vulnerable. As they begin to break down, the terrified and confused population withdraws from reality, unable to acknowledge their fragility and impending collapse. The elites retreat into isolated compounds, whether at Versailles, the Forbidden City, or modern palatial estates. They indulge in unchecked hedonism, the accumulation of wealth, and extravagant consumption. The suffering masses are repressed with greater and greater ferocity. Resources are depleted until they are exhausted. And then the hollowed-out edifice collapses. The Roman and Sumerian empires fell this way. The Mayan elite became, at the end, as the anthropologist Ronald Wright notes in *A Short History of Progress*, " . . . extremists, or ultraconservatives, squeezing the last drops of profit from nature and humanity."[13] This is how all civilizations, including our own, ossify and collapse.

The unrest in the Middle East, the implosion of national economies such as those of Ireland, Italy, and Greece, the increasing anger of a beleaguered working class at home and abroad, the desperate and growing human migrations, and the refusal to halt our destruction of the ecosystem, are the harbingers of our own decline. Our march toward self-annihilation has already obliterated ninety percent of the large fish in the oceans and wiped out half of the mature tropical forests, the lungs of the planet.[14] At this rate, by 2030, only ten percent of the Earth's tropical forests will remain.[15] Contaminated water kills more than six thousand people every day around the globe.[16] Greenhouse gases in the atmosphere are at 390 parts per million (ppm) and climbing,[17] with most climate scientists warning that the level must remain below 350 ppm to sustain life as we know it. The Intergovernmental Panel on Climate Change estimates that the measurement could reach 541 to 970 ppm by 2100. At that point, huge parts of the planet, beset with overpopulation, droughts, soil erosion, freak storms, massive crop failures, and rising sea levels, will be unfit for human existence. And yet we retreat into fantasy. The U.S. Senate, in the summer of 2010, refused to take a vote on a watered-down and largely ineffectual climate bill. The House, in April 2011, voted 184 to 240 against legislation asserting that global warming was real.[18]

The same happened on Easter Island. The inhabitants, when they first settled the sixty-four-square-mile island during the fifth century, found abundant freshwater and woods. Seafood was plentiful. Within five or six centuries, Easter Island's population swelled to some ten thousand people. The natural resources were depleted.

"Forest clearance for the growing of crops would have led to population increase, but also to soil erosion and decline of soil fertility," Paul Bahn and John Flenley write in *Easter Island, Earth Island*:

> Progressively more land would have had to be cleared. Trees and shrubs would also be cut down for canoe building, firewood, house construction, and for the timbers and ropes needed in the movement and erection of statues. Palm fruits [from the initially plentiful Chilean wine palm tree] would be eaten, thus reducing regeneration of the palm. Rats, introduced for food, could have fed on the palm fruits, multiplied rapidly and completely prevented palm regeneration. The overexploitation of prolific sea bird resources would have eliminated these for all but the offshore islets. Rats could have helped in this process by eating eggs. The abundant food provided by fishing, sea birds and rats would have encouraged rapid initial human population growth. Unrestrained human population increase would later put pressure on availability of land, leading to disputes and eventually warfare. . . . Inadequate canoes would restrict fishing to the inshore waters, leading to further decline in protein supplies. The result could have been general famine, warfare and the collapse of the whole economy, leading to a marked population decline.[19]

By the year 1400 the woods were gone. The soil had eroded and washed into the sea. The islanders began to fight over old timbers and were reduced to eating their dogs and the last nesting birds.

"Are the events of three hundred years ago on a small remote island of any significance to the world at large?" Bahn and Flenley ask. "Like the Earth, Easter Island was an isolated system. . . . They carried out for us the experiment of permitting unrestricted population growth, profligate use of resources, destruction of the environment, and boundless confidence in their religion to take care of the future. The result was an ecological disaster leading to a population crash. . . . Do we have to repeat the experiment on this grand scale?" [20]

"There is a feeling of powerlessness," says Julian Martin, a seventy-four-year-old retired high school teacher and the son of a coal miner. He says of those in the decayed coal towns:

> They have no money, very little land and huge trucks carrying one hundred and eighty thousand pounds of coal down a highway over and over. These

trucks can't go on the interstate they are so heavy. They are banned on the interstate. They were against the law in West Virginia, and they just changed the law. Now they are legal. If you grow up in one of these places like Naugatuck, Gilbert, or Krome and you see these huge monster trucks go by and maybe you get in your four-wheeler and get a look at these huge monster earthmover machines, you know you're nobody. This is the blitzkrieg. And someone wants you to fight back against an outfit that can take the tops off of mountains? You don't feel like you're a very big person.

"The coal companies are running people out," he says, as we speak on a gray, rainy afternoon in the town of Logan. "Eventually it will be like Cuba, where the United Fruit Company owned so much property that if you wanted to go from one end of the island to the other, you had to pass through their gates. Southern West Virginia will be owned by the coal companies, or they will abandon it and it will be this big wasteland.

"I'm scared every time I do anything," says Martin, who has joined protesters condemning mountaintop removal. "I am afraid of gettin' killed. And I don't know why I let that bother me. Hell, I'm seventy-four. I've had a good life, an excellent, fantastic life.

"An awful lot of the people in the coal camps are there because they can't get out," he says. "The people who got educations have left. You don't have a core of highly educated leadership, not that it has to be educated. Robert McNamara was educated and see what he did. My dad was uneducated. I was the first one to go to college. These were not stupid people. My grandpa was in the battle of Blair Mountain, he and his brother. They were plenty smart. But the highly talented, creative people have been sucked out of the Appalachians.

"It's a sacrifice zone," he says:

It's so the rest of the country can have electric toothbrushes and leave the lights on all night in parking lots for used cars and banks lit up all night long and shit like that. We have been a national sacrifice zone. Hell, that phrase was created thirty-five, forty years ago. Now it's terminal. There is no way to stop it. I haven't had any hope for a long time. But the only reason I keep goin' is, why the hell not? I'm goin' die. Shit, might as well hold my head up. I don't want Bill Raney, the president of the [West Virginia] Coal Association, to be able to tell his lies without somebody saying, "Bill, shit, that's not true."

These corporations are goin' to strip the whole country. If you face this reality then you become a guerrilla. You blow up the damn thing. I can't go there, because they will put me in the penitentiary, and I don't want to go there. I know they would catch me eventually.

⚜

About half of those living in McDowell County depend on some kind of relief check such as Social Security, Disability, Supplemental Security Income (SSI), Temporary Assistance for Needy Families, retirement benefits, and unemployment to survive. They live on the margins, check to check, expecting no improvement in their lives and seeing none. The most common billboards along the roads are for law firms that file disability claims and seek state and federal payments. "Disability and Injury Lawyers," reads one. It promises to handle "Social Security. Car Wrecks. Veterans. Workers' Comp." The 800 number ends in COMP. Harry M. Caudill, in his monumental 1963 book *Night Comes to the Cumberlands*, describes how relief checks became a kind of bribe for the rural poor in Appalachia. The decimated region was the pilot project for outside government assistance, which had issued the first food stamps in 1961 to a household of fifteen in Paynesville, West Virginia. "Welfarism" began to be practiced, as Caudill wrote, "on a scale unequalled elsewhere in America and scarcely surpassed anywhere in the world."[21] Government "handouts," he observed, were "speedily recognized as a lode from which dollars could be mined more easily than from any coal seam."[22] Obtaining the monthly "handout" became an art form. People were reduced to what Caudill called " . . . the tragic status of 'symptom hunters.' If they could find enough symptoms of illness, they might convince the physicians they were 'sick enough to draw' . . . to indicate such a disability as incapacitating the men from working. Then his children, as public charges, could draw enough money to feed the family."[23]

Joe and I are sitting in the Tug River Health Clinic in Gary with a registered nurse who does not want her name used. The clinic handles federal and state black lung applications. It runs a program for those addicted to prescription pills. It also handles what in the local vernacular is known as "the crazy check"—payments obtained for mental illness from Medicaid or SSI—a vital source of income for those whose five years of welfare payments have run out. Doctors willing to diagnose a patient as mentally ill are important to economic survival.

"They come in and want to be diagnosed as soon as they can for the crazy check," the nurse says. "They will insist to us they are crazy. They will tell us, 'I know I'm not right.' People here are very resigned. They will avoid working by being diagnosed as crazy."

The reliance on government checks, and a vast array of painkillers and opiates, has turned towns like Gary into modern opium dens. The painkillers Oxy-Contin, fentanyl—eighty times stronger than morphine—Lortab, as well as a wide variety of anti-anxiety medications such as Xanax, are widely abused. Many top off their daily cocktail of painkillers at night with sleeping pills and muscle relaxants. And for fun, addicts, especially the young, hold "pharm parties," in which they combine their pills in a bowl, scoop out handfuls of medication, swallow them, and wait to feel the result. A decade ago only about five percent of those seeking treatment in West Virginia needed help with opiate addiction. Today that number has ballooned to twenty-six percent. It recorded ninety-one overdose deaths in 2001. By 2008 that number had risen to three hundred and ninety. Drug overdoses are the leading cause of accidental death in West Virginia, and the state leads the country in fatal drug overdoses.[24] Oxy-Contin—nicknamed "hillbilly heroin"—is king. At a drug market like the Pines it costs a dollar a milligram. And a couple of 60- or 80-milligram pills sold at the Pines is a significant boost to a family's income. Not far behind OxyContin is Suboxone, the brand name for a drug whose primary ingredient is buprenorphine, a semisynthetic opioid. Dealers, many of whom are based in Detroit, travel from clinic to clinic in Florida to stock up on the opiates and then sell them out of the backs of gleaming SUVs in West Virginia, usually around the first of the month, when the government checks arrive. Those who have legal prescriptions also sell the drugs for a profit. Pushers are often retirees. They can make a few hundred extra dollars a month on the sale of their medications. The temptation to peddle pills is hard to resist.

We meet Vance Leach, forty-two, with his housemates, Wayne Hovack, forty, and Neil Heizer, thirty-one, in Gary. The men scratch out a meager existence, mostly from disability checks. They pool their resources to pay for food, electricity, water, and heat. In towns like Gary, communal living is common.

When he graduated from the consolidated high school in Welch in 1987, Leach drifted. He went to Florida and worked for the railroad. He returned home and worked in convenience stores. He held a job for eleven years for

Turner Vision, a company that took orders for satellite dishes. He lost the job when the company was sold. He worked at Welch Community Hospital for six months and then as an assistant manager of the McDowell 3, the Welch movie theater. His struggle with drugs, which he acknowledges but does not want to discuss in detail, led to his losing his position at the theater. He is preparing to start a course to become licensed as a Methodist minister and serves the two local United Methodist churches, neither of which muster more than about a half dozen congregants on a Sunday. The twenty theology classes, which cost $300 a class, are held on weekends in Ripley, about four hours from Gary.

Leach is seated in his small living room with Hovack, who bought the house when his home was destroyed by flooding, and Heizer. Hovack was given $40,000 from the Federal Emergency Management Authority to relocate. Heizer tells us how he almost lost his life from an overdose a few weeks before.

The three men are the sons and grandsons of coal miners. None of them worked in the mines.

"My dad worked with his dad," Heizer says, nodding towards Leach. "My grandfather died in the coal mines in 1965. He had a massive heart attack. Forty-nine years old."

"It was good growin' up in McDowell County twenty-plus years ago," Leach says.

"Except for when the mines would go on strike," adds Hovack. "That was rough. I can remember that."

"Welch used to be a boomin' place," Vance says. "When you went to Welch you really thought you went somewhere."

"Used to be about three *thee-ay-ters* in Welch many, many years ago," Leach says.

"All them stores," says Hovack. "I can remember my mom goin' to take me to Penny's and Collins. An' H&M. But when the U.S. Steel cleaning plant went out, that was it for this county."

"I went to school here in Gary, and when the plant closed down I was 'bout twelve or thirteen and my friends in school would say, 'My dad and mom, we're movin' 'cause they have to go look for work," Hovack says.

"You seen a lot of people depressed after that, wonderin' how they were gonna make it, how they were gonna pay their bills, how they were gonna live, how they were gonna pay their mortgage," says Leach. "It was devastating. A lot of people didn't have a good education, so there wasn't anything else to turn to. The coal mines was all they ever knew. My dad, he didn't finish high school. He quit in his senior year, went right into the mine."

Heizer speaks in the slowed cadence of someone who puts a lot of medication into his body. He recently lost his car after crashing it into a fence. His life with his two roommates is sedentary. The three men each have a television in their bedrooms and two more they share, including the big-screen television that, along with an electric piano for Hovack, were bought with Heizer's first disability check. The men spent the $20,000 from the check in a few days.

"I became disabled back in late 2006," Heizer tells us. "I had degenerative disc disease and I hurt my back. I was workin' at this convenience store. They knew that I had a back injury, but yet they had me come in on extra shifts and unload the truck. Now I've got four discs jus' layin' on top of each other, no cushion be-

tween them. For three years I lived here without an income, and my dad helped support me, and then last November I finally was awarded my disability."

Heizer, who is gay, saw his drug addiction spiral out of control four years ago after his boyfriend committed suicide. He tells us he has been struggling with his weight—he weighs three hundred and twenty-four pounds—as well as diabetes, gout, and kidney stones. These diseases are common in southern West Virginia and have contributed to a steady rise in mortality rates over the past three decades.

OxyContin takes a a few hours to kick in when swallowed. If the pills are crushed, mixed with water, and injected with a syringe, the effect is immediate. Heizer says that after the drug companies began releasing pills with a rubbery consistency, they could not be ground down. Heizer heated the newer pills in a microwave and snorted them—leading to his recent overdose. It took place at

Vance Leach, Neil Heizer, and Wayne Hovack at home in Gary, West Virginia.

his mother's house. He went into renal failure. He stopped breathing. His kidneys shut down. He was Medevac'd to a hospital in Charleston, the capital of West Virginia, where he stayed for four days.

"I was just sittin' around watching TV and started aspiratin'," Heizer says flatly. "The medication was goin' into my lungs. You gurgle with every breath. You are drownin', basically. I remember walkin' down my mom's steps and gettin' in the ambulance. I remember at Welch, they put me on the respirator and then transferred me. After they put me on the respirator, I stopped breathing on my own. And then I remember in Charleston wakin' up an' they had my hands restrained so I wouldn't pull the tubes out. I had a real close call."

The men sit in front of their flat-screen television and chat about friends, classmates, and relatives who died of overdoses. Hovack talks about a niece in her early twenties, the mother of two small children. She recently died of a drug overdose. He tells us about a high-school classmate, an addict living in a shack we can see from the window. The shack has no electricity or running water. The men, who rarely leave the house, mention the high bails being set for selling drugs, with some reaching $50,000 to $80,000. They joke about elderly grandmothers being hauled off to prison for drug dealing.

"I've seen a lot of busts in the county over the last few years, and a lot of the people that have been arrested are elderly people that are sellin' their medication just to live," Vance says. "When I was workin' at the hospital I seen ODs all the time. Young people were comin' in. It's bad. The depression and the pain. I guess some people that hang and live in this area, they just have to turn to somethin'."

"Since the drug problem is so bad you see the crime rate as well," Leach says. "People breakin' into homes, stealin' whatever they can to sell or pawn, just to keep up with their drug habit."

Heizer, seven weeks later, dies of a drug overdose, sitting on the living room couch in front of the big-screen television.

❧❖❧

Prisons are supposed to be the new growth industry. West Virginia has six large federal prisons and thirteen state prisons. Welch has two of the state prisons, one of which, Stevens Correctional Facility, is located in the former

Welch city hospital. Another federal prison is under construction on the rubble left behind from a strip-mining operation. The McDowell County Correctional Center occupies the old courthouse in the center of Welch. Prisons are touted by state officials as bonanzas for the unemployed and underemployed. But prison operators complain that local applicants often cannot pass the proficiency exams or the drug tests. For these reasons, most of the jobs go to people who do not live in the county.[25]

Outside the post office in the town of Sylvester in Boone County, where the Elk Run Coal Company plant has its operations on the edge of town, we meet Harry White, an eighty-year-old retired miner and Korean War veteran. He is wearing a blue baseball cap and a West Virginia University sweatshirt. Like everyone else in the town, he lives in clouds of noxious coal dust.

"You can't even sit outside," he says.

He runs his index finger along the sill of the post office window. It is black with coal dust. He has little time for "scabs," the nonunionized miners that have taken over the work in the mining industry. He believes that a spate of recent mine disasters happened because the unions have been broken and the mining companies are no longer forced to comply with minimal safety standards. His father was a miner and died of black lung disease in 1946.

"He worked that night and came home and died at 3:33 in the morning," he says. "He ran the cut machine that cut the coal. He died on March 3. We buried him on March 5. I started working in the mines on March 7."

White, however, has little time for the environmental activists who come from outside the state to protest mountaintop removal. The activists, often dressed in baggy cotton clothes and not given much to bathing, are a public-relations gift to the coal companies, which tag them and their local supporters as "tree huggers."

"If I was runnin' things I would put them on a ship, send them out to sea, and sink 'em," White says of the activists. "They don't belong here. They never worked a day in their life. They draw a lot of benefits, Social Security, anything they want. They are lazy."

Workers in this country paid for their rights by suffering brutal beatings, mass expulsions from company housing and jobs, crippling strikes, targeted assassinations of union leaders, and armed battles with hired-gun thugs and state militias. Unions created the middle class. They opened up our democracy.

Federal marshals, state militias, sheriff's deputies, and at times even U.S. Army troops, along with the courts and legislative bodies, were repeatedly used to crush organized workers. Striking sugar cane workers were gunned down in Thibodaux, Louisiana, in 1887. Steel workers were shot to death in 1892 in Homestead, Pennsylvania. Railroad workers were murdered in the nationwide Pullman strike of 1894. Coal miners were massacred at Ludlow, Colorado, in 1914 and at Matewan, West Virginia, in 1920.

The Rockefellers, the Mellons, the Carnegies, and the Morgans—the Goldman Sachs and Walmart of their day—never gave a damn about workers. All they cared about was profit. The eight-hour workday, the minimum wage, Social Security, pensions, job safety, paid vacations, retirement benefits, and health insurance were achieved because hundreds of thousands of workers physically fought a system of capitalist exploitation. They rallied around radicals such as Mary Harris "Mother" Jones—arrested at one point in the West Virginia coalfields for reading the Declaration of Independence to a crowd of miners—United Mine Workers' President John L. Lewis, and "Big" Bill Haywood and his Wobblies, as well as Socialist presidential candidate Eugene V. Debs.

"The whole history of the progress of human liberty shows that all concessions yet made to her august claims, have been born of earnest struggle . . . " Frederick Douglass said. "If there is no struggle there is no progress. Those who profess to favor freedom and yet deprecate agitation are men who want crops without plowing up the ground. They want rain without thunder and lightning. They want the ocean without the awful roar of its many waters. The struggle may be a moral one, or it may be a physical one, or it may be both moral and physical, but it must be a struggle. Power concedes nothing without a demand. It never did and it never will. Find out just what any people will quietly submit to and you have found out the exact measure of injustice and wrong which will be imposed upon them, and these will continue till they are resisted with either words or blows, or with both. The limits of tyrants are prescribed by the endurance of those whom they oppress."[26]

Sylvester is one of the few towns in this region that was not built and run by the coal companies. The residents kept out the coal camps and land companies. They built their own homes. They owned their own property. The area has long had a streak of fierce independence. When employees of the Webb Coal Mining Company at Ferndale, Local 1057 went on strike in 1922, company strike-breakers evicted the families of the miners and their furniture from company houses, the usual practice coal companies used against strikers. The miners set up a tent city in what is now Sylvester. They lived in this tent community for eighteen months, which included a harsh winter. A letter from Nellie Susan Miller in the 1996 Sylvester Dog Patch Reunion booklet reads: "Grandpa William Brinigar was among those trying to unionize the mines. His family was put out of their house (on Cabin Creek) and my Dad was born in a tent town of unionizers in Sylvester."

We are sitting with Pauline Canterberry and Mary Miller, both in their eighties, at the dining room table of Miller's home in Sylvester. Each has grown children who moved away years ago.

Through the back window we can see, on the ridge above the house, the Elk Run coal processing plant. The large white dome dominates the gray landscape. The Massey Energy Coal Company uses nonunionized labor and has presided over a series of deadly mine disasters due to its poor safety record. In 1981, Massey, operating through a subsidiary company named Elk Run Mining, opened an underground mine four hundred feet from the town. Elk Run asked the DEP for a permit to put in a coal processing plant on the bluff above the town. The women, along with most of the town, knew that because the winds nearly always blow west to east, the coal dust would saturate the community.[27]

"In nineteen and ninety-six, the permit came out for that," Canterberry says. "It takes a lot of water to operate a preparation plant, 'cause all that coal has to be washed. That's what goes into your slurry impoundments. We have an impoundment beyond this hill here that has two billion gallons of slurry in it. It's nothing but black toxic waste. It has over sixty chemicals in it."

"And if the impoundment broke," I ask, "where would the slurry go?"

"It could break two or three different ways," Canterberry says. "If it broke from the face of it, because the face of it comes this way, it would come out and hit the river there. But there's a mountain in front, so it wouldn't go on, it would hit it and it would split. Now you look around here and you see there's no escape routes outta here."

"We have three up this valley that are like loaded guns," she continues. "These hills are like honeycombs. They were mined in the early 1900s. They were mined in the '20s. They were mined again in the '40s. They were mined in the '60s. When they're minin' coal, you're supposed to, by law, leave so much coal to secure the mountain, you know, that it will hold up. But they don't do that, they'll go just as far as they can. And they could break through anywhere. There's a lot of weak spots in these mountains."

The women organized a petition against the permit. It was signed by seventy-five percent of the town. A hearing was held at the local elementary school on November 3, 1996. The room was packed with angry townspeople. But the DEP ignored them. The coal processing plant was built. Huge belt lines to transport the coal were installed. Mounds of coal heaped up around the plant.[28]

"They started the plant, April of nineteen and ninety-seven, and within a month, we were literally *covered* with coal dust," Canterberry says.

The processing plant was worked twenty-four hours a day, seven days a week, spewing black grit and dust. Huge eighteen-wheeler trucks, up to thirty-five thousand of them a year, roared through the town with loads of coal. Houses, lawn furniture, cars, grass, and clotheslines were coated in the grit. No one would sit outside. Backyard cookouts and barbecues ended.[29]

"We didn't even want to walk down the street because it blew in our face," Canterberry says.

The town filed complaint after complaint for two years. The complaints were ignored. The residents watched in horror as a massive slurry impoundment grew to the size of a small lake above the town. Should it break its banks, the impoundment would wipe out Sylvester in a matter of minutes. By April 2000, Elk Run, confronted with the evidence and complaints of the townspeople in a hearing before the DEP, agreed to install a screen to help contain the dust. A system to sprinkle the coal with water was installed, although residents say it is rarely used due to the cost.[30]

"Children would come in off the school ground covered with coal dust," Miller says. "The school cooks had to rewash the pots and cooking utensils every morning to get off the coal dust. They put everything in plastic bags the night before to keep them clean. The school was finally closed, mainly because of the coal dust."

The citizens were granted a hearing in October 2000 with the Office of Surface Mining. The board of five ordered Elk Run to halt the emissions of coal dust, but nothing changed. The two women, distraught at the inaction, went to the state legislature to try to get a bill passed that would limit the amount of coal dust that could be released in the air. The Division of Air Quality killed the bill.[31]

The DEP suggested that the women collect dust samples and take videos to illustrate the problem. The two women collected the data and videos for two years.

"We had a team of about eight that took turns going," Canterberry says. "Two and a half years. Every eight days. Faithful. Faithful. Come sleet, snow, rain, hail, or sunshine we did the samples faithfully, filmed, dated, and stored them in Ziploc. The DEP never asked for them."

The women got a lawyer in Charleston in 2000 to take their case. They convinced one hundred and sixty four residents, three-quarters of the town, to join a lawsuit against Massey Energy. They asked for compensation, punitive

Mary Miller and Pauline Canterberry, Sylvester, West Virginia.

damages, and a cessation of the coal dust emissions. The pressure—and the election of a new governor, who appointed Matt Crum, a more responsive head of the DEP—saw Massey install a dust-monitoring system in the town. The two women and other townspeople took daily readings of the system. When their data did not match the data collected by Massey Energy, the company removed the system.[32]

On October 29, 2001, townspeople filmed a heavy cloud of coal dust as it left the preparation plant at Elk Run and drifted in a dark mass over the town. Dust on the homemade film is seen drifting downward, coating the elementary school playground, cars, houses, lawns, and the road in black grit. When the film was sent to the DEP, Massey was ordered to close the plant or cover it with a dome. The company spent $1.5 million to construct the dome. The dome has been ruptured twice. Its presence has reduced but not ended the daily emissions. It was clear the plant was going to stay. The townspeople bringing the lawsuit had appraisals made of their homes. Most homes had decreased in value by eighty to ninety percent due to the coal dust and mountaintop removal.[33]

When the townspeople's lawsuit finally got into court, much of their evidence was tossed out. They were told they could not involve Massey Energy in the lawsuit because Massey was not responsible for Elk Run Mining, even though Elk Run was solely owned by Massey. The court would not let the townspeople submit as evidence thirty-two violations the company had received for contaminating Sylvester's drinking water. Judge Lee Schlaegel dismissed the violations as nothing more than "parking tickets." But the court did rule that the plant was releasing too much coal dust and required the company to pay comprehensive damages along with the trial expenses, court costs, and attorney fees. The company was told it could not run more than seven thousand coal trucks through the town a month. It had been running thirty-five thousand. The company was ordered to purchase a vacuum sweeper and clean the town streets once a week. It was told to install dust monitors to measure the amount of released coal dust.[34]

The ruling made little improvement. The coal trucks still spewed dust and chewed up the highways, the plant still released clouds of dust, the water was still polluted, and the air was still filled with carcinogens. Four years after the suit, the townspeople got the company to establish a warning system to alert residents if the massive sludge impoundment broke.

Massey, the third-largest coal company in the country, has, over the past decade, leveled an area the size of Delaware—1.4 million acres—and left behind a poisoned and dead landscape. Coal companies like Massey rack up appalling safety and environmental violations. Yet for such companies, it is less expensive to pay the fines than comply with the strictures of the Clean Water Act or mine safety standards. The EPA office in West Virginia rarely enforces the fines, and when Massey was fined for violations over a six-year period by the federal EPA office, the company paid $20 million,[35] less than one percent of what was required under the law. The Sylvester lawsuit brought the town $100,000. In the next six months, Massey amassed another four thousand violations.

"Our politicians are so indebted to the coal industry, for favors, through campaigns, by the time they run for office, that they can't make decisions solely on their own," says Canterberry. "Massey had given a donation of $4 million to the politicians in West Virginia."

Elk Run's coal dust containment dome, Sylvester, West Virginia.

"Not only coal mining, but timberin', and gas—there's gas in these mountains—and yet we're the poorest state in the nation. Something's wrong. Something's drastically wrong," Canterberry says. "But you know why they want to keep the people down and under their thumb. What, the first thing they do when you go to the doctor is that they want to throw dope atchya.

"When people moved into this town, it was as near to Camelot as you'd want it to be," Canterberry continues. "You knew that everybody else would look after your children the same as you did, and you looked after their children. All the children that grew up here will tell you the same thing. But they all had to leave because there was no work or anything here for them. Mary's children ran away from here, my children went away from here 'cause I told them, 'There's nothing here for you.' "

"There's a lotta sickness around here," Miller says. "We've had a lot of people that's got kidney problems . . . "

"Bronchitis . . . " Canterberry adds.

"Dialysis . . . There's a lot of Alzheimer's . . . " Miller says.

"And cancer is rampant here," Canterberry says. "What was it, two weeks ago, four died in one week with cancer? You look at our prayer list for church, it lists cancer, cancer, cancer, cancer, cancer. Kidney problems, dialysis. We never used to have that here. We'd swim in that river, as clean as any well water you'd ever want to drink. But it sure isn't now."

From 2000 to 2010, Don Blankenship was chairman and CEO of Massey Energy. He is the personification of the coal companies' indifference to human life. Blankenship refused to recognize unions or hire unionized miners. His retirement was triggered in part by the death of twenty-nine miners on April 5, 2010, in an explosion at Massey's Upper Big Branch Mine, which had accumulated four hundred and fifty-eight safety violations that year.[36] It was the worst mine disaster in forty years.[37]

Blankenship grew up in poverty—he had lived for a time in a trailer—in Stopover, Kentucky, where his divorced mother ran a convenience store and gas station for forty years. He trained as an accountant at a local college and clawed his way to the top of Massey.

When Massey coal slurry contaminated the wells near Blankenship's palatial hilltop home, the company built a water line to his house from a neighboring town, bypassing all of Blankenship's neighbors. A photograph of Blankenship vacationing on the French Riviera with West Virginia Supreme

Coal trucks on the mountain roads of southwest West Virginia.

Court Justice Spike Maynard was taken shortly before November 2007, when Maynard voted with the majority in a three-to-two decision to reverse a $76 million judgment against Massey Energy. The photograph was published in 2008 in the *New York Times*.[38]

In 2004, Blankenship helped rid the state of a West Virginia Supreme Court Justice, Warren McGraw, whom he considered too friendly to workers. Blankenship contributed $3 million to the And For The Sake of the Kids PAC, which highlighted a case in which McGraw had been part of a three-to-two majority that had freed a mentally disturbed child molester, who then went to work in a school. McGraw was defeated and replaced by Blankenship crony Brent Benjamin.[39]

"It's like a jungle, where a jungle is survival of the fittest," Blankenship told a documentary filmmaker in the 1980s. "Unions, communities, people—everybody's gonna have to learn to accept that in the United States you have a capitalist society, and that capitalism, from a business standpoint, is survival of the most productive."[40]

❧❦❧

The destruction of the water supply has left households dependent on bottled water. Joe and I drive up a narrow mud road in Prenter, where the water was poisoned by mine waste a few years ago. We park next to a small, dilapidated house with a tattered Marine Corps flag flapping from the front fence. We knock on the door. Patty Sebok, who was raised on the other side of the road, answers it. We enter her living room, leaving our muddy boots by the door. She says that when she was a child, the water in her parents' home was oddly colored and had a strange odor. She finally moved out of the holler when the water became so fetid she could not drink it. The state piped in water for some of the residents in the lower end of the holler after several, including Sebok, made repeated trips to the state capital carrying glass jars filled with the murky water from their wells.

"It was what they call iron water," she says, "turns everything red, spots it yellah, that rusty look. But, everybody always said, 'Well, you know, that's just the geographical nature of living around here.'"

She and the other residents in the impoverished hollow in Prenter were unaware that thousands of gallons of contaminated coal slurry were being pumped by the mining companies into abandoned mine shafts around them and leeching into the groundwater.

"Everybody had health problems," she says, "but you know how it is. You're busy with your life. You're going through your work, taking care of your family, doing whatever. Unless it's real close family, people just weren't talking about all these things and connectin' the dots."

Neighbors around her were dying in alarming numbers from brain tumors and cancer. Kidney stones were so frequent that she, and many residents in the holler, had to have their gallbladders removed.

"The water smells like a cross between rotten eggs and sewer," Sebok says. "So I've been told that's sulfur. It dries your hair. It dries your skin. It stains even clear glass yellah. And if it does that to hard surfaces, what does it do to the inside of the body?"

"A lot of people didn't want to believe their water was bad because they are coal mining families," she says. "They just didn't want to hear it, because, I mean, it's a hard choice when you gotta make a living, or you gotta say your water is bad from the company you're working for. They're scared."

Her son, Ryan, twenty-three, has just returned from training for the Marine Corps Reserve. He passes through the room with a quick nod. By the time he was five, Ryan's teeth were so decayed from the water she took him to a dentist to have them capped.

"People said to me, 'Well, I wouldn't waste all that money on that, I'd just get 'em pulled,' and I said, 'What's he supposed to do until he's seven or eight?'" she says. " 'He won't have any teeth, you know?' "

"It seems like there is a military tradition here," says Joe. "A lot of people go into the military. Is there a sense of patriotism here?"

"Oh, sure," she says.

"For what?" Joe asks. "The United States?"

"For our freedoms," she says. "But yet, we have to fight for water here, and for medical care. You have to fight everybody here. And it's either fight, get out, shut up, lie down, die. What are you gonna do?"

"What do you think the coal companies want to do?" I ask.

"Smash it, grab it, run with the profit, just as fast as they can," she says.

We find Ken Hechler, ninety-four years old, slightly bent with age and dependent on a walker, in his cluttered basement apartment across from the state capitol in Charleston. Hechler was one of the few honest politicians in the state.

He refused money from the coal companies as a member of the U.S. House of Representatives for eighteen years and as the Secretary of State for West Virginia for sixteen years. And when he got out of politics, he did not sell his services to corporations or lobbying firms. He remains a fixture at rallies to oppose mountaintop removal, as well as those to defend the rights of miners. He now attends in his wheelchair. He is a throwback to an older time, when the liberal wing of the Democratic Party stood with working men and women and defied big business.

Hechler has a mischievous sense of humor, quick wit, and an amazing recall for dates, facts, and information, along with a deep disgust for the coal companies and corporations that are destroying his state and the nation.

He was drafted into the Army in 1942, passing the medical exam by memorizing the eye chart to mask his poor eyesight. At the conclusion of the war, with the rank of major, he was assigned to interview many of the captured senior Nazi commanders, several of whom would be executed or commit suicide following the Nuremberg Trials, including Hermann Göring.

He returned from Europe and worked as President Harry Truman's speech writer and then ran for Congress in West Virginia, serving in the House from 1959 to 1977. Hechler was elected the Secretary of State for West Virginia from 1985 to 2001.

"Coal industry has deep pockets, and they buy off members of the legislature, members of Congress, even judicial officials, by contributing big bucks to their campaigns," he says. "Every governor that we've had, ever since a renegade man named [William C.] Marland, who first introduced a severance tax on coal, which caused the legislature to reject it. They virtually ran him out of office. And he turned to alcohol. He left the state, and somebody discovered he was driving a taxicab in Chicago. He was the only farsighted governor that was doing things for the people and for the state that made sense. Every other governor we've had, Democrat or Republican, failed. Two of them went to prison."

By the time Hechler arrived in West Virginia, the glory days of the United Mine Workers Union of America under John Lewis had ended. By the 1960s the union was headed by Tony Boyle, who Hechler calls "corrupt and murderous." Boyle saw the union as a route to personal enrichment.

"Boyle fought me every step of the way on my efforts to bring an end to the excessive amount of coal dust in the mines," Hechler says:

Then when a candidate ran against him named Jock Yablonski, he sent out a contract and had Yablonski, his wife, and his daughter murdered, around Christmas-New Year 1969. He served a life term and died in prison, as well as the three triggermen. The first inkling I got of Boyle's ineptitude was, you know, we had a major disaster on the 20th of November 1968, which killed seventy-eight miners at Farmington. Whenever there was a mine disaster Lewis used to go down into the mines and emerge with a blackened face and denounce the industrial murder that had occurred. He was a great hero among the miners for that reason: he always stood up for them. Boyle came to Farmington the day after the disaster in a long black limousine, in a new suit with a rose in his buttonhole. And, in front of the widows of that disaster, he said, "This happens to be one of the best companies so far as cooperation with the union is concerned." Immediately his reputation went downhill. His people contacted me after the disaster and said, "We want you to introduce two bills in Congress, one that has to do with black lung, and a second that has to do with safety. And after you introduce the black lung bill, we will quietly bury it and just support the safety bill." And I said, "You're absolutely wrong. Now's the time to get both of these together in one measure," which I eventually succeeded in doing.

Heckler's hearing aid begins to beep because the battery is low. He gets up and rummages through a cluttered desk drawer to find a replacement.

"Why didn't they want to support the black lung bill?" I ask.

"They thought it couldn't pass," he says:

And I didn't think it could pass at first until I began to raise hell. You know, I started out in Congress as an activist but found that wasn't enough, so I became an agitator and I found *that* wasn't enough so I became a hell-raiser, and that was effective. That was probably the proudest thing I ever did in my life, to get that bill through and pretty much the way I wrote it, even though I was not a member of the committee. I used effective tactics. For example, the widows of the Farmington disaster asked me to meet with them right after the disaster, and I thought it was primarily to console them on the loss of their husbands. But one of them stuck her finger in my chest and said, "You're a Congressman, why don't you do something about this?" And I said,

"Will you help me?" I said, "I'll pay your way to Washington to lobby the members of the House and Senate from non-coal-mining states, and tell them how important it is that these stringent health and safety measures be enacted, because the efforts to protect the safety and health of coal miners have always failed in the past." The coal industry had so much lobbying power it prevented stringent measures. Congress had always been affected by the demands of the coal industry. The coal industry has never invested a cent into improving safety, but they have invested millions into increasing production. Doctors, many of whom were partially on the payroll of coal companies, were saying that not only is coal dust not harmful but in some cases it might even prevent pneumonia or tuberculosis. It took great courageous heroes like Dr. Donald Rasmussen and Dr. I. E. Buff and Dr. Hawey Wells, three rebels who challenged the medical industry and pointed out that coal dust is what caused the incurable disease which has killed and disabled so many miners.

When President Richard Nixon contemplated vetoing the bill, Hechler called a press conference. He announced that if the bill was not signed into law there would be a nationwide coal strike.

"Hell," he says, laughing, "I didn't know if there would actually be a coal strike, but it scared Nixon into signing it."

"What do you think the future will be like?" I ask.

"Pretty bad," Hechler answers. "Getting worse. You know, I was very active in the civil-rights movement. We had a period in our history when I thought we were going upward. Working for Harry Truman was a great thrill because he never allowed anybody to take a poll. He said that polls give you a temporary snapshot of perhaps ill-informed public opinion that hasn't been corrected through education, but they don't tell you the difference between justice and injustice. That was his moral compass when he was deciding whether to sign or veto a bill. He was way ahead of his time on civil rights, so at that time I was very optimistic about the future of the nation, but I'm sorry to say that I'm not optimistic now."

~✦~

Joe and I made our way through the underbrush up the slope of Blair Mountain with Kenny King. King is part of a group that is trying to save the mountain, slated to be destroyed for its coal seams. Blair was the site of the largest civil uprising and armed insurgency in the United States since the Civil War. In late August and early September 1921, as many as fifteen thousand armed miners, angered by a series of assassinations of union leaders and their chief supporters, as well as mass evictions, blacklists, and wholesale firings by coal companies, for five days faced militias and police, who were equipped with heavy machine guns and held back advancing miners from behind a trench system still visible on the ridge above us.

At the time of the uprising, thousands of miners and their families, thrown out of company housing because of union activity, were living in tent encampments along the Tug River. The incident that would set off the rebellion happened on May 19, 1920. Agents from the Baldwin-Felts Detective Agency— hired company goons referred to derisively by the miners as "gun thugs"— arrived in the town of Matewan to evict miners and their families from company houses. The local sheriff, Sid Hatfield, had turned down the usual coal company enticements to turn against the union. When Hatfield now tried to arrest the company-hired agents, a gun battle broke out, leaving ten dead, including Matewan's mayor.[41] Hatfield was indicted on murder charges but was acquitted in January 1921, which infuriated the mine owners. They had Hatfield charged after his acquittal with dynamiting a coal tipple. When Hatfield and his young wife, as well as deputy and friend Ed Chambers and his wife, walked up the courthouse steps in Welch for the new trial, they were assassinated by a group of Baldwin-Felts agents standing at the top of the stairs.[42] The killings triggered the armed rebellion, with many of the Winchester rifles and handguns allegedly supplied by the United Mine Workers Union. The coal operators hastily organized militias and hired private planes to drop homemade explosives on the miners. General Billy Mitchell sent Army bombers to carry out aerial surveillance of the miners. It was only when the U.S. Army was ordered into the coalfields that the miners gave up. By the time the five days of shooting ended, perhaps one hundred miners were dead. The state of West Virginia indicted 1,217 miners for complicity in the rebellion, including charges of murder and treason. Many miners spent several years in prison. The union was effectively broken. It was not reconstituted until 1935, when the Roosevelt administration legalized union organizing.[43]

Kenny King searches for evidence of the Battle of Blair Mountain.

The physical eradication of Blair Mountain, part of the methodical destruction of southern West Virginia, will obliterate not only a peak, but also one of the most important physical memorials to the long struggle for justice. The battle marked a moment when miners came close to breaking the stranglehold of the coal companies. And its neglected slopes, soon perhaps to be blasted into rubble, are a reminder of the relentless assault of corporations.

"The mountains that have been destroyed still exist in the mind of God," novelist Denise Giardina said at the memorial service in Beckley for the fiery activist Judy Bonds, who died at fifty-eight of cancer:

I said that as a way of addressing my own grief about what we have lost. Perhaps the most disheartening thing in this struggle against mountaintop removal is not the power of the coal industry. It is that if President Obama should issue a proclamation this very afternoon saying that mountaintop removal would no longer be allowed, we would still have lost five hundred mountains, mountains that aren't coming back. And yet. And yet I said that years ago, and I repeat it today. Those mountains still exist in the mind of God. Wherever God is, those mountains are. And our friend Judy Bonds, whose loss we grieve today, still exists in the mind of God. Wherever God is, Judy is. She is surely among those lovely mountains she fought so hard to protect. And where those mountains are now, where Judy is, no coal company can reach.

How many thousands of lives were lost in these mines and hollers for profit? How many families were left after mine accidents without fathers, sons and brothers? How many miners suffered and choked to death from black lung disease so shareholders and coal owners could enjoy a life of luxury and opulence? How many of the poor here have died of cancer? How many mountains have to be destroyed to make a few people rich? And why did we let them do it?

In a small coal museum in Madison, West Virginia, Joe and I find a copy of a note taken from the body of Jacob L. Vowell, who died in a mine explosion on May 19, 1902. He was the husband of Ellen and the father of Elbert and four other children. The explosion took the lives of one hundred and eighty-four miners.

"Ellen, darling, goodbye for us both," the shaky handwriting reads. "Elbert said the Lord has saved him. We are all praying for air to support us, but it is getting so bad without air. Ellen, I want you to live right and come to heaven. Raise the children the best you can. Oh How I wish to be with you, goodbye. Bury me and Elbert in the same grave by little Eddy. Goodbye. Ellen, goodbye Lily, goodbye Jemmie, goodbye Horace. Is 25 minutes after two. There is a few of us alive yet. Jake and Elbert. Oh God for one more breath. Ellen remember me as long as you live. Goodbye darling."

4

DAYS OF SLAVERY

Immokalee, Florida

※

In America today we are seeing a race to the bottom, the middle class is collapsing, poverty is increasing. What I saw in Immokalee is the bottom in the race to the bottom.

—SENATOR BERNIE SANDERS

R ODRIGO ORTIZ, A TWENTY-SIX-YEAR-OLD FARMWORKER—A SHORT man in a tattered baseball cap and soiled black pants that are too long—stands forlornly in the half-light in front of the La Fiesta Supermarket on South 3rd Street in Immokalee, Florida. He is waiting for work in the tomato fields. Ortiz is on the lowest rung of the $50 billion, labor-intensive fresh produce industry in the United States. The supermarket, which opens at 3:30 A.M. to sell tacos to the workers, is a whitewashed, single-story cement block building. Workers inside the supermarket, which has brightly colored piñatas hanging from the ceiling and ads in Spanish for MoneyGram International and prepaid phone cards, are lined up before a grill, where two short-order cooks scrape their spatulas noisily on the greasy metal griddle covered with frying strips of beef.

Hoping for work in the La Fiesta parking lot, Immokalee, Florida.

On the walls outside the front door, where knots of workers congregate, are painted the words *Check Cashing, Grocery, Carnicería, Taquería, Panadería,* and *Tortillería,* along with a sign posted by the Collier County Sheriff's Office: "Consumption of Alcoholic Beverages in public is a violation of county ordinance. Violators will be prosecuted."

The parking lot is jammed with a few hundred workers seeking a day's employment—referred to in Spanish as *el labor*—from crew leaders who operate school buses painted white and blue with logos such as "P. Cardenas Harvesting," "Antonio Juarez & Sons New Generation," and "Efrain Juarez and Sons." Diesel fumes from the running bus engines fill the air. Groups of men and a few women, speaking softly in Spanish and Creole, cluster on the asphalt or sit at picnic tables. Roosters crow as the first light of dawn appears above the flat, dull horizon. Crew leaders have backed up pickup trucks to a large ice machine on the wall of the supermarket. They take turns shoveling ice into ten-gallon plastic orange containers. They lug the containers to the trucks. The pickers carry the water from the melted ice into the sweltering, humid fields, where temperatures soar to 90 degrees and above.

Harvesting tomatoes and other produce from the nation's agricultural fields is arguably the worst job in the country.[1] Florida produces about forty percent of the nation's fresh domestic tomatoes.[2] There are weeks with no work and no wages. Once it starts to rain, field-workers are packed onto the buses and sent home. They can travel one or two hours on a bus and be prevented from beginning work for a few more hours because of the dew on the plants. Workers must bend over plants for hours in blazing temperatures. They are exposed to toxic chemicals and pesticides. They often endure verbal and physical abuse from crew leaders. Women suffer sexual harassment. The U.S. Department of Labor estimates that the agriculture industry has a death rate seven times higher than the average rate of most industries.[3] The meager pay, along with endemic wage theft and systemic minimum wage violations, keep the majority of workers below the poverty line.

The average annual income for farmworkers is between $10,000 and $12,499, according to the 2005 Department of Labor's National Agricultural Workers Survey, about a third of the national average. A laborer must pick almost two-and-a-quarter tons of tomatoes a day to earn minimum wage. This is twice what they had to pick thirty years ago for the same amount of money.[4] Half the people in Immokalee live below the poverty line. Two-thirds of the children who enter kindergarten never graduate from high school.[5] And on any one morning as many as half of the laborers who wait in the collection spots walk away without a job.

Ortiz is not fortunate. The last buses leave by 7:00 A.M. He walks forlornly to the overcrowded trailer he shares with nine other men. He worries that this week he may not get the $50 he needs to pay his landlord.[6]

"*Esta semana solo trabajé tres días*"—"I only had three days of work this week," Ortiz says. "I don't know how I will pay my rent."

Ortiz sends about $100 home to Mexico every month to support elderly

Waiting to be taken to the fields.

parents. He hovers between impoverishment and homelessness, never sure when he is going to be pushed over the line.

⚜

The food supply chain reaches from the squalid trailer parks and fields upward to the lavish suites of a handful of global corporations, such as Walmart, which buys tens of millions of pounds of tomatoes a year. Chains such as McDonald's or Burger King, along with supermarkets such as Walmart, Giant, Stop & Shop, Trader Joe's, and Publix, have the purchasing power of tens of thousands of restaurants.

"Walmart makes farmworkers poor," read a recent statement from the Coalition of Immokalee Workers (CIW), an organization that advocates on behalf of farmworkers. "But not just Walmart—all the major retail food brands that have grown at meteoric rates over the past thirty years have used the same volume purchasing strategy to drive their profits and growth at the expense of the workers who make that growth possible."[7]

The United Food and Commercial Workers, in a report titled "Ending Wal-Mart's Rural Stranglehold," quoted John Tyson of Tyson Foods, Inc., who, when confronted by an activist farmer on the low price paid for meat to the farm, answered: "Walmart's the problem. They dictate the price to us and we have no choice but to pay you less."[8]

The suppliers and growers, beset by the rising costs of pesticides, fertilizer, and chemicals, along with the diesel fuel that runs their farm equipment and pumping stations, have few other ways to save money. In 1992, according to U.S. Department of Agriculture statistics, the farm share of the U.S. consumer dollar spent on tomatoes was 40.8 percent. This meant that forty cents of every dollar spent at the cash register on tomatoes went back to the farmer in 1992. By the end of the decade, that number had fallen to 20.5 percent.[9] Growers have lost half of their share of the retail price to the retailers. Wages in the fields have remained stagnant over the past three decades, and in real terms have declined.

David Sanchez, missing several teeth and wearing a brown camouflage baseball cap that reads "Air Force," waits in the lot outside the supermarket for work. Sanchez is fifty-five, considerably older than most field-workers. He came to Immokalee from Texas as a child with his parents and nine siblings. They lived in work camps in the fields. The children accompanied their parents to the fields.

He bears the scars of the fields, including a bad back—a common ailment among workers, who spend up to twelve hours a day bent over plants and ferrying thirty-two-pound buckets of green tomatoes to a waiting truck.

"The worst is when you lift that plastic mulch," he says in English, of the rows of plastic that cover the tomato beds. "You pick up that plastic and you can't even breathe. It burns your eyes. You be cryin' all day long. Sometimes they give you a paper mask, but the fumes go right through it. The fumes knock you out."

The arid, sandy soil in southern Florida is devoid of plant nutrients. Growers saturate the soil with chemical fertilizers. More than one hundred herbicides and pesticides are used to prevent fungal diseases, weeds, disease spores, and nematodes. These chemicals often accompany the produce to supermarket shelves. Some are highly toxic, known to cause damage to the brain and nervous systems. But they are effective in the relentless war against the rapacious armies of potato, flea, and blister beetles, along with vine borers, squash bugs, spider mites, stinkbugs, loopers, and hornworms. Growers can spend about $2,000 an acre on chemical fertilizers and pesticides. They often fumigate rows before planting with methyl bromide, a chemical that even in small concentrations can cause death in humans and is one of the leading causes of the depletion of the ozone layer. Methyl bromide is banned for use on most crops but is permitted on tomatoes, strawberries, eggplants, and peppers. It is injected into the tomato beds and trapped under a layer of green polyethylene plastic mulch.[10] Workers such as Sanchez, who have to lift up the mulch, routinely complain of eye and respiratory ailments, rashes, open sores, nausea, and headaches.[11] The Environmental Protection Agency (EPA) and the National Institute for Occupational Safety and Health show that upward of twenty thousand farmworkers suffer from acute pesticide poisoning every year.[12]

USDA studies found traces of thirty-five pesticides on conventionally grown fresh tomatoes for sale in the United States. Three of those chemicals found in high concentration are known carcinogens, six are neurotoxins, fourteen are endocrine disruptors, and three cause reproduction problems and birth defects.[13] Tomatoes are harvested before they are ripe. They are gassed in packing plants with ethylene into an artificial ripeness.[14] By the time the tomato reaches the dinner plate, as Barry Estabrook points out in his book *Tomato-land*, it is largely devoid of taste, robbed of most core nutrients, and carrying residues of poison. The rapid turnover of workers in the fields, which can be as high as forty percent a year, has made it hard to track the effects of the chemicals and the pesticides on those who harvest the plants. But anecdotal evidence points to severe health impairments, including high rates of cancer.

Sanchez rubs his right hand up and down his left forearm.

"Pretty soon your arm hair falls out," he says. "You go home and you have to use Clorox to get the green dust off your skin and out of your hair. You sneeze all day long. You can't get that smell out of you.

"We know we are not supposed to be workin' when they spray," he says. "We all have to watch a video that shows workers wearing protective gloves. We sign a paper saying we know the regulations, but every time the growers spray around us and break the regulations we don't say nothin'. We need the job. I don't complain. If I complained then the next day I wouldn't have a job."

Sanchez stands next to the crew leader, Rudy Rivera, a friend who often gives him work. Rivera owns an old school bus repainted blue and white, with worn brown vinyl seats, and the words *R. Rivera Harvesting* on the side. The top halves of the windows by each seat are open. Most of the workers inside are asleep, heads tilted back and mouths agape. Rivera ticks off his bus expenses: "$7,000 to buy it, $9,000 to paint it, $4,000 for insurance, $370 for tires, $30 a day for diesel.

"I usually look for men who are around eighteen, nineteen, or twenty years old," he says. "When there is heavy work I don't take women. They can't do it. When we lay the plastic or we have to shovel, I want men. When you lay down the sticks and use the air hammer, I want men. I only use women when I do the planting and picking."

Rivera came to the United States from Mexico at the age of fourteen with an uncle who helped shepherd him across the border.

"We walked for fifteen days," he says. "I had huge blisters on my feet. I was cryin' and cryin'. I told my uncle to let me go down to the highway and go home. He refused to let me go. He told me to be a man."

Rivera started work in the fields as a boy. He was caught five years later by the Immigration and Naturalization Service (INS) and deported.

"When I showed up at my house, my mother burst into tears," he says of his return to Mexico. "She hadn't heard from me in five years. She didn't know if I was alive. Then I crossed the border again and went back to work."

Rivera is one of the crew leaders for B.F. Stanford, a small farmer who has been in Florida for nearly five decades. Joe and I drive out early one morning to Stanford's property. Stanford, sixty-eight, sits in the cab of a pickup truck with the window rolled down. It is early in the day, but in the intense Florida humidity the air is already oppressive. Nestled amid the breaks in the fields are fifty white beehives, rented each year so the bees will pollinate the crops. A handful of egrets, spoonbills, and pink flamingos flock around the edges of the irrigation canals. Stanford says he hangs on financially by his fingertips. His son, who worked for many years with a large grower, has recently returned to help his father. They scoff at the idea of cracking down on undocumented farm help, saying no farm would be able to stay in business. The economic downturn has seen a rash of thefts on the farms, from diesel fuel to the equipment locked in sheds.

B. F. Stanford.

Stanford was robbed last season when the lock on his shed was cut one night and his equipment stolen.

The growers are also struggling to compete with the cheaper produce imported from Mexico.

"Mexico will put the American farmers out of business," says Stanford. "They don't follow the same rules. No one says what the Mexicans can and can't spray. The labor is cheap. And the big corporations like Six L's are already moving their production over the border. The small farmers are getting killed. The cost of fertilizer, the plastic boxes, the paper, the labor, and the fuel keeps going up and we have about the same prices for our produce as we had fifty years ago. NAFTA [the North American Free Trade Agreement] was the breaking point. Then you really saw the banks go in and take homes and equipment. Then you saw a lot of the smaller operations close. I went out of business once. I had to sell all my equipment and start over."

"They should shut Mexico down," he snaps.

The workers in Stanford's fields are a mix of Haitians and Hispanics. They stand amid rows of cucumbers, holding red or orange buckets. The workers wear yellow gloves. The farm also grows watermelons.

Stanford is not pleased with the labor imported into his fields.

"I put my heart and soul into that crop, and every day they go and tear it up," he says. "The labor don't care."

"Everybody get a row," says Rivera, in English to the Haitians and in Spanish to the Latinos. "You move. The bucket moves. And all phones off."

"*Asegúrate que esté gordo, no delgado*"—"Make sure it's fat, not thin," he says to a worker bent over the plant.

"What's up?" he says to a worker who is standing. "You pickin' today?"

"No," the worker answers. "Dumpin'."

The worker in charge of dumping climbs onto the back of a blue flatbed truck. The truck bed is piled with white plastic pallets to collect the produce. As a worker brings a full bucket to the dumper, or *dumpeador*, they are given a chip. Each chip adds ten cents to the worker's hourly minimum wage and is given out as an inducement to work quickly. There are gradations among the workers. Laborers, or pickers, the lowest position in the fields, harvest the crop. Walkers go up and down the rows checking if the vegetables or fruit (the tomato is technically a fruit) are picked at the proper time and have the required size and shape. The *dumpeadores*, who have a status above the field-walkers, stand in the back of the trucks and are handed the produce buckets. And then there are the crew leaders, who select the workers every morning, drive them to the fields in their buses, and oversee the work. The crew leaders, most of whom inherit the positions from their fathers, decide who works and who does not. They distribute the pay. And with that power can come abuse.

Sexual favors, according to numerous women who work in the fields, are sometimes demanded in exchange for work. Most women, who make up only about ten percent of the work force, will not go into the fields unless a male relative accompanies them.

"I worked for two years in the fields," says María Vences, a Mexican immigrant who runs a small grocery with her two sons in Immokalee. "The crew leaders were always trying to get me into their truck to give them sexual favors. When I refused they would say, 'OK, no more work for you.' There are women who do it. They don't get paid. They just get to keep their job."

The workers, coming home in the late afternoon from *el labor* in their rubber boots, their shirts stained green from the tomato plants, skirt any *bolillos*—white Americans. Conversations, when we can open them up, are routinely monosyllabic, with the eyes of those being questioned darting back and forth and feet shifting in discomfort. When Joe and I enter trailer parks, workers hastily closet themselves inside. They refuse to answer our knocks, even when they knew we saw them swing the doors shut. Contact with the outside world, especially the white world, can mean deportation, a personal and economic catastrophe. Relatives in small villages in Mexico, Honduras, or Guatemala depend on the $100 a month sent back by wire. Homes are often put up as collateral so workers can raise the hefty transportation fees demanded by the *coyotes*, the traffickers who smuggle undocumented immigrants into the United States. Families face ruin if the workers they depend upon are deported. The INS, known as *la migra*, is a powerful incentive to remain silent and unseen. And the hostility of many growers to the Coalition of Immokalee Workers means that undocumented workers who take outspoken stands can not only be blacklisted, but also threatened with exposure to the INS.

Picking cucumbers.

When you fall on hard times in the fields, there is usually no one to catch you. There is no extended family to bail you out or provide you with some food and a place to sleep. There are no social services or union to save you from destitution.

Abel Matiaz, unsteady on his feet from too much drink, sways and lurches through the undergrowth making his way toward the patch of ground where he spends his nights.

"*Yo no estoy trabajando en ningún lado. Yo no estoy recogiendo tomates*"— "I'm not working anywhere," he says. "I'm not picking tomatoes."

Matiaz is twenty-five. He wears a worn black Metallica sweatshirt with a large rip in the back right shoulder. The cuffs of his gray pants are soiled and stained. His hands and face are darkened and weathered from the sun. He is missing a few teeth. He came to the United States at the age of fourteen. He walked with his uncle for six days from the Mexican border into Arizona to escape detection by border patrols. Three days after arriving in Phoenix he was hidden with other undocumented immigrants in the back of a truck and driven to the tomato fields in Florida. He has remained in the United States ever since, moving to North and South Carolina for the summer harvests, and back to Immokalee in the winter to pick tomatoes.

Matiaz and the other transient laborers who sleep in the woods wake in the dark at 4:00 A.M. and walk to the parking lot in front of the La Fiesta Supermarket. But the last few days have not been good. By 7:00 A.M. he and dozens of others have left without work. He was unable to pay his landlord the $50 weekly rent for a dilapidated trailer he shared with nine other workers two weeks ago. Rents in the trailer parks, dominated by three local families who collectively fix the price, are astronomical. A trailer that should be condemned brings in a monthly rent of $2,000. The enclosed trailer encampments, usually surrounded by cyclone fencing, are named for the colors the owners paint them or the street where they are located—Camp Rojo, Camp Blanco, and Camp Colorado. Most workers have no car and need to be close to the collection points. Those who can't pay the $50 a week sleep outside.

Matiaz pushes creepers and vines out of the way.

"I went to the parking lot this morning at four," he says, "but there was no work. I don't have any money so I sleep in the bushes. The last time I worked was three days ago. I made $20. But we only got four hours in the fields. I used $15 to buy a phone card and the rest for a soda and something to eat."

"*Mosquitos, serpientes, gusanos, insectos. Es terrible*"—"Mosquitos, snakes, bugs, insects," he mutters to himself. "It's awful."

He stops in a clearing where the grass and vegetation are matted down. There are discarded beer bottles, papers, and trash.

"Here," he says, sweeping his arm out over the encampment. "Sometimes there are fifty of us at night."

He stumbles over to the edge of a tree and shows us where he sleeps. He has no blanket or sleeping bag. A local Catholic church gave the squatters tents, but fifteen days ago the police raided the encampment and confiscated them.

"I had a tent for a little while for myself," he says, pointing to a patch where it had been set up.

He sees a log and lowers himself slowly and unsteadily to sit. He pulls the neck of his sweatshirt up over his face and the hood down over his bloodshot eyes to show us how he sleeps.

"*Hace frío en la noche. Hace* fucking *frío*"—"It's cold at night," he says. "It's *fucking* cold," he adds, using the English word.

A rooster begins to crow.

"My father abandoned me," he says. "My mother died when I was young. I had to look for work as a boy. I have a few belongings, some clothes and a television. My friend has them. He is keeping them until I get work again. I had a girlfriend, but she left me for someone else. Now she wants to come back. She calls me on the phone and says, 'I love you. I love you.' But I told her, 'No.' I don't want her back. She can stay where she is.

"I wanted to be an American, to raise myself above all this," he says, his thoughts trailing off as he stares into the woods.

We head back down the narrow path, again pushing the creepers out of our faces. We walk along the side of the road, past the Guadalupe Center in the Catholic church, where we had found Matiaz at the lunchtime soup kitchen. He had been seated with other migrants, including mothers with children, spooning up soup served by church volunteers. It is the only meal he and most of those in the center eat daily. He says he will continue to trudge from his encampment to the parking lot until he finds work. He hopes to get enough steady work to earn the $50 to sleep on a mattress on the floor of his old trailer, which comes with holes in the floorboards, a single showerhead for the ten men, and scurrying rats and cockroaches. And then, he hopes, he can retrieve his few clothes and his television.

We walk with Matiaz along a sandy rut on the edge of a potholed asphalt road. We pass some boarded-up buildings, a collection of trailers with garbage strewn out front, and a woman balancing a bag of groceries with one hand on her head. Old bottles, cans, newspapers, plastic bags, and cardboard lie scattered in the overgrown grass. There are tiny check-cashing shops nestled along the streets. They charge steep fees to migrants who do not have bank accounts or who want to wire money back home. There are little *tiendas* with crates of oranges and tomatoes out front for sale. There are old vans and minibuses, *servicios de transporte*, which rumble down the road as part of the informal system of local transportation. Tickets for the *servicios de transporte* are sold in shops

A trailer park for workers, Immokalee, Florida.

that cater to workers. Chickens and roosters root around in the dirt yards. It looks, sounds, and feels like a small village in Mexico.

Matiaz, at least when he is sober, is the model worker in the corporate state. He has no job protection or security, no benefits, no medical coverage, no over-time, no ability to organize, no Social Security, no food stamps, no legal protec-tion, and when his employers do not need him he is left without an income, a place to live, or something to eat.

The hardships Matiaz and other farmworkers endure refute the economist David Ricardo's classic economic theory of the Iron Law of Wages. Wages, the eighteenth-century economist insisted, would never fall below subsistence level in the free market because at that point the worker would no longer be able to sustain him or herself. The free market would, by its own accord, drive wages down to this subsistence level and no lower.[15] Ricardo's theory was never fully put to the test within the industrialized nation state. The supply of trained and competent workers was not unlimited. Workers formed unions and demanded workplace standards, including the minimum wage—although when the federal minimum-wage law was enacted in 1938, farmworkers were excluded from the provisions and would be for three decades.[16] But in our globalized economy, where the labor pool stretches from Mexico to Asia and where industry can move easily across borders, Ricardo's theory has been exposed as yet another absurdity held up by the proponents of laissez-faire capitalism.

The determining factor in global corporate production is poverty. The poorer the worker and the poorer the nation, the greater the competitive advantage. With access to vast pools of desperate, impoverished workers eager for scraps, unions and working conditions no longer impede the quest for larger and larger profits. And when corporations no longer need these workers, they are cast aside and left to sleep in the woods or on heating grates. They become dependent on the charity of others. Once the workers in the tomato fields get older, losing the agility and endurance of the young, most crew leaders refuse to hire them. Many head back to Mexico, Haiti, or Guatemala as poor as when they arrived.

The worst is not life as a serf. It is life as a slave. And, as Douglas Molloy, the chief assistant U.S. attorney in Fort Myers, has said, Florida has been "ground zero for modern slavery"[17] in America.

Slavery in its many guises and configurations has been a feature of the Florida economy for centuries. The Spanish *conquistadores*, who settled in Florida, enslaved indigenous peoples to tend their crops. This practice ended when the native population was largely exterminated. Once Great Britain took control of Florida in 1763, African American slaves were imported to work the rice and indigo fields. When Spain regained control of Florida following the American Revolution, the northeastern coast became one of the centers for the trafficking of human beings, especially when in 1807 the Congress banned the international slave trade.

The Seminole Indians, who had been pushed southward into Florida, joined by African Americans who had escaped slavery, mounted three protracted and devastating wars with the U.S. Army between 1814 and 1858 in a bid for freedom. The United States committed more than forty thousand troops[18] to quell the rebellions that took the lives of fifteen hundred U.S. soldiers.[19] Small remnants of the Seminoles and their African American allies, after suffering military campaigns that razed their settlements and slaughtered their women and children, retreated into the swamps of the Everglades rather than surrender.[20]

By the time Florida returned to American control in 1821, huge numbers of African American slaves were working the cotton and sugar plantations. On the eve of the Civil War, nearly forty-four percent of the state's total population was enslaved. There were fewer than one thousand free African Americans in Florida when the Civil War began.[21] Little changed for African Americans following the war as white plantation owners turned to violence, legal constraints, and debt peonage, to keep African Americans impoverished and trapped in the fields. They were slaves in all but name. Florida had the highest per capita lynching rate in the country between 1882 and 1930, with at least two hundred and sixty-six murders.[22] Lynchings were public spectacles that drew thousands of white onlookers. They were also public service announcements to the black community. They cemented into place the reign of terror.

In his book *Trouble in Mind: Black Southerners in the Age of Jim Crow*, Leon F. Litwack describes an 1893 lynching in Fort White, Florida. Trains ferried in additional participants and spectators from surrounding cities. After a mock trial, the lynching began.

"They sawed at the victim's throat, cut off both his ears, cut out one eye, stuffed handkerchiefs in his mouth to stifle his 'awful screams,' " Litwack writes. "Stabbing him repeatedly, the lynching came close to cutting out his backbone. He was then dragged two blocks before the crowd emptied their guns into his body."[23]

African American men, arrested on usually bogus charges of vagrancy, were part of the vast convict-lease system. Counties and states in the South leased groups of black convicts, who could be held in bondage for years, to farm owners. Many never survived long enough to finish their terms. As Litwack writes:

> What convict labor demanded of blacks physically and emotionally not only resembled slavery but in many instances exceeded its worst abuses and routines. "We go from can't to can't," a Florida convict turpentine worker said. "Can't see in the morning to can't see at night." Awakened before dawn, the convicts were marched rapidly to the fields in chains, where they worked until dinner (for which they received some forty minutes) and then continued to work until after sundown or "as long as it was light enough for a guard to see how to shoot." The fourteen or more hours they worked each day, the pace demanded of them, the savage beatings meted out to slackers, the dangerous conditions they often confronted, along with the quality of their food, shelter, and medical care, made survival a triumph in itself.[24]

"Before the war, we owned the negroes," a planter said in 1883. "If a man had a good nigger, he could afford to take care of him; if he was sick, get a doctor. He might even put gold plugs in his teeth. But these convicts: we don't own 'em. One dies, get another."[25]

In the 1920s, labor contractors, known as crew leaders, rounded up poor, itinerant workers and began to ship them north to harvest the summer crops and then back south again for the winter crops. These migrant workers, largely African American, were left out of the labor protections put in place later by the New Deal, including collective bargaining, part of a backroom deal Franklin Roosevelt made with white Southern politicians, who wanted African-Americans kept out of unions.[26] Collective bargaining among agricultural laborers, while not illegal in Florida, is unprotected under the state labor laws. Workers who attempt to form a union can be summarily fired.[27]

"We used to own our slaves," a grower said in Edward R. Murrow's 1960 television exposé *Harvest of Shame*. "Now we just rent them."[28]

Despite the termination of the convict-lease system in 1923 by Florida and Alabama—the last two states to end the practice—incidents involving slavery and forced labor continue to be uncovered. African Americans have been largely replaced in the fields by workers, many of them undocumented, from Mexico, Central America, and Haiti. Lack of legal status, inability to speak English, and fear of deportation make them easier to abuse and exploit. Debt peonage is the instrument of control. For the agricultural workers, it often begins in the form of a transportation fee. Workers, newly arrived in the United States and without money, are told they can "owe" the $1,000 it costs for a ride to a job in Florida. They are then informed that they cannot leave until the debt is repaid.

⚜

Immokalee is a town filled largely with desperately poor single men. Among their few diversions are local bars such as the Chile Caliente, where their meager pay evaporates. Bar owners bring in women from Miami and Fort Myers by van on the weekends to dance with patrons for $5 a dance. The night Joe and I are at the Chile Caliente, the women, in tight shorts, grind in high heels all the way down to the floor and up again like seasoned strippers. The men can flirt with the women as long as they buy them the bar's overpriced drinks, of which the women get a cut from the house. The height of the harvesting season in the winter sees two or three brothels open up in dilapidated house or trailers.

Sexual exploitation parallels the exploitation in the fields. Clients at the seasonal brothels pay $20 to the brothel managers, or *ticketeros*, at the door. The patrons are handed a poker chip. They enter and wait on an old couch. They carry their chip to one of the prostitutes when it is their turn. The women keep condoms, a roll of paper towels, and lubricants next to them. They lie passively on mattresses sectioned off by sheets or plastic garbage bags. Clients get no more than ten, at most fifteen minutes. Most of the women are paid $7 to $10 per customer. The night's wages are determined by the number of chips the women turn in at the end of the night to the *ticketero*. On a busy night they can have sex with twenty to thirty men. Some women are as young as fourteen, and Collier County Sheriff officials told us of women arrested as old as sixty. Many of the women were lured to the United States by promises of jobs in hotels, cleaning services, restaurants, or in private homes as domestics. The women are told they can pay off the smuggling fee, often as much as $2,000, once they start work. But the debt, magically, never diminishes. It is constantly augmented by charges for food and rent deducted by the brothel owners from the paychecks, as well as the cost of any abortions. The women are trapped, like enslaved field workers, in a cycle of endless exploitation.

Crew leaders, like the brothel owners, often swiftly pile on the debt in farm camps. Workers are charged for rent, food, wine, beer, and cigarettes, leaving them beholden to the crew leader until the debt is paid off, a near impossibility, since it is the crew leader who sets the inflated price, collects the wages, sells the purchased items to the workers, and keeps the accounts. Owners note down the mounting sums owed by workers, siphoning money each week from wages, supposedly to pay off a portion of the debt, a practice few of the workers can challenge since many cannot read and have no access to police or courts.

These debt peonage operations are often large. Miguel Flores of La Belle, Florida, and Sebastian Gomez, of Immokalee, were sentenced in 1997 to fifteen years each in federal prison on slavery, extortion, and firearms charges. They

Dancing in Immokalee.

oversaw a workforce of four hundred men and women who harvested the fields in Florida and South Carolina. The workers, mostly indigenous Mexicans and Guatemalans, were forced to work ten to twelve hours a day, six days a week, for as little as $20 dollars a week, all under the supervision of armed guards. Those who attempted to escape were beaten, pistol-whipped, and at times shot. The crew leaders charged the workers exorbitant prices for food. Female workers, according to one victim, were routinely raped. Flores told the workers that if they ever spoke about their experiences he would cut out their tongues. This case was only one of the few that have been uncovered, due in part to the Coalition of Immokalee Workers, which convinced a dozen witnesses to come forward.[29]

More than a thousand men and women in the state of Florida have been freed by law enforcement over the past fifteen years from slave camps.[30] There have been nine federal prosecutions for modern-day slavery since 1997. And there are other operations that law enforcement officials say remain undetected. Workers are routinely "sold" to crew leaders, cheated out of pay, beaten, or pistol-whipped if they complain or are sick. They are kept in gated enclosures at night, at times chained to prevent escape, and warned that their families in Mexico or Central America will pay the consequences if they flee and report the abuse to authorities. Child labor laws are often ignored. The body of an undocumented farm worker periodically appears on the side of the road or floating in one of the irrigation canals, a reminder to other workers of what happens when you attempt to challenge the bosses.

On the north side of Immokalee behind cyclone fencing are two rows of gray wooden huts, rented out to farm laborers for the inflated sum of $55 dollars a week per person. There is a collective shower house and laundry center, also painted slate gray, with a vending machine for soft drinks. Joe and I wander among the huts looking for a man known as Don Paquito, the nickname for José Hilário Medel. Workers eating lunch at the Guadalupe Center told us that he could usually be found outside the Monterrey bodega or sleeping under a mango tree near the rental shacks. A woman, who informs us she has "full-blown AIDS," says the landlord who oversees the rental huts chased Don Paquito off the property a couple of hours before. She says he will be back. I give her my cell phone number. She calls later in the afternoon to say Don Paquito is with her.

Don Paquito is a soft-spoken, diminutive man less than five feet tall with a broad, darkened face and a wispy black moustache. He is missing several teeth. He is shabbily dressed. An old baseball cap sits backward on his head. His eyes are bloodshot. One of his worn sneakers is missing a lace. He is a gentle, broken soul whose life has been marked by horrible poverty, abuse, and tragedy. He has retreated into the fog of alcoholism. He was held as a slave, forced to work in Florida's citrus and tomato fields, then trucked in the summer to the fields in North and South Carolina by members of the Navarrete family, who occupied a beige stucco house at 209 Seventh Street on the south side of town. Don Paquito and the other workers held by the Navarretes harvested on some of the largest farms in Florida, including Pacific Tomato Growers in Palmetto, and Immokalee-based Six L's, a company controlled for four generations by the Lipman family. Six L's packs and ships fifteen million twenty-five pound boxes of tomatoes a year from its huge warehouse outside Immokalee.[31]

Cesar Navarrete, at the time twenty-seven, and his brother, Geovanni Navarrete, then twenty-two, were the enforcers. Each received a twelve-year federal prison sentence in 2008 for enslaving Mexican and Guatemalan tomato pickers. They beat workers for disobedience if they tried to run away, if they were sick, or if they expressed a reluctance to work. The Navarrete brothers, who often carried pistols, routinely made the men work seven days a week. The family would pocket most and sometimes all of the men's paychecks. The workers were charged $20 a week by the Navarretes to sleep inside locked sheds, vans, or an old furniture truck, where they had no choice but to urinate and defecate in a corner. Their beds were plywood boards on top of milk crates. They were charged for the cheap bottles of booze their overseers sold to them on credit. They were charged $50 a week for food, usually rice, beans, and stale tortillas, provided by the mother, Virginia Navarrete, who was also sentenced to jail. They could never repay their debts. And that was the idea.

"*Yo estaba trabajando construcción en Naples*"—"I was working construction in Naples," Don Paquito says as we sit on a stoop. "Cesar Navarrete found me in Naples. He offered me a job and a place to live. I did not know I was being kidnapped. We were locked inside the trucks at night. They made us pay $5 to use the garden hose for a bath, and the water was always cold. We had money taken out of our pay for food, which wasn't fit for animals, and for rent. It was horrible."

He reaches into the pocket of his dirty trousers and carefully pulls out a worn plastic bag wrapped around his personal documents.

He hands me his Employment Authorization card with his name, José Hilário Medel, and his birth date, February 9, 1963. The card was given to him after he agreed to testify against the Navarrete family. His testimony, however, came with a stiff price. He was blacklisted by the crew leaders. No one would give him a job. He was threatened and for a while went into hiding. And he became destitute.

"The crew chiefs know me," he says. "I don't get work. I sleep outside, sometimes in front of the Catholic church on 9th Street with about eighteen other workers, sometimes . . . there."

Don Paquito.

He points to two large mango trees in a lot surrounded by bottles, cans, plastic bags, and cardboard.

"I've been robbed three times," he says, almost as an afterthought. "I don't have anything anymore. I have a blanket. Sometimes the people in the rental park let me use their water. I eat one meal a day at the Guadalupe Center. I have five children in Mexico, in my village. But I haven't seen them since I came here six years ago. I used to send them money so they could go to school."

In November 2007 three workers punched their way through the ventilator hatch of the van where they were locked up at night. The men were free for the first time in two and a half years.

A week later, on November 21, 2007, the Collier County Sheriff's Department mounted a pre-dawn raid on the house where the remaining eleven workers, including Don Paquito, were being held.

Most of the workers refused to testify, in part fearing reprisals against their families in Mexico or Central America. The workers, the Sheriff's Office found, were covered with bruises and marks from repeated beatings. One of the workers had an open gash from a knife. Another had swollen and numb hands from having his arms chained behind him at night.

"They were treated like animals," said Marysol Schloendorn, the victims' advocate for the Collier County Sheriff's Office. She took part in the raid:

> There was garbage and feces in the yard where the workers lived. One worker had his feet chained to a pole. They were sleeping in old vehicles on boards. And when we went into the house and seized the family's money, we saw the family was not rich, but they had televisions, running water, clean clothes, and trucks outside. Many of the workers did not want to be considered victims, especially as men. I think it comes from the macho culture. It was only as we did more and more interviews that they came to accept what had happened to them.

The indictment delivered against six members of the Navarrete family in Fort Myers by the U.S. District Court in 2008 sets out in clinical detail the abuses endured by the workers for nearly three years. The court estimated that the Navarrete family had stolen about $240,000 in wages from the laborers they held in captivity.[32] In the section of the indictment titled "Overt Acts," some of the charges against the family included:

- In or about May 2005, defendant Cesar Navarrete stopped paying his workers then told LMD and other workers that if they went to work for anyone else he would find them, beat them and their new employer.

- On an unknown date, at the Navarrete property in Collier County, Florida, defendant Cesar Navarrete grabbed AL and locked him in the back of a yellow truck for approximately four hours because AL wanted to leave his employment.

- On or about June 2007, in DeSoto County, Florida, on a morning when LMD did not want to work, defendants Cesar Navarrete and Geovanni Navarrete picked up LMD, threw him in the back of a truck, beat LMD in the body, head, and mouth, causing him injury and pain.

- In or about July or August 2007, in Walterboro, South Carolina, defendant Geovanni Navarrete, and others known to the grand jury, chained PSG's feet together and to a pole to prevent him from leaving their employment.

- In or about September 2007, in North Carolina, defendant Geovanni Navarrete struck APS near his eye, causing him serious injury to this eye.

- In or about November 2007, defendant Cesar Navarrete, and others known to the grand jury, hit and kicked RRC because he left the Navarrete property without permission and went to the Coalition of Immokalee Workers office.

- On or about November 19, 2007, in Collier County, Florida, defendants Cesar Navarrete and Geovanni Navarrete, and others known to the grand jury, beat LMD then locked him, JHM, JVD, and two other workers in the back of a box truck to prevent them from leaving and to ensure they would be available for work the following morning.[33]

Hundreds of thousands of poor from Mexico and Central America have fled northward to escape mounting poverty and unemployment. Plots of land and farms have been abandoned following severe droughts, hurricanes, earthquakes, and sudden, severe drops in the price of coffee, on which much of the Guatemalan economy depends. The Mexican poor have joined this tidal wave courtesy of Bill Clinton's NAFTA, which permitted the huge agrobusinesses in the United States to flood the Mexican market with cheap corn. This swiftly bankrupted millions of small Mexican farmers, perhaps two million of whom joined the surge of undocumented immigrants into the United States. These are the rumblings of a new world order, one in which a mad scramble for diminishing resources, a world where workers at home and abroad are forced, out of desperation and sheer vulnerability, into a global serfdom.

⚞⚟

Joe and I are in Laura Germino's small office in the Coalition of Immokalee Workers's one-story stucco building. The building is across the street from the parking lot where workers gather each morning in Immokalee. She and her husband, Greg Asbed, helped form the coalition in the mid-'90s while they were working for Florida Rural Legal Services. Germino and Asbed, who met as students at Brown University, each spent time in the developing world—Germino as a Peace Corps volunteer in Burkina Faso and Asbed in Haiti. It would be good training for Immokalee, especially Asbed's command of Creole.

"In the Ron Evans case," Germino says, referring to a 2007 case in which Evans kept indebted workers enslaved behind a chain-link fence topped with barbed wire, "they would recruit from homeless shelters, or from centers where people were trying to recover from substance abuse. And then they would promise people—homeless people, mind you—a job and a roof over their heads. What more would you want, right? It's a reasonable thing to want. And so people would then end up in North Florida, or the Carolinas, with Ron Evans in this kind of situation that you're seeing here in the photo."

She pulls down from her bookshelf a photo of Evans's encampment, with its coils of barbed wire and "No Trespassing" sign. Evans worked for grower Frank Johns, the former chairman of the Florida Fruit & Vegetable Association, the powerful lobbying arm of the state agricultural industry.

"This was up in Palatka, north Florida," Germino says:

It shows one of the more classic styles of holding people against their will back since the '60s. This is a high fence and barbed wire. And it was normally closed. There is an interview with an older man named Jewel, and he talks about how Evans at the end of the workday would take up everyone's shoes, so that it would be harder for them to leave at night. Evans was sentenced to thirty years back in 2007. But he'd been practicing since at least the '80s. One of the misconceptions is that people look at farmwork as a snapshot of today. They don't wind back the video to get the whole time, the evolution.

Germino stresses that slavery will not disappear until the growers and the corporations that buy the produce are forced to comply with basic labor standards. The agricultural industry, she said, has long enslaved citizens as well as noncitizens. The problem did not begin with the arrival of undocumented workers to the fields.

"There's this invisible hand of this corporate buyer asking for high volume at low price," she says:

I don't want them to be forgotten about. It's like the movie *The Burning Season*, about Carlos Mendes. There is the middleman who does the actual violence, but it's the oil people living in Rio or whatever that are behind the destruction of the forests. There's a lot of talk about factors that make people vulnerable, for example, immigrant workers, why they end up here? They come because you've been spit out by the global economy by NAFTA. They don't come for adventure. They are vulnerable and fall prey to a boss who holds people in forced labor. These are the sending factors. But the more important question is about the receiving country factors. I can understand a trafficker wanting to take advantage of these people. But why does it happen here? This is the question everybody in the U.S. has to ask. Why are there conditions here that allow slavery to take root? There will always be vulnerable people. There will always be homeless people. But why are such people enslaved here?

"What needs to be eliminated is the sweatshop, the exploitative conditions," Germino continues:

Forced labor doesn't happen in isolation. It doesn't happen in a vacuum. It is part of a continuum, the end of a whole range of labor violations. It doesn't fall out of the sky. It has to have conditions like soil in which it can take root. If you eliminate that from U.S. soil, you eliminate forced labor. Agriculture has always had that soil, at least up until now, in the tomato industry. In Florida in the past two or three hundred years, there's never been a time without slavery, or a form of forced labor. It's changed. It's no longer chattel slavery, or plantation slavery. It's not legal anymore. But it still happens. When they passed the Emancipation Proclamation it continued in different forms, as you saw in the turpentine camps up in north Florida. Agriculture has always had it. And what's interesting is that other industries are actually now more prone to it, industries that didn't used to have it. This shows you that when any industry devolves from being an industry with a fulltime work force with benefits and overtime, pensions, or whatever, to a subpoverty minimum-wage workforce—not salaried, day labor—you start seeing more cases of forced labor. We are starting to see labor trafficking in the garment industry and in hotels and construction. It devolves. I'm surprised it hasn't happened in meatpacking, where salaries have also gotten lower and the benefits have gotten worse. I had hoped that agriculture would become more like other industries, but I fear that in our race to the bottom other industries are beginning to resemble agriculture.

The advances made by the Coalition of Immokalee Workers on behalf of the tomato workers, however, are among the few bright spots in the nation's agricultural fields, advances made outside the formal structures of power by the workers themselves.

"What is happening in the tomato industry is huge and promising," Germino says. "It is something new and genuinely exciting. I've been doing this for twenty years. I don't get excited easily about something."

Joe and I wait in the coalition's small parking lot one Sunday morning to travel with a group of laborers to picket a Publix supermarket in Sarasota. The Coalition is trying to get tomato buyers to sign a deal, known as the Fair Food Agreement, which has already been accepted by the giants in the fast-food industry. If the supermarket chains, including Publix, Trader Joe's, Walmart, Kroger, and Ahold brands Giant and Stop & Shop, sign the agreement, the wages of the farmworkers could nearly double. The agreement could also significantly alleviate the draconian conditions that permit forced labor, crippling poverty, and egregious human-rights abuses, including slavery, in the nation's tomato fields. If the campaign fails, however, the gains made by farmworkers could be threatened.

Supermarkets are huge buyers of tomatoes and wield great influence, if they choose to, over conditions in the field.

The campaign has been resisted. The corporations have mounted a public-relations blitz to denounce the agreement. The supermarket chain Publix sent an employee posing as a documentary filmmaker into the coalition. And the activities of the coalition are closely monitored.

"Publix has a cabal of labor relations, human relations, and public-relations employees who very frequently descend from corporate headquarters in Lakeland, Florida—or one of their regional offices—and show up at our demonstrations," says Marc Rodrigues, who works with the Coalition. "They watch us with or without cameras. They constantly attempt to deflect us. If we attempt to speak to consumers or store managers, these people will intercept us and try to guide us away. These people in suits and ties come up to us and refer to us by our first names—as if they know us—in a sort of bizarre, naked attempt at intimidation."

The coalition organized a nationwide boycott in 2001 that forced several major fast-food chains including Yum Brands, McDonald's, Burger King, Subway, Whole Foods Market, Compass Group, Bon Appétit Management Company, Aramark, and Sodexo to sign the Fair Food Agreement, which demands more humane labor standards from their Florida tomato suppliers and a wage increase of a penny or more for each pound of tomatoes harvested. But if the major supermarkets do not also sign this agreement, growers who ignore the agreement will be able to continue selling tomatoes to the supermarkets. This could leave at least half of all the fields without protection, making uniform enforcement of the agreement difficult, if not impossible.

"Supermarkets such as Trader Joe's insist they are responsible and fair," says Gerardo Reyes, a farmworker and coalition staff member, whom we meet in the coalition's office:

They use their public relations to present themselves as a good corporation. They sell this idea of fairness, this disguise. They use this more sophisticated public-relations campaign, one that presents them as a friend of workers, while at the same time locking workers out of the discussion and kicking us out of the room. They want business as usual. They do not want people to question how their profits are created. We have to fight not only them but this sophisticated public-relations tactic. We are on the verge of a systemic change, but corporations like Trader Joe's are using all their power to push us back.

Three protestors going to Sarasota, including a mother with her young son, ride with us. They sit together in the back seat. The woman, whom we will call Ana, begins to recount in Spanish her journey north. I translate for Joe as we drive to Sarasota. Ana talks to us, at times breaking down, for more than three hours, including about a half hour in the parking lot of a local church before we join the demonstrators. It is a story that, with a few variations, we could have heard from most of the workers around us.

"I was in a private school because the vocational training I wanted wasn't in the public schools. I was studying to be a house decorator.

"My parents were now five hours away... My father helped me pay for school, but I had to pay for the books."

Ana washed dishes to earn money and began cleaning the houses of the wealthy, too, but found, "I no longer had time to go to school."

She left her studies and began cleaning homes full time.

"The first time I went in one of those houses of the rich I got very emotional because I saw all those things the rich people had...

"[M]y girlfriends and I [hoped maybe one day] we could have a home like this with a washer and a dryer because in our town we didn't even have electricity.

"[Their] children would have parties and we would have to arrive early to clean... but then they didn't want us to stay. They would call us when we had to clean up.

"We would... stay in the home until two or three in the morning...

THE WORST WAS TO SEE HOW THEY WOULD THROW AWAY FOOD BECAUSE IN MY LITTLE PUEBLO THERE WERE DAYS WHEN WE DIDN'T EVEN HAVE FRIJOLES.

J. SACCO 12·11

At 16, Ana married a man she met in Guatemala City, who happened to come from the same village she did. They moved back to the country and in with her father.

He lived in a one-room house and on property that had been granted by a Spanish priest, who had bought a large farm, divided it among the people, and set up a coffee-growing cooperative.

The cooperative found buyers for the crop and divided the profits among its members.

PEOPLE WERE ABLE TO EXPAND THEIR HOUSES... AND RENT LAND TO GROW BEANS AND CORN.

SO WE BEGAN TO EAT MUCH BETTER THAN WE ATE BEFORE.

Ana had her first child, and now "we wanted a house of our own." Her husband decided to go to the United States to earn the money.

He hooked up with a couple of acquaintances who claimed to know the route, and together they made the journey to the U.S. border.

HE STAYED IN THE UNITED STATES FOR ONE YEAR, AND EVERY TWO WEEKS HE SENT US 3,000 QUETZALS.*

Ana was now able to pay off food debts, but also—

HE TOLD ME TO SAVE THE MONEY SO I COULD PAY A COYOTE TO [GUIDE ME] TO THE UNITED STATES.

* AT THAT TIME 1,000 QUETZALS WAS ABOUT $125

But Ana would not be able to take her daughter.

"The idea was to come for one or two years and return home...

"It was very hard to leave my daughter. I told her it would be for a little while and then I would be back."

When she had the required sum—40,000 quetzals—she joined a group of 40 Guatemalans attempting to reach the United States. They moved by public transportation from safe house to safe house.

Because they did not have papers they were smuggled across the river at the Mexican border on truck tires.

The river was not wide, she says, "but it was deep.

"Each tire had someone to pole it across. The coyotes paid the men to take us across."

"In the days we hid, and if we could we hid where there was some shade.

"When we crossed, everyone was carrying a gallon of water, and we had to be careful we didn't drink too much.

"We were supposed to sleep during the day, but pretty much you don't sleep because you have to watch out for patrols.

"It was three nights to get across."

The group arrived at a destination in Texas, and from there Ana was taken to Phoenix.

Her husband was now in Pennsylvania working in the blueberry fields, and she flew to Philadelphia to be reunited with him.

"It had been over a year since I'd seen my husband.

"I didn't know how the airport worked, and I couldn't find [him]."

J. SACCO 12-11

Resistance came, as it often does, when workers found the courage to stand up to abuse, breaking the cycle of fear that keeps the system in place. One of those workers was Lucas Benitez, now thirty-six with two small children. He crossed the border into the United States at the age of seventeen from the impoverished Mexican state of Guerrero. He began as a migrant field-worker. He sent money home to support his parents and five brothers and sisters. He was driving tomato stakes into the ground one day when he found himself ahead of the other workers.

"*Mi error fue trabajar rápido*"—"My error was to work quickly," he said when we spoke with him in Spanish one afternoon in the Coalition's office. "I got ahead of the other workers, and thought I was being smart and could finish early and take a rest. The crew leader came over and told me to go back and work with the others. I told him I had finished my row. I should be able to wait. He yelled at me to go back and raised his fist. I picked up a stake and held it like a weapon."

Benitez remembers that those around him looked the other way or turned their backs. The crew leader backed off.

"*Él estaba sorprendido*"—"He was surprised," Benitez says. "He was used to hitting workers that did not defend themselves. He didn't try and hit me. But he told me not to come to work the next day. He said I wouldn't have a job."

Benitez became an organizer. He began meeting other disaffected workers at night in the local Catholic church. These gatherings, which included Haitians who spoke only Creole, along with Mexicans and Central Americans, some of whom spoke the indigenous tongues of Mixtec, Kanjobal, Mam, K'iche' or Tzotzil and only rudimentary Spanish, would become the Coalition of Immokalee Workers. They gathered to study the abuse and slavery in the fields. And they discussed ways to resist. Translators such as Asbed kept the various ethnicities in communication.

Benitez is sitting on a couch in the outer office where the meetings of the coalition are held. The walls around him are covered with posters, framed newspaper articles in Spanish and English, and signs from past protests. There is one poster with a caricature of a crew leader labeled "Don Tomato," shouting: "I'm the Law! I'm the Boss!" and a placard reading "*No Más Abusos*"—"No More Abuses." On the far end of the room is a small food pantry where workers can buy staples such as rice and beans at reduced prices to help counter the gouging that typifies most of the town's bodegas.

"These conditions are hereditary," Benitez says in Spanish. "They exist and have existed for generations. First you had slaves. Then you had freed slaves. Then you had poor whites and sharecroppers. Now you have immigrants. It is all part of a continuum we have to break."

It was clear from the beginning, he says, that whatever organization arose, it could not revolve around a single leader. It would be too easy to decapitate. The model for organization would have to be consensus.

"What happened in Immokalee is similar to what is happening in the rest of the country with the Occupy movements," he says:

We began because we were desperate. We didn't see a solution through the system itself. We knew we had to change the balance of power between the workers and the corporations. And this is happening all over the world.

Lucas Benitez.

Many people are desperate. They work hard and have nothing to show for it. You see in these Occupy movements young people who burned their eyelashes off studying and have no job and huge debts. There are differences. We are poor. We are isolated. But like the Occupy movements we are organic, we are responding to corporate power. We, too, are nonhierarchical. Everyone has a voice. There are no designated leaders.

In 1995 the growers attempted to reduce wages from $4.25 an hour to $3.85 an hour, and add 10 cents a bucket as an incentive. The reduced wage and incentive to earn a dime a bucket, in fact, was a swindle. If the worker was paid the proposed $3.85 an hour and the 10 cents incentive per bucket, they would make about $50 for a day, not $90, for the same two hundred buckets. To get the point across to the workers, the Coalition drew pictures of turtles working in the fields and told workers earning $3.85 an hour and a dime a bucket to work as slowly as possible to conserve their strength. The wage reduction, on top of the verbal and physical abuse, enraged the workers. They gathered each morning in the supermarket parking lot and blocked the buses from entering the lot.

"This was a huge surprise for the crew leaders," Benitez says:

They never thought Mexicans, Guatemalans, Salvadorans, Hondurans, and Haitians would get together and strike. The crew leaders were frantic. They kept asking the workers: "Who told you to do this? Who is organizing this?" The strike lasted for a week. No buses could pick up workers. And after a week the growers said they would implement the $4.25 an hour, and some started to pay $5.50 and $4.75 an hour. When we heard this, we climbed on top of the cab of a truck to tell the workers. It was just like a General Assembly in the Occupy movements. We asked the crowd, "What should we do? Are you ready to go back to work?" And they said, "Yes." We didn't trust the promises of the growers. The next week we checked everyone's pay to make sure the agreement was real.

The victory by the some three thousand migrant workers[34] awakened a workforce that had, until that moment, been submissive. A Coalition of Immokalee Worker staff salary is commensurate with farmworker income, meaning minimum wage with no health insurance or benefits. And the coalition representatives usually live in trailers and run-down houses in Immokalee along with the workers.

"We realized that the only way there would be real change was when we yelled and fought for ourselves," he says. "We discovered that we could not wait for someone from the outside to come and save us. We were our own saviors."

A year later, in 1996, a sixteen-year-old Guatemalan named Edgar stumbled into the Coalition's office splattered with blood.

"His nose was so red and his face was so swollen he looked like a clown," Benitez says. "His shirt was saturated with blood."

Edgar said he had taken a drink of water in the fields without permission. The crew leader savagely beat him, telling the other workers that if they disobeyed him they would also be beaten. The boy fled.

That night nearly two hundred workers crammed themselves into the Coalition's office.

"We discussed the problem," Benitez says. "We were frustrated. When we took cases like this to the police or the Department of Labor, they never responded. Nothing ever changed. We met for four or five nights trying to figure out what to do. People were angry. Finally, we decided to march to the crew leader's house."

A crowd of about three hundred workers left the Coalition's offices and made their way through the dusty, poorly-lit streets. Other farmworkers joined them. The crowd swelled to five hundred. Police descended on the marchers with riot gear and twenty-eight vehicles. The crowd, holding Edgar's blood-stained shirt above their heads, stood outside the crew leader's home and chanted: *"Golpear a uno es golpear a todos"*—"When you beat one of us, you beat all of us."

"But the biggest impact occurred the next morning," Benitez says. "When the buses came to the parking lot, no one would get on the buses owned by the crew leader who had beaten Edgar. His buses were boycotted for the entire season. We broke the crew leader. He was wiped out. And he was one of the biggest."

The coalition decided that if the cause of farmworker poverty lay with the market power of highly consolidated retail food chains, then the solution would be found there as well. It designed its Campaign for Fair Food and built coalitions with student groups, faith communities, and the labor movement to carry out protests outside of major fast-food chains and supermarkets. It pressured the nine multibillion-dollar retail food chains to sign the agreement, which calls on buyers to pay a Fair Food premium to support a raise in workers' wages, support the Fair Food Code of Conduct that regulates conditions in the fields, purchase only from participating growers, and shift purchases away from any grower who fails to comply with the Fair Food Code. The agreement includes an education program in the fields in which workers learn of their rights under the Fair Food Code. There is now a participatory Complaint Investigation and Resolution Process, or grievance system, through which workers can identify abusive bosses and workplace conditions and eliminate them, without fear of retaliation. They can also work to eliminate "cupping"—the forced overfilling of buckets, until now a standard practice in the industry that can reduce a worker's piece-rate wages by as much as ten percent. The agreement also created Worker Health and Safety Committees to create a space for discussion of workers' concerns, ranging from pesticide poisoning to sexual harassment. And it brought concrete changes in the fields, from the provision of shade to prevent heat-related illnesses to the institution of time clocks, so that workers are paid for all the hours they are on the job. All this is new to the produce industry in Florida. If the major supermarkets can be pressured to sign the agreement it will be one of the most significant victories for farmworkers in decades.

⚜

Immokalee is dotted with tiny, hole-in-the-wall coffee shops and *tiendas*. I sit in one at the end of the day where the food items are listed on pink, orange, and green poster board on the wall behind the counter. The full-throated blast of a Mexican *telenovela* reverberates from a television mounted on the wall. I read the items on the poster board. *Pan con bistec* costs $5.59. *Huevo con chorizo* costs $1.25. There is a glass case with a few Krispy Kreme doughnuts. When the *telenovela* concludes, an announcer with frizzy blond hair begins to read the horoscopes.

"Virgo," she says in Spanish, lips heavy with gloss, eyes coated in blue eyeshadow, "will have interesting experiences."

The woman behind the counter tells me she lives in a trailer with her husband and two sons, ages ten and five. She is undocumented. She said her greatest fear is deportation. She cannot get a driver's license. She drives to her work without one.

"*Si yo estoy parado por la policía, me van a deportar*"—"If I am stopped by the police, they're going to deport me," she says.

She came to work in the fields as a young woman with her father and two brothers.

"I wouldn't get on a bus to go work in the fields unless I was with one of them," she says. "You can't be alone there as a woman. If I went to the bathroom I always went with another woman."

Her father, who because of his age is no longer able to find work, went back to Mexico. One brother is working construction in North Carolina. Another is employed on a poultry farm. Her husband still works in the harvest—*el labor.* She has a job now in the coffee shop. She hopes to keep it and stay out of the fields.

"I could not put my boys to bed when I worked in the fields," she says:

I was not there when they woke up. They slept every night in a trailer with other children whose parents went to find work at 5:00 in the morning with the crew leaders. Our boys were taken to school by a woman who charged parents $25 a week for the service. Now I have this job, but for how long? Now I can put them to bed and take them to school, but for how long? And what will happen when my husband gets too old to work in the fields? Poverty here. Poverty at home. It is a vice. We sacrifice our lives for our boys, but we wonder if their future will be any different.

5

DAYS OF REVOLT

Liberty Square, New York City

⚜

Ideas that have outlived their day may hobble about the world for years, but it is hard for them ever to lead and dominate life. Such ideas never gain complete possession of a man, or they gain possession only of incomplete people.

—ALEXANDER HERZEN

It is impossible to predict the time and progress of revolution. It is governed by its own more or less mysterious laws. But when it comes, it moves irresistibly.

—VLADIMIR ILYICH LENIN

THERE COMES A MOMENT IN ALL POPULAR UPRISINGS WHEN THE DEAD ideas and decayed systems, which only days before seemed unassailable, are exposed and discredited by a population that once stood fearful and supine. This spark occurred on September 17, 2011, in New York City when a few hundred activists, who were easily rebuffed by police in their quixotic attempt to physically occupy Wall Street, regrouped in Zuccotti Park, four blocks away. They were disorganized at first, unsure of what to do, not even convinced they had achieved anything worthwhile, but they had unwittingly triggered a global movement of resistance that would reverberate across the country and in the capitals of Europe. The uneasy status quo, effectively imposed for decades by the elites, was shattered. Another narrative of power took shape. The revolution began.

The devastation on Pine Ridge, in Camden, in southern West Virginia, and in the Florida produce fields has worked its way upward. The corporate leviathan has migrated with the steady and ominous thud of destruction from the outer sacrifice zones to devour what remains. The vaunted American dream, the idea that life will get better, that progress is inevitable if we obey the rules and work hard, that material prosperity is assured, has been replaced by a hard and bitter truth. The American dream, we now know, is a lie. We will all be sacrificed. The virus of corporate abuse—the perverted belief that only corporate profit matters—has spread to outsource our jobs, cut the budgets of our schools, close our libraries, and plague our communities with foreclosures and unemployment. This virus has brought with it a security and surveillance state that seeks to keep us all on a reservation. No one is immune. The suffering of the other, of the Native American, the African American in the inner city, the unemployed coal miner, or the Hispanic produce picker is universal. They went first. We are next. The indifference we showed to the plight of the underclass, in Biblical terms our neighbor, haunts us. We failed them, and in doing so we failed ourselves. We were accomplices in our own demise. Revolt is all we have left. It is the only hope.

There is a mysterious quality to all popular uprisings. Astute observers know the tinder is there, but never when it will be lit. I had watched this dynamism in the Middle East in late 1987. The brutality of the Israeli occupation of the Palestinian territories, which included extrajudicial killings, mass detentions, mass incarcerations, house demolitions, deportations, and crippling poverty in the West Bank and Gaza, was sending out waves of rage, especially through the young, whose dignity, hopes, and dreams were being crushed in the concrete hovels of the Palestinian refugee camps. But none of us expected that a general uprising would be ignited on December 8, 1987, after four Palestinians from the Jabalia refugee camp were killed in a traffic accident involving an Israeli truck. Rioting erupted throughout the occupied territories, including East Jerusalem, followed by commercial strikes, boycotts, and mass demonstrations by tens of thousands of people, including women and children. The Palestine Liberation Organization (PLO), the largest and best organized of the Palestinian resistance groups, was as surprised as the Israelis.

In November 1989, I was in Leipzig, East Germany, covering the street protests which had been started by a few intrepid church leaders. Leipzig, the country's second-largest city and once a major industrial center, was in a state of decay that mirrored what we found in Camden and southern West Virginia. There were streets where all the houses were unoccupied. Roofs had caved in. The glass in the windows, along with the pipes, had been pilfered. The roads in the city were cratered with potholes. The hills outside Leipzig were coated in black coal dust from the lignite mines that produced more than two-thirds of East Germany's electricity. The air was fetid, and the rivers and reservoirs were polluted with staggeringly high levels of mercury and other toxins. There were abnormally high rates of respiratory ailments, birth defects, cancer, and skin diseases.

Like Occupy of 2011, the opposition in Leipzig of 1989, which came together under a group formed that September called New Forum, had nothing that could be called a platform or a specific list of demands. At first, it requested only a "dialogue" with the East German government. It held sparsely attended candle-light vigils in which protestors held up signs calling for peace, disarmament, and protection of the environment. New Forum applied for legal status and was denied. But a few days after the denial, one hundred and fifty thousand people, with little prompting, signed a petition calling for talks between the protestors and the regime. The central group of activists, usually no more than a few dozen, had been demonstrating for years. Now they were joined by hundreds and then thousands of others. On September 18, 1989, when fifteen thousand people attended a march, making it the largest unofficial demonstration in East Germany since 1953, the police and plainclothes internal security force known as the Stasi arrested around a hundred people. Police vans holding the arrested protestors plowed into the crowd, injuring about a dozen demonstrators. A split at that point opened up within the ruling elite between those who wanted to use harsher forms of violence to crush the movement and those who feared that increased force would plunge the country into chaos and street fighting.

On October 9, with one of the largest demonstrations expected to date, Erich Mielke, the secret police chief, unilaterally issued a secret directive to shoot "troublemakers." An elite paratroop regiment was sent to Leipzig and took up positions outside the city center and the railway station, along the route of the march. That evening more than seventy thousand people gathered. It was only at the last minute that the regime lost its nerve, ordering the paratroopers, some of whom were weeping and visibly distressed, to retire.[1] "This was the turning point," Victor Sebestyen writes in his book *Revolution 1989*, "when the people knew that the regime lacked the will or the strength to maintain power."[2] Communist dictator Erich Honecker, who had ruled for eighteen years, lasted in power another week.

No one, including the leaders of the opposition, expected such a swift and stunning collapse. I was with the leaders of the opposition on the afternoon of November 9, 1989. They said they hoped that within a year there would be free access back and forth across the Berlin Wall. A few hours later, the wall, at least as an impediment to human traffic, did not exist. East Germany's internal security apparatus had been one of the most pervasive, feared, and intrusive in the world. There was a Stasi officer or regular informer by the mid-1980s for every sixty-three East Germans.[3] But the corruption, cynicism, rank opportunism, and deep disenchantment within the institutions of control proved fatal.

The rebellion that same year in Prague, as in East Germany, was led not by the mandarins in the political class but by marginalized artists, writers, clerics, activists, labor leaders, and intellectuals such as Václav Havel, whom I and other reporters met with most nights during the Velvet Revolution in the dingy confines of the Magic Lantern Theater. These rebels, no matter how bleak things appeared, had kept alive the possibility of resistance. Their lonely stances and protests took place over forty years of Communist rule. They were pushed to the margins, usually ignored, or periodically denounced and ridiculed by the monolith of state media. The state sought to erase most of their names from national consciousness. Havel was better known abroad than within his own country. Many of these rebels spent years in jail. They were dismissed, when they were even acknowledged, as cranks, foreign agents, fascists, or misguided and irrelevant dreamers. But they persisted. They nurtured and preserved the embers of rebellion. They were to prove that no act of resistance, however solitary, hopeless, and futile it appears in the moment, is useless. These acts keep alive the possibility of resistance and finally hope.

I was in Prague's Wenceslas Square with hundreds of thousands of Czechoslovakians on a cold winter night in 1989, as the singer Marta Kubišová approached the balcony overlooking the square. Kubišová had been banished from the airwaves in 1968 after the Soviet invasion for her anthem of defiance, "Prayer for Marta." Her entire catalogue, including more than two hundred singles, had been confiscated and destroyed by the state. She had disappeared from public view. That night her voice, heard in a public place for the first time in decades, flooded the square. Around me were throngs of students from Charles University, most of whom had not been born when she became a nonperson. They began to sing the words of the anthem along with her. There were tears running down their faces. It was then that I understood the intrinsic power of all acts of rebellion. It was then that I knew the Communist regime was finished.

"The people will once again decide their own fate," the crowd sang in thunderous unison with Kubišová.

Kubišová had been the most popular recording star in the country. She was reduced, after being purged, to assembling toys in a factory. The playwright

Havel was in and out of jail. Jiří Dienstbier, one of the country's most prominent foreign correspondents, was blacklisted after the 1968 uprising. He was working as a janitor when I arrived in Prague and had to leave opposition meetings periodically to tend the boiler at the building where he was employed. He became the country's foreign minister after the fall of communism.

The long, long road of sacrifice, tears, and suffering that led to the collapse of these regimes stretched back decades. Those who made change possible were those who had discarded all notions of the practical. They did not try to reform the Communist Party. They did not attempt to work within the system. They did not know what, if anything, their protests would accomplish. But through it all they held fast to moral imperatives. They did so because these values were right and just. They expected no reward for their virtue, and they got none. They were marginalized and persecuted. And yet these poets, playwrights, actors, clerics, singers, and writers finally triumphed over state and military power. They drew the good to the good. They triumphed because, however cowed and broken the masses around them appeared, their message of defiance did not go unheard. It did not go unseen. The steady drumbeat of rebellion embodied in their lives exposed the rot, lies, and corruption of the state.

The walls of Prague were covered that chilly winter with posters depicting Jan Palach, a university student who set himself on fire in Wenceslas Square on January 16, 1969, to protest the crushing of the country's democracy movement. He died of his burns three days later. The state swiftly attempted to erase Palach and his act of defiance from national memory. There was no mention of it in state media. Police broke up a funeral march by Charles University students. The Communist authorities exhumed Palach's body from its grave, which had become a shrine, cremated his remains, and shipped them to his mother with the provision that his ashes could not be placed in a cemetery. But it did not work. His revolt remained a rallying cry. His sacrifice spurred the students in the winter of 1989 to act. Shortly after I left for Bucharest, the Red Army Square in Prague was renamed Palach Square. Ten thousand people went to the dedication.[4]

In his book *Anatomy of a Revolution*, the historian Crane Brinton laid out the common route to revolution. The preconditions for successful revolution, Brinton argued, are:

- discontent that affects nearly all social classes;

- widespread feelings of entrapment and despair;

- unfulfilled expectations;

- a unified solidarity in opposition to a tiny power elite;

- a refusal by scholars and thinkers to continue to defend the actions of the ruling class;

- an inability of government to respond to the basic needs of citizens;

- a steady loss of will within the power elite itself together with defections from the inner circle—a crippling isolation that leaves the power elite without any allies or outside support

- a financial crisis.

Our corporate elite, as far as Brinton was concerned, has amply fulfilled these preconditions. But it is Brinton's next observation that is most worth remembering. Revolutions always begin, he wrote, by making impossible demands that, if met, would mean the end of the old power configurations. The second stage, the one we have entered now, is the unsuccessful attempt by the power elite to quell the unrest and discontent through physical acts of repression.

At 1:00 A.M. on November 15, 2011, the New York City Police Department raided and shut down the two-month-old Occupy Wall Street encampment in Zuccotti Park. By that time the power elite had lost control of the narrative. The vision and structure of Occupy Wall Street had been imprinted into the minds of thousands of people who passed through the park, renamed Liberty Square by the protesters. The greatest gift the Occupation movement gave us was a blueprint for how to fight back. It recaptured the communitarian spirit of Native American tribes, forming a society where no one was turned away, where food and resources were shared rather than hoarded by a few, and where all had a say in decisions. The Occupy leadership, to protect against personality cults, was consciously horizontal rather than vertical. And its unequivocal denunciation of the corporate state gave it ideological ties to the revolutions in Eastern Europe. This blueprint, this example of another way to form and organize community, was soon transferred to cities and parks across the country and beyond the boundaries of the United States. The Occupy movement serves as a template, much as the Paris Commune of 1871, which only lasted seventy-two days, served as the physical model for nineteenth-century anarchists such as Mikhail Bakunin, who took part in the Commune, as did Karl Marx and Friedrich Engels. The Commune was also decentralized, libertarian, and characterized by improvisation and direct action. And its vision of an egalitarian society was one that, as Paul Avrich wrote, had been articulated by rebels and dissenters since the Middle Ages. Similar social experiments would rise up in Russia at the inception of the revolution, in Germany following World War I, in Barcelona in 1936, in Budapest in 1956, and in Prague in 1968.[5]

"Some defeats are really victories," said the German socialist Karl Liebknecht shortly before his murder in 1919, "while some victories are more shameful than defeats."[6]

Welcome to the revolution. The elites have exposed their hand. They have shown they have nothing to offer. They can destroy but they cannot build. They can repress but they cannot lead. They can steal but they cannot share. They can talk but they cannot speak. They are as dead and useless to us as the water-soaked books, tents, sleeping bags, suitcases, food boxes, and clothes that were dumped into garbage trucks after the New York City police raid that November night. They have no ideas, no plans, and no vision for the future.

Our decaying corporate regime has strutted in Portland, Oakland, Los Angeles, Philadelphia, and New York, sending its baton-wielding cops to clean up "the mess." The state always employs the language of personal hygiene and public security in the effort to make us disappear. They think we will all go home and accept their corporate nation, a nation where crime and government policy have become indistinguishable, where nothing in America, including the ordinary citizen, is deemed by those in power worth protecting or preserving, where corporate oligarchs awash in hundreds of millions of dollars are permitted to loot and pillage the last shreds of collective wealth, human capital, and natural resources, a nation where the poor do not eat and workers do not work, a nation where the sick die and children go hungry, a nation where the consent of the governed and the voice of the people is a cruel joke.

Get back into your cages, they are telling us. Return to watching the lies, absurdities, trivia, celebrity gossip, and political theater we feed you in twenty-four-hour cycles on television. Invest your emotional energy in the vast system of popular entertainment. Run up your credit card debt. Pay your loans. Be thankful for the scraps we toss. Chant back to us our platitudes about democracy, greatness, and freedom. Vote in our rigged corporate elections. Send your young men and women to fight and die in useless, unwinnable wars that provide huge profits for corporations. Stand by mutely as our legislators plunge us into a society without basic social services while Wall Street speculators loot and pillage.

The rogues' gallery of Wall Street crooks—such as Lloyd Blankfein at Goldman Sachs; Howard Milstein at New York Private Bank & Trust; the media tycoon Rupert Murdoch; David and Charles, the Koch brothers; and Jamie Dimon at JPMorgan Chase & Co.—no doubt think the Occupy movement has passed. They think it is back to the business of harvesting what is left of America to swell their personal and corporate fortunes. But they have no concept of what is happening around them. They are as mystified and clueless about these uprisings as the courtiers at Versailles or the Forbidden City, or the inner sanctums of the communist elites in Eastern Europe, who never understood until the very last days that their world was collapsing. Michael Bloomberg, the billionaire mayor of New York, enriched by a deregulated Wall Street, is unable to grasp why people would spend two months sleeping in a park and demonstrating in front of Goldman Sachs. He says he understands that the Occupy protests are "cathartic" and "entertaining," as if demonstrating against the pain of being homeless and unemployed is a form of therapy or amusement. But now, he says, it is time to let the adults handle the affairs of state. Democratic and Republican mayors, along with their parties, have sold us out.[7] But for them this is the beginning of the end.

The elites, and their mouthpieces in the media, were puzzled from the start over what the Occupy Wall Street movement wanted. They asked: "Where is the list of demands? Why don't they present us with specific goals? Why can't they articulate an agenda?" The lack of specific demands and goals was not initially deliberate, but was ultimately inevitable. The Occupy movement understood that it could not work within the system. All energy directed toward reforming political and state structures was wasted. They were not pleading with Congress for electoral reform. They were not looking for a viable candidate. They knew that electoral politics was a farce. They had no faith in the political system or the two major political parties. Anyone who trusts in the reformation of our corporate state fails to recognize that those who govern, including Barack Obama, are as deaf to public demands and suffering as the old communist regimes. The Occupy movement knew the media would not amplify their voices. So they created media of their own. They knew the economy serves the oligarchs, so they formed their own communal system. They found another way to be heard and build a society.

Kevin Zeese is one of the activists who first called for the Occupy movements. We met on a snowy afternoon in Washington at Skewers, a small Middle Eastern restaurant. Zeese and others, including public health-care advocate Dr. Margaret Flowers, set up the Occupy encampment on Freedom Plaza in Washington, D.C. They got a four-day permit in the fall of 2011 and used the time to create an infrastructure—a medic tent, a kitchen, a legal station, and a media center—that would be there if the permit was not extended. The National Park Service did grant them an extended permit, but finally ordered the encampment shut down at the end of January 2012.

"We do have a grand strategy," says Zeese, who was the spokesman for Ralph Nader's 2004 presidential campaign. "Nonviolent movements shift power by attacking the columns that hold the power structure in place. Those columns are the military, police, media, business, workers, youth, faith groups, NGOs, and civil servants. Every time we deal with the police, we have that in mind. The goal is not to hit them, hit them, hit them, and weaken them. The goal is to pull people from those columns to our side. We want the police to know that we understand they're not the 1 percent. The goal is not to get every police officer, but to get enough police so that you have a division.

"We do this with civil servants," he went on. "We do whistle-blower events. We go to different federal agencies with protesters blowing whistles and usually with an actual whistle-blower. We hand out literature to the civil servants about how to blow the whistle safely, where they can get help if they do, why they should do it. We also try to get civil servants by pulling them to our side.

"One of the beautiful things about this security state is that they always know we're coming," Zeese says. "It's never a secret. We don't do anything as a secret. The EPA, for example, sent out a security notice to all of its employees—advertising for us [by warning employees about a coming protest]. So you get the word out.

"Individuals become the media," he says. "An iPhone becomes a live-stream TV. The social network becomes a media outlet. If a hundred of us work together and use our social networks for the same message we can reach as many people as the second-largest newspapers in town, the *Washington Examiner* or the *Washington Times*. If a thousand of us do, we can meet the circulation of the *Washington Post*. We can certainly reach the circulation of most cable news TV shows. The key is to recognize this power and weaken the media structure.

"We started an Occupy house in Mount Rainier in Maryland," Zeese says. "Its focus is Occupy the Economy. This is the U.N.'s year of the co-op. We want to build on that. We want to start worker-owned co-ops and occupy our own co-ops. These co-ops will allow Occupiers to have resources so that they can continue occupying. It will allow them to get resources for the community. It will be an example to the public, a public where a high percentage of people are underemployed and unemployed although they have a lot of skills. People can band together in their community and solve a problem in the community. They can create a worker-owned collaborative of some kind. They can develop models of collective living.

"We looked at polling on seven key issues and found supermajorities of Americans—sixty-plus percent—were with us on issues including health care, retirement, energy, money in politics," he says. "We are more mainstream than Congress. We aren't crazy radicals. We are trying to do what the people want. This is participatory democracy versus oligarchy. It's the elites versus the people. We stand with the majority."

The Washington encampment, like many Occupy encampments, has had to deal with those society has discarded—the homeless, the mentally ill, the destitute, and those whose lives have been devastated by substance abuse. This created a huge burden for the organizers, who decided that they were not equipped or able to deal with these wider, societal problems. The encampment in Washington's Freedom Plaza enforces strict rules of behavior, including an insistence on sobriety, in order to ensure its own survival. Other Occupy movements will have to do the same.

"We don't want to become a soup kitchen or a homeless shelter," Zeese says. "We're a political movement. These are problems beyond our ability. How do we deal with this? Let's feed the Occupiers first, and those who are just squatting here for free get food last, so if we have enough food, we feed them. If we don't, we can't. We always fed people, of course. We usually have enough peanut butter and jelly sandwiches for everyone. But as we debated this issue, we stated talking about things like, 'How about a Freedom Plaza badge, or a Freedom Plaza wristband, or a Freedom Plaza card?' None of those ideas were passed. What we ended up developing was a set of principles. Those principles included in them participation. You can't be there because you want a [tent] or free food. You have to be there to build the community and the movement. You have to participate in the general assemblies.

"The first principles, of course, were nonviolence and non-property destruction," he says. "We don't accept violent language. When you're violent you undermine everything. If the protesters in [Manhattan's] Union Square, who were pepper-sprayed, had been throwing something at the police, you would not have had the movement. It was because they were nonviolent and didn't react when they were being pepper-sprayed that the movement grew. At U.C. Davis, when those cops just walked down the line and sprayed, the nonviolent reaction by those kids was fantastic."

"We constantly kept hearing in the beginning, what are our demands, what are our demands, is our demand to meet with Obama?" Zeese says. "We said: 'Oh no, that would just be a waste. If we meet with Obama, he'll just get a picture opportunity out of that. We won't get anything.' You don't make demands until you have power. If you make demands too soon, you don't demand enough and you can't enforce the demand that you get. So if you get promised an election, you can't enforce that the ballots are counted right, for example. We realized late into our discussions—we had six months of planning, so four months into it—'we don't have the power to make a demand.' That was very hard for a lot of our people to accept.

"Instead of making demands, we put up what we stood for, what principles we wanted to see," Zeese says. "The overarching demand was end corporate rule, shift power to the people. Once you make that as your demand, as your pinnacle, you can pick any issue—energy, health care, elections—and the solution becomes evident. For health care, it's get the insurance companies out from between doctors and patients; on finance, it's break up the big banks so that six banks don't control sixty percent of the economy, and break them up into community banks so that the money stays at home rather than going to Wall Street; energy is to diversify energy sources so people can build and have their own energy on their roof and become energy producers. The overarching goal was: End corporate rule, shift power to the people. We developed a slogan: 'Human needs before corporate greed.' After that, everything fell into place for us."

When the congressional supercommittee was meeting, the Occupy Washington movement formed its own supercommittee. The Occupy Super Committee, which managed to get its hearing aired on C-SPAN, included experts on the wealth divide, fair taxation, the military budget, job creation, health care, and democratizing the economy as well as giving voice to the ninety-nine percent. A report titled "The 99%'s Deficit Proposal: How to Create Jobs, Reduce the Wealth Divide and Control Spending," resulted from the Occupy hearing. The report made evidence-based recommendations Zeese knew would not be considered by Congress, but still he saw the report as foundational for the movement.

"History shows the demands made by those in revolt are never initially considered by government," he says. "Our job is to make the politically impossible the politically inevitable."

This rebellion will not stop until the corporate state is extinguished. It will not stop until there is an end to the corporate abuse of the poor, the working class, the elderly, the sick, children, or those being slaughtered in our imperial wars and tortured in our black sites. It will not stop until foreclosures and bank repossessions stop. It will not stop until students no longer have to go into debt to be educated, and families no longer have to plunge into bankruptcy to pay medical bills. It will not stop until the corporate destruction of the ecosystem stops, and our relationships with one another and the planet are radically reconfigured. And that is why the elites, and the rotted and degenerate system of corporate power they sustain, are at once terrified and befuddled. That is why they keep asking what the demands are. They don't understand.

"Something is happening here," Bob Dylan sang in "Ballad of a Thin Man." "But you don't know what it is,/ Do you, Mister Jones?"

The corporate state, if it understood the depth of the suffering and rage of tens of millions of Americans, would institute profound reforms to mitigate the poverty and despair. The $1 trillion in student debt, which now surpasses credit card debt, would be forgiven.[8] There would be a moratorium on foreclosures and bank repossessions, which took the homes of seven million people between 2008 and 2011 and was expected to dispossess another two million in 2011.[9] There would be a $1 trillion jobs program targeted at those under the age of twenty-five. And this is the minimum. The New Deal in the 1930s, for all the vicious assaults it endured from business interests and right-wing politicians, was in fact the mechanism that saved capitalism, which had come perilously close to collapse. The misguided attempt by the corporate state to physically eradicate protests and the Occupy encampments without addressing the issues that brought people into the streets is a dark and ominous sign. The rage will find other nonviolent organizing outlets. Or it will eventually descend into violence.

The political philosopher Sheldon Wolin uses the term *inverted totalitarianism* in his book *Democracy Incorporated* to describe our political system. In inverted totalitarianism, the sophisticated technologies of corporate control, intimidation, and mass manipulation, which far surpass those employed by previous totalitarian states, are effectively masked by the glitter, noise, and abundance of a consumer society. Political participation and civil liberties are gradually surrendered. Corporations, hiding behind this smokescreen, devour us from the inside out. They have no allegiance to the country.

The corporate state does not find its expression in a demagogue or charismatic leader. It is defined by the anonymity and facelessness of the corporation. Corporations, who hire attractive and eloquent spokespeople like Barack Obama, control the uses of science, technology, education, and mass communication. They control the messages in movies and television. And they use these tools of communication to bolster tyranny. Our systems of mass communication, as Wolin writes, "block out, eliminate whatever might introduce qualification, ambiguity, or dialogue, anything that might weaken or complicate the holistic force of their creation, to its total impression."[10]

The result is a monochromatic system of information. Celebrity courtiers, masquerading as journalists, officially anointed experts and specialists, identify our problems and patiently explain the parameters. All who argue outside the imposed parameters are dismissed as irrelevant cranks, extremists, or members of a radical left. Prescient social critics are banished. Acceptable opinions, as Dorothy Parker once said of Katherine Hepburn's emotional range as an actor, run the gamut from A to B. The culture, under the tutelage of these corporate courtiers, becomes a world of cheerful conformity, as well as an endless and finally fatal optimism. We busy ourselves buying products that promise to change our lives, make us more beautiful, confident, or successful, as we are steadily stripped of rights, money, and influence. All messages we receive through these systems of communication, whether on the nightly news or talk shows like *The Oprah Winfrey Show*, promise a brighter, happier tomorrow. And this, as Wolin points out, is "the same ideology that invites corporate executives to exaggerate profits and conceal losses, but always with a sunny face."[11] We have been entranced, as Wolin writes, by "continuous technological advances" that "encourage elaborate fantasies of individual prowess, eternal youthfulness, beauty through surgery, actions measured in nanoseconds: a dream-laden culture of ever-expanding control and possibility, whose denizens are prone to fantasies because the vast majority have imagination but little scientific knowledge."[12]

Our manufacturing base has been dismantled. Speculators and swindlers have looted the U.S. Treasury and stolen billions from small shareholders who had set aside money for retirement or college. Civil liberties, once guaranteed under our Constitution, have been stripped away. Basic services, including public education and health care, have been handed over to the corporations to exploit for profit.

But the façade is crumbling. And as more and more people realize that they have been used and robbed, we move from Aldous Huxley's *Brave New World* to George Orwell's *1984*. In Orwell's novel most of the citizens in Oceania did not live there. The Inner Party composed about two percent of the population. The Outer Party composed another thirteen percent. The remaining one hundred million people were outcasts or "proles." A similar configuration of wealth and power, one replicated by most centralized totalitarian systems of authority, is now our own. The well-paying jobs are not coming back. The largest deficits in human history[13] mean that we are trapped in a debt peonage system that will be used by the corporate state to eradicate the last vestiges of social protection for citizens, including Social Security. The state, dominated by two corporate parties, has devolved from a capitalist democracy to a stark neofeudalism. The elites have squandered the country's wealth on two of the costliest and most useless wars in American history while blithely pretending the environmental crisis does not exist. News and entertainment bleed into each other to become indistinguishable. There is constant reporting on the foibles of those in shows such as *Jersey Shore*, *Keeping Up with the Kardashians* or *The Real Housewives of Beverly Hills*. But as our predicament becomes more apparent, anger is replacing the corporate-imposed cheerful conformity and chatter of celebrity gossip. The bleakness of our postindustrial pockets, where more than fifty million Americans live in poverty and tens of millions in a category called "near poverty,"[14] coupled with the lack of credit to save families from foreclosures, bank repossessions, and bankruptcy from medical bills, means that inverted totalitarianism no longer works.

And the global elite know it. They have lost all sense of proportion. They wage vast and expanding wars and proxy wars against desperate groups of fanatics who have no conventional military and little more than box cutters and assault rifles. They build ever more elaborate walls and security systems to protect themselves, including the vast internal security apparatus of the U.S. Department of Homeland Security, with some one million employees. The elites are lashing out with such disproportionate force, fury, and viciousness against peaceful protestors, many of whom come out of the middle class, as well as Muslims in the Middle East, that they are turning ever greater numbers of an alienated mass, at home and abroad, against them.

We, like those who opposed the long night of communism, no longer have any mechanisms within the formal structures of power that will protect or advance our rights. We, too, have undergone a coup d'état carried out not by the stone-faced leaders of a monolithic Communist Party, but by our largely anonymous corporate overlords. George Orwell wrote that all tyrannies rule through fraud and force, but that once the fraud is exposed they must rely exclusively on force. We have now entered the era of naked force. The internal security and surveillance state, justified in the name of the war on terror, will be the instrument used against us. The corrosion of the legal system, begun by George W. Bush and codified by Barack Obama's Democratic administration, means we can all be denied habeas corpus. The warrantless wiretapping, eavesdropping, and monitoring of tens of millions of citizens, once illegal, is now legal. The state has given itself the power to unilaterally declare U.S. citizens as enemy combatants and torture or assassinate them, as Barack Obama did when he in September 2011 ordered the killing of the American-born Islamist cleric Anwar al-Awlaki in Yemen.[15] The state can deny U.S. citizens suspected of what it vaguely defines as "terrorist" activities the right to a trial. It can turn these citizens over to the military, which can hold them without charges indefinitely. Our country's capacity for draconian control in the face of widespread unrest means we will be no different from other totalitarian regimes throughout history. Police forces in major cities have been transformed into paramilitary units with assault rifles, helicopters, and armored vehicles. Almost certainly, if the pressure mounts, as I expect it will, these militarized police forces will become ubiquitous and people will be killed.

The corruption of the legal system—the ability of the state to make legal what was once illegal—is always the precursor to totalitarian rule. The timidity of those tasked with protecting our Constitutional rights—the media, elected officials, judges, the one million lawyers in this country, and the thousands of law school professors and law school deans—means there is no internal mechanism with which to decry or prevent abuse. Occupy encampments were violently shut down by police in major cities, including St. Louis, Salt Lake City, Denver, Portland, Oakland, Philadelphia, Los Angeles, and New York City. Voices tasked with defending the rule of law and the right of dissent and nonviolent protest remained silent. If peaceful protest is not defended, if it is effectively thwarted by the corporate state, we will see widespread anger and frustration manifest in an ascendant militancy, rioting, the destruction of property, and violence.

"Do you begin to see, then, what kind of world we are creating?" Orwell wrote in *1984*. "It is the exact opposite of the stupid hedonistic Utopias that the old reformers imagined. A world of fear and treachery and torment, a world of trampling and being trampled upon, a world which will grow not less but more merciless as it refines itself."

Despotic regimes, in the end, collapse internally. Once the foot soldiers ordered to carry out acts of repression and violence to protect the elite no longer obey orders, disgraced regimes swiftly crumble. They never appear that fragile from the outside. In the fall of 1989, the massive machinery of the Communist Party in then-Eastern Germany, and the expansive internal security network of the Stasi, seemed to those of us who were there, including those leading the street protests, unassailable. And yet as soon as peaceful protests rocked the country, the East German state crumbled within weeks. The Romanian dictator Nicolae Ceaușescu, referred to as the *Conducător* or "Leader," ruled through terror and a state-sponsored personality cult. He stood on a balcony in Palace Square in Bucharest on December 20, 1989, before a crowd of one hundred and ten thousand people bused in from factories and offices or press-ganged off the streets of the capital by the Securitate, the state security apparatus. Ceaușescu, with his wife Elena at his side, walked out and stood before the crowd at 12:31 in the afternoon and began to speak into a bank of four microphones. The rally of adulation for the leader began the way countless events in the past had begun. There were cheers and applause. But eight minutes into his speech, there were faint sounds of booing and catcalls and a steady chant of TI-MI-ȘOA-RA, the name of the city where the regime had launched a bloody crackdown on protestors. Ceaușescu looked first confused and then frightened as crowds for the first time began to shout him down with the words: "Ceauşescu, we are the People!" and "Down with the Killer!" He stopped speaking and hastily ended his speech. He and his wife attempted to flee the city in a helicopter, but they were captured and executed four days later by a firing squad. Victor Stănculescu, the army general whom Ceauşescu had depended on to crush protests, was the one who oversaw his Christmas Day execution.[16] Tunisia's Ben Ali and Egypt's Hosni Mubarak lost power once a passive and cowed population found its voice and these dictators could no longer count on the security forces or the military to fire into crowds.

⤞✦⤝

We may feel powerless in the face of the ruthless corporate destruction of our nation, our culture, and our ecosystem. But we are not. We have a power, as the Occupy encampments demonstrated, that terrifies the corporate state. Any act of rebellion, no matter how few people show up or how heavily it is censored, chips away at corporate power. Any act of rebellion keeps alive the embers for larger movements that follow us. It passes on another narrative. It will, as the state consumes itself, attract larger and larger numbers. Perhaps the full-blown revolution will not happen in our lifetimes. But if we persist, we can keep this possibility alive. If we do not, it will die.

The process of defection among the ruling class and security forces is slow and often imperceptible. And the protestors can encourage and invite defections by rigidly adhering to nonviolence, refusing to respond to police provocation, and showing verbal respect for the blue-uniformed police, no matter how unbearable they can be while wading into crowds and using batons as battering rams. As the Polish dissident Adam Michnik correctly observed: "A revolution that begins by burning down Bastilles, will in time build new Bastilles of its own."[17] Some of the first cracks in the edifice may have opened in Oakland, California. When Oakland Mayor Jean Quan ordered police to clear the encampment of Occupy Oakland, mayoral deputy Sharon Cornu and the mayor's legal adviser and longtime friend, Dan Siegel, resigned in protest. What the media initially saw as a victory for establishment political forces turned out to be a major embarrassment for the Quan administration. "Support Occupy Oakland, not the 1% and its government facilitators," Siegel tweeted after his resignation.[18]

The Occupy Wall Street activists in New York and the encampments that soon followed across the country and in foreign capitals had internalized what Czechoslovakian dissident Havel articulated in his 1978 essay "The Power of the Powerless." Havel wrote a reflection on the mind of a greengrocer who, as instructed, puts up a poster "among the onions and carrots" that reads: "Workers of the World—Unite!" The poster is displayed, Havel writes, partly out of habit, partly because everyone else does it, and partly out of fear of the consequences of not following the rules. The greengrocer would not, Havel writes, display a poster saying: "I am afraid and therefore unquestioningly obedient."

> . . . that one day something in our greengrocer snaps and he stops putting up the slogans merely to ingratiate himself. He stops voting in elections he knows are a farce. He begins to say what he really thinks at political meetings. And he even finds the strength in himself to express solidarity with those whom his conscience commands him to support. In this revolt the greengrocer steps out of living within the lie. He rejects the ritual and breaks the rules of the game. He discovers once more his suppressed identity and dignity. He gives his freedom a concrete significance. His revolt is an attempt to live within the truth . . .

This attempt to "live within the truth" brings with it ostracism and retribution. But punishment is imposed in bankrupt systems because of the necessity for compliance, not out of any real conviction. And the real crime committed is not the crime of speaking out or defying the rules, but the crime of exposing the charade:

> By breaking the rules of the game, he has disrupted the game as such, he has exposed it as a mere game. He has shattered the world of appearances, the fundamental pillar of the system. He has upset the power structure by tearing apart what holds it together. He has demonstrated that living a lie is living a lie. He has broken through the exalted façade of the system and exposed the real, base foundations of power. He has said that the emperor is naked. And because the emperor is in fact naked, something extremely dangerous has happened: by his action, the greengrocer has addressed the world. He has enabled everyone to peer behind the curtain. He has shown

everyone that it is possible to live within the truth. Living within the lie can constitute the system only if it is universal. The principle must embrace and permeate everything. There are no terms whatsoever on which it can coexist with living within the truth, and therefore everyone who steps out of line denies it in principle and threatens it in its entirety.[19]

Those who do not carve out spaces separate from the state and its systems of power, those who cannot find room to become autonomous, or who do not "live in truth," inevitably become compromised. In Havel's words, they "are the system." The Occupy movement, by naming corporate power and refusing to compromise with it, by forming alternative systems of community and society, embodies Havel's call to "live in truth." It does not appeal to the systems of control, and for this reason it is a genuine threat to the corporate state.[20]

Movements that call on followers to "live in truth" do not always succeed. They failed in Nicaragua, El Salvador, and Guatemala in the 1970s and 1980s, as well as in Yugoslavia in the 1990s, triggering armed insurgencies and blood-drenched civil wars. They have failed so far in Iran, the Israeli-occupied territories, and Syria. China has a movement modeled after Havel's Charter 77 called Charter 08. But the Chinese opposition has been effectively suppressed, although its principal author, Liu Xiaobo, currently serving an eleven-year prison term for "incitement of subversion of state power," was awarded the Nobel Prize.[21] Power elites that stubbornly refuse to heed popular will and resort to harsher and harsher forms of state control can easily provoke counterviolence. The first Palestinian uprising, which lasted from 1987 to 1992, saw crowds of demonstrators throw rocks at Israeli soldiers, but it was largely a nonviolent movement. The second uprising, or intifada, which erupted in 2000 and endured for five years, with armed attacks on Israeli soldiers and civilians, was not. History is dotted with brutal fratricides spawned by calcified and repressive elites. And even when these nonviolent movements do succeed, it is impossible to predict when they will spawn an uprising or how long the process will take. As Timothy Garton Ash noted about the revolutions in Eastern Europe, in Poland it took ten years, in East Germany ten weeks, in Czechoslovakia ten days.[22]

Karl Marx wrote that bourgeois revolutions, despite their drama and even ecstasy, are by nature short-lived. They reach a zenith and then are absorbed back into the society. Proletarian revolutions, however:

. . . constantly criticize themselves, constantly interrupt themselves in their own course, return to the apparently accomplished, in order to begin anew; they deride with cruel thoroughness the half-measures, weaknesses, and paltriness of their first attempts, seem to throw down their opponents only so the latter may draw new strength from the earth and rise before them again more gigantic than ever, recoil constantly from the indefinite colossalness of their own goals—until a situation is created which makes all turning back impossible, and the conditions themselves call out: "Hier ist die Rose, hier tanze"[23]—["Here is the rose; dance here"].

Ketchup, a petite twenty-two-year-old from Chicago with wavy red hair and bright red-framed glasses, arrived in Zuccotti Park in New York City on September 17, 2011. She had a tent, a rolling suitcase, forty dollars worth of food, the graphic version of Howard Zinn's *A People's History of the United States*, and a sleeping bag. She had no return ticket, no idea what she was undertaking, and no acquaintances among the stragglers who joined her that afternoon to begin the Occupy Wall Street movement. She decided to go to New York after reading the Canadian magazine *Adbusters* calling for the occupation, although she noted when she got to the park that *Adbusters* had no discernible presence.

The lords of finance in the looming towers surrounding the park, who toy with money and lives, who make the political class, the press, and the judiciary jump at their demands, who destroy the ecosystem for profit and drain the U.S. Treasury to gamble and speculate, took little notice of Ketchup or any of the other scruffy activists on the street below them. The elites consider everyone outside their sphere marginal or invisible. And what significance could an artist who paid her bills by waitressing have for the powerful? What could she and the others in Zuccotti Park do to them? What threat can the weak pose to the strong? Those who worship money believe their buckets of cash, like the $4.6 million JPMorgan Chase gave to the New York City Police Foundation, can buy them perpetual power and security. Masters all, kneeling before the idols of the marketplace, blinded by their self-importance, impervious to human suffering, bloated from unchecked greed and privilege, they did not know they were about to be taught a lesson in hubris.

In those first hours there was nothing but confusion, uncertainty, and an energy that buzzed through the streets like an electric current.

Ketchup in Liberty Square.

"We get to the park," Ketchup says of the first day:

There's madness for a little while. There were a lot of people. They were using megaphones at first. Nobody could hear. Then someone says we should get into circles and talk about what needed to happen, what we thought we could accomplish. And so that's what we did. There was a note-taker in each circle. I don't know what happened with those notes, probably nothing, but it was a good start. One person at a time, airing your ideas. There was one person saying that he wasn't very hopeful about what we could accomplish here, that he wasn't very optimistic. And then my response was that "well, we have to be optimistic, because if anybody's going to get anything done, it's going to be us here." People said different things about what our priorities should be. People were talking about the one-demand idea. Someone called for AIG executives to be prosecuted. There was someone who had come from Spain to be there, saying that she was here to help us avoid the mistakes that were made in Spain. It was a wide spectrum. Some had come because of their own personal suffering or what they saw in the world.

"After the circles broke I felt disheartened because it was sort of chaotic," she said. "I didn't have anybody there, so it was a little depressing. I didn't know what was going to happen."

John Friesen, twenty-seven, tall and lanky with a long, dirty-blond ponytail, a purple scarf, and an old green fleece, was also one of the first to arrive in the park. Joe and I find him sitting on the concrete edge of Zuccotti Park one morning, leading a coordination meeting, a gathering that took place every morning with representatives of each of Occupy Wall Street's roughly forty working groups.

"Our conversation is about what it means to be a movement and what it means to be an organization," he says to the circle. A heated discussion follows, including a debate over whether the movement should make specific demands.

We look for him later and see him on a low stone wall surrounding a flower bed in the park. He decided to come to New York City, he said, from the West Coast for the tenth anniversary of 9/11. He found a ride on Craigslist while staying at his brother's home in Champaign, Illinois.

"It was a television event when I was seventeen," he says of the 2001 attacks.

"I came here for the ten-year anniversary. I wanted to make it real to myself. I'd never been to New York. I'd never been to the East Coast."

Once he reached New York City, he connected with local street people to find "assets." He slept in parks and on the street. Arriving on the first day of the occupation in Zuccotti Park, he found other "traveler types" whose survival skills and political consciousness were as developed as his own.

In those first few days, he says, "it was the radicals and the self-identifying anarchists" who set up the encampment. Those who would come later, usually people with little experience in Dumpster diving, sleeping on concrete, or depending on a McDonald's restroom, would turn to revolutionists like Friesen for survival. Zuccotti Park, like most Occupied sites, schooled the uninitiated.

"The structure and process carried out by those initial radicals," he says with delight of the first days in the park, "now have a wide appeal."

The park, like other Occupied sites across the country, became a point of integration, a place where middle-class men and women were taught by those who have been carrying out acts of rebellion for years. These revolutionists bridged the world of the streets with the world of the middle class.

"They're like foreign countries almost, the street culture and the suburban culture," Friesen says:

> They don't understand each other. They don't share their experiences. They're isolated from each other. It's like Irvine and Orange County [home of the city of Irvine]; the hearsay is that they deport the homeless. They pick them up and move them out. There's no trying to engage. And it speaks to the larger issue, I feel, of the isolation of the individual. The individual going after their individual pursuits, and this façade of individuality, of consumeristic materialism. This materialism is about an individuality that is surface-deep. It has no depth. That's translated into communities throughout the country that don't want anything to do with each other, that are so foreign to each other that there is hardly a drop of empathy between them.

The Occupy movements fused the elements vital for revolt. They attracted small groups of veteran revolutionists whose isolated struggles, whether in the form of squatter communities or acts of defiance such as the tree-sit protest in Berkeley that ran from December 1, 2006, to September 9, 2008, to save an oak grove on the University of California campus,[24] are often unheeded by the wider culture. The Occupy movements, like the movements in Eastern Europe, were nurtured in numerous small, dissident enclaves. Bands of revolutionists in cities such as New York, Oakland, Chicago, Denver, Boston, San Francisco, Eugene, Portland, Los Angeles, and Atlanta severed themselves from the mainstream, joined with other marginalized communities, and mastered the physical techniques of surviving on the streets and in jails.

"It's about paying attention to exactly what you need, and figuring out where I can get food and water, what time do the parks close, where I can get a shower," Friesen says.

Friesen grew up in an apolitical middle-class home in Fullerton in southern California's Orange County, where systems of power were obeyed and rarely questioned. His window into political consciousness began inauspiciously when

John Friesen in Liberty Square.

he was a teenager, with the Beatles, The Doors, and Crosby, Stills, Nash & Young. He found in the older music "a creative energy" and "authenticity" that he did not hear often in contemporary culture. He finished high school and got a job in a LensCrafters lab and "experienced what it's like to slave away trying to make glasses in an hour." He worked at a few other nine-to-five jobs but found them "restrictive and unfulfilling." And then he started to drift, working his way up to Berkeley, where he lived in a squatter encampment behind the U.C. Berkeley football stadium. He used the campus gym to take showers. By the time he reached Berkeley he had left mainstream society. He has lived outside the formal economy since 2005, the last year he filed income taxes. He was involved in the tree-sit protest and took part in the occupations of university buildings and the demonstration outside the Berkeley chancellor's campus residence to protest fee hikes and budget cuts, activities that saw him arrested and jailed. He spent time with the Navajos on Black Mesa in Arizona and two months with the Zapatista Army of Liberation in Mexico.

"What I saw in the Zapatistas was a people pushed to the brink of extinction and forgetting," he says. "Their phrases ring true: 'Liberty! Dignity! Democracy!' 'Everything for Everyone! Nothing for Ourselves!' The masks the Zapatistas wear check egos. People should be united in their facelessness. This prevents cults of personality.

"I have no interest in participating in the traditional political process," he says:

It's bureaucratic. It's vertical. It's exclusive. It's ruled by money. It's cumbersome. This is cumbersome, too, what we're doing here, but the principles that I'm pushing and that many people are pushing to uphold here are in direct opposition to the existing structure. This is a counterpoint. This is an acknowledgement of all those things that we hate, or that I hate, which are closed and exclusive. It is about defying status and power, certification and legitimacy, institutional validation to participate. This process has infected our consciousness as far as people being allowed [to participate] or even being given credibility. The wider society creates a situation where people are excluded. People feel like they're not worth anything. They're not accepted. The principles here are horizontal in terms of decision-making, transparency, openness, inclusiveness, accessibility. There are people doing sign language at the general assembly now. There are clusters of deaf people that come together and do sign language together. This is an example of the inclusive nature that we want to create here. And as far as redefining participation and the democratic process, my understanding of American history is that it was a bunch of white males in power, mostly. This is radically different. If you're a homeless person, if you're a street person, you can be here. There's a radical inclusion that's going on.

The park, especially at night, became a magnet for the city's street population. The movement provided food along with basic security, overseen by designated "peacekeepers" and a "de-escalation team" that defuses conflicts. Those like Friesen who span the two cultures of the middle class and the homeless and destitute, served as the interlocutors. But even Friesen, by the end, was burned out as he and the other facilitators lost control of the park. The arrival in the cold weather of individual tents, along with numerous street people with mental impairments and addictions, tore apart the community. Drug use, as well as assaults and altercations, became common. When the final assault by the police took place on November 15, 2011 Friesen, who with a few protestors had chained themselves around the kitchen, said he at once half hoped for the encampment's dissolution. As he and the other stalwarts in lock-down around the kitchen area were cut loose and arrested he looked at the names on the police badges, addressed the officers by name, and told them that they had a choice in life about their own actions.

"You're dealing with everyone's conditioning, everyone's fucked-up conditioning, the kind of I'm-out-for-me-and-myself, that kind of instinct," he says. "People are unruly. People are violent. People make threats.

"We are trying to sort this out, how to work together in a more holistic approach versus just security-checking someone—you know, like tackling them," he says:

Where else do these people have to go, these street people? They're going to come to a place where they feel cared for, especially in immediate needs like food and shelter. We have a Comfort committee. I've never been to a place where there's a Comfort committee. This is where you can get a blanket and a sleeping bag, if we have them. We don't always have the resources. But everyone is being taken care of here. As long as you're nonviolent, you're taken care of. And when you do that, you draw all sorts of people, including those people who have problematic behavior.

"This is a demand to be heard," he says of the movement. "It's a demand to have a voice. People feel voiceless. They want a voice and participation, a renewed sense of self-determination, but not self-determination in the individualistic need of just-for-me-myself. But as in 'I recognize that my actions have effects on the people around me. I acknowledge that, so let's work together so that we can accommodate everyone.'"

Friesen says that digital systems of communication helped inform new structures of communication and new systems of self-governance.

"Open-source started out in the '50s and '60s over how software is used and what rights the user has over the programs and tools they use," he says. "What freedoms do you have to use, modify, and share software? That's translated into things like Wikipedia. We're moving even more visibly and more tangibly into a real, tangible, human organization. We modify techniques. We use them. We share them. We decentralize them. You see the decentralization of a movement like this."

Revolutions need their theorists, but such upheavals are impossible without practical revolutionists like Friesen, who haul theory out of books and shove it into the face of reality. By the end of the nineteenth century, practical anarchists such as Mikhail Bakunin were as revered by revolutionists as Karl Marx. Bakunin's entire adult life was one of fierce physical struggle, from his role in the uprisings of 1848, where, with his massive bulk and iron determination, he manned barricades in Paris, Austria, and Germany, to his years in the prisons of Czarist Russia and his dramatic escape from exile in Siberia.

Bakunin had little time for Marx's disdain for the peasantry and the *Lumpenproletariat* of the urban slums. Marx, for all his insight into the self-destructive machine of unfettered capitalism, viewed the poor as a conservative force, those least capable of revolutionary action. Marx saw them as a social force that would be made irrelevant by the growth of capitalist forces and caustically referred to them as a "sack of potatoes."[25] Bakunin, however, saw in the "uncivilized, disinherited, and illiterate" a pool of revolutionists who would join the working class and turn on the elites who profited from their misery and enslavement. Bakunin proved to be the more prophetic. The successful revolutions that swept through the Slavic republics, Russia, Spain, and China, and those movements that battled colonialism in Africa and the Middle East as well as military regimes in Latin America, were largely spontaneous uprisings fueled by the rage of a disenfranchised rural and urban working class and dispossessed intellectuals. Revolutionary activity, Bakunin correctly observed, was best entrusted to those who had no property, no regular employment, and no stake in the status quo. Finally, Bakunin's vision of revolution, which challenged Marx's rigid bifurcation between the proletariat and the bourgeoisie, carved out a vital role for these rootless intellectuals, the talented sons and daughters of the middle class who had been educated to serve within elitist institutions, or expected a place in the middle class, but who had been cast aside by society. The discarded intellectuals—unemployed journalists, social workers, teachers, artists, lawyers, and students—were for Bakunin a valuable revolutionary force: "fervent, energetic youths, totally déclassé, with no career or way out." These déclassé intellectuals, like the dispossessed working class, had no stake in the system and no possibility for advancement. The alliance of an estranged class of intellectuals with dispossessed masses creates the tinder, Bakunin argued, for successful revolt. This alliance allows a revolutionary movement to skillfully articulate grievances while exposing and exploiting, because of a familiarity with privilege and power, the weaknesses of autocratic, tyrannical rule.[26]

"It's funny that the cops won't let us use megaphones, because it's to make our lives harder, but we actually end up making a much louder sound [with the "people's mic"] and I imagine it's much more annoying to the people around us," Ketchup says of the first day in the park:

I had been in the back, unable to hear. I walked to different parts of the circle. I saw this man talking in short phrases and people were repeating them. I don't know whose idea it was, but that started on the first night. The first general assembly was a little chaotic because people had no idea . . . "a general assembly, what is this for?" At first it was kind of grandstanding about what were our demands. Ending corporate personhood is one that has come up again and again as a favorite and. . . . What ended up happening was, they said, "OK, we're going to break into work groups."

"People were worried we were going to get kicked out of the park at 10 P.M.," she goes on, speaking of the first night. "This was a major concern. There were tons of cops. I've heard that it's costing the city a ton of money to have constant surveillance on a bunch of peaceful protesters who aren't hurting anyone. With the people's mic, everything we do is completely transparent. We know there are

undercover cops in the crowd. I think I was talking to one last night, but it's like, what are you trying to accomplish? We don't have any secrets.

"The undercover cops are the only ones who ask, 'Who's the leader?'" she says. "Presumably, if they know who our leaders are, they can take them out. The fact is we have no leader. There's no leader, so there's nothing they can do.

"There was a woman [in the medics unit]," she says. "This guy was pretending to be a reporter. The first question he asks is, 'Who's the leader?' She goes, 'I'm the leader.' And he says, 'Oh yeah, what are you in charge of?' She says, 'I'm in charge of everything.' He says, 'Oh yeah? What's your title?' She says, 'God.'

"So it's 9:30 P.M. and people are worried that they're going to try and rush us out of the camp," she says:

> At 9:30 they break into work groups. I joined the group on contingency plans. The job of the Bedding group was to find cardboard for people to sleep on. The Contingency group had to decide what to do if they kick us out. The big decision we made was to announce to the group that if we were dispersed, we were going to meet back at 10 A.M. the next day in the park. Another group was arts and culture. What was really cool was that we assumed we were going to be there more than one night. There was a food group. They were going Dumpster diving. The direct action committee plans for direct, visible action like marches. There was a security team. It's security against the cops. The cops are the only people we think might hurt us. The security team keeps people awake in shifts. They always have people awake.

The working groups make logistical decisions, and the general assembly makes large policy decisions. Working groups blossomed in the following days. The Media working group was joined by a Welcome working group for new arrivals. There was a Sanitation working group that included members who went around the park on skateboards as they carried brooms. A Legal working group was formed with lawyers, along with an Events working group, an Education working group, Medics, and a Facilitation working group, which trained new facilitators for the general assembly meetings. There was a Public Relations working group, and an Outreach working group, for like-minded communities as well as the general public. There was an Internet working group and an Open-Source Technology working group. The nearby McDonald's became the

The people's mic at work in Washington Square Park.

principal bathroom for the park after Burger King banned protesters from its facilities.

Caucuses also grew up in the encampment, including a "Speak Easy caucus."

"That's a caucus I started," Ketchup says. "It is for a broad spectrum of individuals from female-bodied people who identify as women to male-bodied people who are not traditionally masculine. I was just talking to a woman named Sharon who's interested in starting a caucus for people of color.

"A caucus gives people a safe space to talk to each other without people from the culture of their oppressors present," she says. "It gives them greater power together, so that if the larger group is taking an action that the caucus felt was specifically against their interests, then the caucus can block that action. Consensus can potentially still be reached after a caucus blocks something, but a block, or a 'paramount objection,' is really serious. You're saying that you are willing to walk out.

"We've done a couple of things so far," she says:

So, you know the live stream? The comments are moderated on the live stream. There are moderators who remove racist comments, comments that say, 'I hate cops' or 'Kill cops.' They remove irrelevant comments that have nothing to do with the movement. There is this woman who is incredibly hardworking and intelligent. She has been the driving force of the finance committee. Her hair is half-blond and half-black. People were referring to her as "blond-black hottie." These comments weren't moderated, and at one point whoever was running the camera took the camera off her face and did a body scan. So, that was one of the first things the caucus talked about. We decided as a caucus that I would go to the moderators and tell them this is a serious problem. If you're moderating other offensive comments, then you need to moderate these kinds of offensive comments.

The heart of the movement became the two daily meetings, held in the morning and the evening. The assemblies, which usually lasted about two hours, started with a review of process, which was open to change and improvement, so people were clear about how the assembly worked. Those who wanted to speak raised their hand to get "on stack."

"There's a stack-keeper," Ketchup says. "The stack-keeper writes down your name or some signifier for you. A lot of white men are the people raising their hands. So, anyone who is not apparently a white man gets to jump stack. The stack-keeper will make note of the fact that the person who put their hand up was not a white man and will arrange the list so that it's not dominated by white men. People don't get called up in the same order as they raise their hand."

When someone spoke, their words were amplified by the people's mic. The crowd indicated approval, indifference, or disapproval silently through hand signals.

"Putting your fingers up like this," she says, holding her hands up and wiggling her fingers, "means you like what you're hearing, or you're in agreement. Like this," she said, holding her hands level and wiggling her fingers, "means you don't like it so much. Fingers down, you don't like it at all; you're not in agreement. Then there's this triangle you make with your hand that says 'point of process.' So, if you think that something is not being respected within the process that we've agreed to follow, then you can bring that up.

"You wait till you're called," she says:

These rules get abused all the time, but they are important. We start with agenda items, which are proposals or group discussions. Then working group report-backs, so you know what every working group is doing. Then we have general announcements. The agenda items have been brought to the facilitators by the working groups because you need the whole group to pay attention. Like last night, Legal brought up a discussion on bail: "Can we agree that the money from the general funds can be allotted if someone needs bail?" And the group had to come to consensus on that. [It decided yes.] There's two co-facilitators, a stack-keeper, a timekeeper, a vibes-person making sure that people are feeling OK, that people's voices aren't getting stomped on, and then if someone's being really disruptive, the vibes-person deals with them. There's a note-taker—I end up doing that a lot because I type very, very quickly. We try to keep the facilitation team one man, one woman, or one female-bodied person, one male-bodied person. When you facilitate multiple times, it's rough on your brain. You end up having a lot of criticism thrown your way. You need to keep the facilitators rotating as much as possible. It needs to be a huge, huge priority to have a strong facilitation group.

Overleaf: Liberty Square, New York City.

"People have been yelled out of the park," she says. "Someone had a sign the other day that said 'Kill the Jew Bankers.' They got screamed out of the park. Someone else had a sign with the n-word on it. That person's sign was ripped up, but that person is apparently still in the park.

"We're trying to make this a space that everyone can join," she adds. "This is something the caucuses are trying to really work on. We are having workshops to get people to understand their privilege."

But perhaps the most important rule adopted by the protesters is nonviolence and nonaggression against the police, no matter how brutal the police become.

"The cops, I think, maced those women in the face and expected the men and women around them to start a riot," Ketchup says of an attack the first week. "They want a riot. They can deal with a riot. They cannot deal with non-violent protesters with cameras."

There are no excuses left. Either you join the revolt or you stand on the wrong side of history. You either obstruct through civil disobedience, the only way left to us, the plundering by the criminal class on Wall Street and accelerated destruction of the ecosystem that sustains the human species, or become the passive enabler of a monstrous evil. You either taste, feel, and smell the intoxication of freedom and revolt, or sink into the miasma of despair and apathy. You are either a rebel or a slave.

To be declared innocent in a country where the rule of law means nothing—where the poor and working men and women are reduced to joblessness and hunger, where war, financial speculation, and internal surveillance are the only real businesses of the state, where habeas corpus no longer exists, where you, as a citizen, are nothing more than a commodity to corporate systems of power, one to be used and discarded—is to be complicit in this radical evil. To stand on the sidelines and say, "I am innocent" is to bear the mark of Cain. It is to do nothing to reach out and help the weak, the oppressed and the suffering, to save our besieged planet.

Ask the environmental activist Tim DeChristopher. He was sentenced in July 2011 in a Salt Lake City courtroom by U.S. District Judge Dee Benson to two years in federal prison and ordered to pay a $10,000 fine for "disrupting" a Bureau of Land Management auction in 2008. The auction, orchestrated by the Bush administration, was held to sell federal land to the oil and natural gas industry. The auction was later overturned and declared illegal. As Bidder No. 70,

DeChristopher drove up the prices of some of the bids and won more than a dozen parcels for $1.8 million.[27]

"The rules are written by those who profit from the status quo," DeChristopher says to me shortly before he goes to prison. "If we want to change that status quo we have to step outside of those rules. We have to put pressure on those within the political system to choose one side or another."

It became clear during the selection of the jury that he did not stand a chance. As the prospective jurors entered the court, activists handed them a pamphlet printed by the Fully Informed Jury Association. It said that jurors had a right to come to any decision based on the evidence and their consciences.

"When the judge and the prosecutor found that out, the prosecutor, especially, flipped his shit," DeChristopher says:

He insisted that the judge tell the jurors that this information was not true. The judge pulled most of the jurors into the chambers and questioned them one at a time. He talked about what was in the pamphlet. He said that regardless of what the pamphlet said, it was not their job to decide if this is right or wrong, but to listen to what he said was the law and follow that even if they thought it was morally unjust. They were not allowed to use their conscience. They were told they would be violating their oath if they decided this on conscience rather than the evidence that he told them to listen to. I was sitting in that chamber and could see one person after another accept this notion. I could see it in their faces, that they had to do what they were told even if they thought it was morally unjust. That is a scary thing to witness in another human being. I saw it in one person after another brought in the courtroom, sitting at the end of a long table in front of the paternalistic figure of the judge with all the majesty around him. They accepted it. They did not question it. It gave me a really good understanding of how some of the great human atrocities happened with the consent of the population, that people can accept what is happening, that it is not their job to question whether any of this is right or wrong.

"As a native of West Virginia," DeChristopher told the court when he was sentenced,

I have seen from a young age that the exploitation of fossil fuels has always gone hand in hand with the exploitation of local people. In West Virginia, we've been extracting coal longer than anyone else. And after one hundred and fifty years of making other people rich, West Virginia is almost dead last among the states in per capita income, education rates and life expectancy. And it's not an anomaly. The areas with the richest fossil fuel resources, whether coal in West Virginia and Kentucky, or oil in Louisiana and Mississippi, are the areas with the lowest standards of living. In part, this is a necessity of the industry. The only way to convince someone to blow up their backyard or poison their water is to make sure they are so desperate that they have no other option. But it is also the nature of the economic model. Since fossil fuels are limited resources, whoever controls access to that resource in the beginning gets to set all the terms. They set the terms for their workers, for the local communities, and apparently even for the regulatory agencies. A renewable energy economy is a threat to that model. Since no one can control access to the sun or the wind, the wealth is more likely to flow to whoever does the work of harnessing that energy, and therefore to create a more distributed economic system, which leads to a more distributed political system. It threatens the profits of the handful of corporations for whom the current system works, but our question is which segment of the public are you tasked with protecting. I am here today because I have chosen to protect the people locked out of the system over the profits of the corporations running the system. I say this not because I want your mercy, but because I want you to join me.

The state is determined to crush all resistance. It is terrified this will spread. It has its long phalanxes of police on motorcycles, rows of white paddy wagons, black helmeted foot soldiers with shields and batons hunting for you on the streets with pepper spray and orange plastic nets. It has its *agents provocateurs* spurring groups such as Black Bloc anarchists—named because they dress in black, obscure their faces, move as a unified mass, seek physical confrontations with police, and destroy property—on to vandalism and violent clashes with police. The Black Bloc's thought-terminating cliché of "diversity of tactics" opens the way for hundreds or thousands of peaceful marchers to be discredited by a handful of hooligans. It turns attention away from the mandarins of power to the security apparatus that serves them. The state could not be happier. Police and security operatives planted within Occupy slander and discredit the most effective organizers and attempt to funnel energy back into the dead game of electoral politics.

The corporate state understands and welcomes the language of force. It uses confrontational tactics and destruction of property to justify draconian forms of control and to frighten the wider population away from supporting the Occupy movement. Once the Occupy movement is painted as a flag-burning, rock-throwing, angry mob, it is finished. If it becomes isolated from the mainstream, which it represents, it can be crushed.

This is a struggle to win over the wider public and those within the structures of power, including the police, who are possessed of a conscience. It is not a war. Nonviolent movements, on some level, embrace police brutality. The continuing attempt by the state to crush peaceful protesters who call for justice delegitimizes the power elite. It prompts a passive population to respond. It brings some within the structures of power to our side and creates internal divisions that will lead to paralysis within the systems of power. Martin Luther King kept holding marches in Birmingham because he knew Public Safety Commissioner "Bull" Connor was a thug who would overreact.

Fear is the psychological weapon of choice for totalitarian systems of power. *Make people afraid. Get them to surrender their rights in the name of national security. Demonize all who dissent. And then finish off the few who aren't afraid enough.*

The National Defense Authorization Act (NDAA), signed into law on December 31, 2011, authorizes the military, for the first time in more than two hundred years, to carry out domestic policing. The military can detain, without trial, any U.S. citizen deemed to be a terrorist or an accessory to terrorism. And suspects can be shipped by the military to our offshore penal colony in Guantánamo Bay until "the end of hostilities." It is a catastrophic blow to civil liberties.

Why, a decade after the start of the "war on terror," do these draconian measures need to be implemented? Why do U.S. citizens need to be specifically singled out for military detention and denial of due process, when under the 2001 Authorization to Use Military Force, the president can apparently find the legal cover to serve as judge, jury, and executioner to assassinate U.S. citizens, as he did with the cleric Anwar al-Awlaki in Yemen? Why is this bill necessary, when the government routinely ignores our Fifth Amendment rights—"No person shall be deprived of life, liberty, or property, without due process of law"—as well as our First Amendment right of free speech? How much more power do they need to fight "terrorism"?

The FBI, the CIA, the director of national intelligence, the Pentagon, and the attorney general did not support the NDAA. FBI director Robert Mueller said he feared the bill would actually impede the bureau's ability to investigate terrorism since it would be harder to win cooperation from suspects held by the military.

"The possibility looms that we will lose opportunities to obtain cooperation from the persons in the past that we've been fairly successful in gaining," he told Congress.

But it passed anyway. And I suspect it passed because the corporations, seeing the unrest in the streets, knowing that things are about to get much worse, worrying that the Occupy movement will expand, do not trust the police to protect them. They want to be able to call in the Army. And now they can.

Major cities such as New York and Chicago are not far behind. Rahm Emanuel, the mayor of Chicago, amended various provisions of the Chicago Municipal Code so that nearly all street protests in the city center will be forced to purchase liability insurance, obtain a permit, and register sound equipment, signs, banners, and contingents within the march. The new provisions increase the number of surveillance cameras and closes parks and beaches to the public at night. They mandate heavy increases in fines for "resisting or obstructing the performance of a police officer" and makes no distinction between active and passive. The mayor said he needed the harsh security measures, which he describes as temporary, to contain protesters during the NATO summit in May.[28] The G8 summit, which was also supposed to have been held in Chicago in May, was hastily moved to the more secure and remote site of Camp David. But few expect these provisions to be rescinded.

These security measures are designed to ensure the pillage continues unimpeded by popular discontent. In the seventeenth century, speculation was a crime. Speculators were hanged. Today they run the state and the financial markets. They write the laws. They make the rules. They disseminate the lies that pollute our airwaves. They know, even better than you, how pervasive the corruption and theft have become, how gamed the system is against you. Corporations have cemented into place a thin oligarchic class and an obsequious cadre of politicians, judges, and journalists who live in their little gated Versailles while 3.6 million Americans are thrown out of their homes,[29] a number expected to rise to ten million.[30] A million people a year go bankrupt because they cannot pay their medical bills, and forty-five thousand die from lack of proper care.[31] In this system, real joblessness is at least 15.6 percent,[32] and the citizens, including students, spend lives toiling in debt peonage, working dead-end jobs, when they have jobs, in a world devoid of hope.

"The Party seeks power entirely for its own sake," Orwell wrote in *1984*:

> We are not interested in the good of others; we are interested solely in power. Not wealth or luxury or long life or happiness: only power, pure power. What pure power means you will understand presently. We are different from all the oligarchies of the past, in that we know what we are doing. All the others, even those who resembled ourselves, were cowards and hypocrites. The German Nazis and the Russian Communists came very close to us in their methods, but they never had the courage to recognize their own motives. They pretended, perhaps they even believed, that they had seized power unwillingly and for a limited time, and that just round the corner there lay a paradise where human beings would be free and equal. We are not like that. We know that no one ever seizes power with the intention of relinquishing it. Power is not a means; it is an end. One does not establish a dictatorship in order to safeguard a revolution; one makes the revolution in order to establish the dictatorship. The object of persecution is persecution. The object of torture is torture. The object of power is power.

Corporations are disemboweling every last social service program funded by the taxpayers, from education to Social Security, because they want that money themselves. Let the sick die. Let the poor go hungry. Let families be tossed in the street. Let the unemployed rot. Let children in the inner city or rural wastelands learn nothing and live in misery and fear. Let the students finish school with no jobs and no prospect of jobs. Let the prison system, the largest in the industrial world, expand to swallow up all potential dissenters. Let torture continue. Let teachers, police, firefighters, postal employees, and social workers join the ranks of the unemployed. Let the roads, bridges, dams, levees, power grids, rail lines, subways, bus services, schools, and libraries crumble or close. Let the rising temperatures of the planet, the freak weather patterns, the hurricanes, the droughts, the flooding, the tornadoes, the melting polar ice caps, the poisoned water systems, and the polluted air degrade until the species dies.

Who the hell cares? If the stock values of ExxonMobil or the coal industry or Goldman Sachs are high, life is good. Profit. Profit. Profit. They have their fangs deep in your neck. If you do not shake them off very, very soon, they will kill you. And they will kill the ecosystem, dooming your children and your children's children. They are too stupid and too blind to see that they will perish with the rest of us. So either you rise up and supplant them, either you dismantle the corporate state for a world of sanity, a world where we no longer kneel before the absurd idea that the demands of financial markets should govern human behavior, or we are frog-marched toward self-annihilation.

The Occupy movements are the physical embodiment of hope. They returned us to a world where empathy is a primary attribute. They defied the profit-driven hierarchical structures of corporate capitalism. They know that hope has a cost, that it is not easy or comfortable, that it requires self-sacrifice and discomfort and finally faith. In Zuccotti Park and throughout the country, they slept on concrete every night. Their clothes were soiled. They ate more bagels and peanut butter than they ever thought possible. They tasted fear, were beaten, went to jail, were blinded by pepper spray, cried, hugged each other, laughed, sung, talked too long in general assemblies, saw their chants drift upward to the office towers above them, wondered if it is worth it, if anyone cared, if they would win.

A society is in serious trouble when its political pariahs have at the core of their demands a return to the rule of law. This inversion, with our political and cultural outcasts demanding a respect for law, highlights the awful fact that the most radical and retrograde forces within the body politic have seized control. All conventional forms of dissent, from electoral politics to open debates, have been denied us. We cannot rely on the institutions that once made piecemeal and incremental reform possible. The only route left is to disconnect as thoroughly as possible from the consumer society and engage in acts of civil disobedience and obstruction. The more we sever ourselves from the addictions of fossil fuel and the consumer society, the more we begin to create a new paradigm for community. The more we engage in physical acts of defiance—as Bill McKibben and others did in front of the White House to protest the building of the Keystone XL pipeline—the more we can keep alive a new, better way of relating to one another and the ecosystem.

We must stop being afraid. We have to turn our backs for good on the Democrats, no matter what ghoulish candidate the Republicans offer up for president. All the public disputes between candidates in the election cycle are a carnival act. On the issues that matter, there is no disagreement among the Republicans and the Democrats. We have to defy all formal systems of power. We have to create monastic enclaves where we can retain and nurture the values being rapidly destroyed by the wider corporate culture and build the mechanisms of self-sufficiency that will allow us to survive.

In William Shakespeare's play *Coriolanus*, the Roman consul is deposed by the mob. Coriolanus, whatever his faults, turns on those who thrust him from power with a valediction we should deliver to our ruling elites and all those who remain in their service.

> BRUTUS: There's no more to be said, but he is banish'd
> As enemy to the people and his country.
> It shall be so.
>
> ALL [PLEBEIANS]: It shall be so, it shall be so.
>
> CORIOLANUS: You common cry of curs, whose breath I hate
> As reek a' th' rotten fens, whose loves I prize
> As the dead carcasses of unburied men
> That do corrupt my air, I banish you!
> And here remain with your uncertainty!
> Let every feeble rumor shake your hearts!
> Your enemies, with nodding of their plumes,
> Fan you into despair! Have the power still
> To banish your defenders, till at length
> Your ignorance (which finds not till it feels,
> Making not reservation of yourselves,
> Still your own foes) deliver you as most
> Abated captives to some nation
> That won you without blows! Despising,
> For you, the city, thus I turn my back;
> There is a world elsewhere.[33]

Faces appeared to me moments before protestors from Occupy Wall Street and I were arrested on a windy November afternoon in front of Goldman Sachs. They were not the faces of the smug Goldman Sachs employees, who peered at us through the revolving glass doors and lobby windows, a pathetic collection of middle-aged fraternity and sorority members. They were not the faces of the blue-uniformed police with their dangling plastic handcuffs, or the thuggish Goldman Sachs security personnel, whose buzz cuts and dead eyes reminded me of the Stasi. They were not the faces of the demonstrators around me, the ones with massive student debts and no jobs, the ones weighed down by their broken dreams, the ones whose anger and betrayal triggered the street demonstrations and occupations for justice. They were not the faces of the onlookers—the construction workers, who seemed cheered by the march on Goldman Sachs, or the suited businessmen, who did not. They were faraway faces. They were the faces of children dying. They were tiny, confused, bewildered faces I had seen in the southern Sudan, Gaza, the slums of Brazzaville, Nairobi, Cairo, Delhi, and the wars I covered. They were faces with large, glassy eyes above bloated bellies. They were the small faces of children convulsed by the ravages of starvation and disease.

I carry these faces. They do not leave me. I look at my own children and cannot forget them, these other children who never had a chance. War brings with it a host of horrors, but the worst is always the human detritus that war and famine leave behind, the small, frail bodies whose tangled limbs and vacant eyes condemn us all. The wealthy and the powerful, the ones behind the glass at Goldman Sachs, laughed and snapped pictures of us as if we were an odd lunchtime diversion from commodities trading, from hoarding and profit, from the collective sickness of money worship, as if we were creatures in a cage, which in fact we soon were.

Goldman Sachs' commodities index is the most heavily traded in the world. The financial firm hoards futures of rice, wheat, corn, sugar, and livestock and jacks up commodity prices by as much as two hundred percent on the global market so that poor families can no longer afford basic staples and literally starve. Hundreds of millions of poor in Africa, Asia, the Middle East, and Latin America do not have enough to eat in order to feed this mania for profit. The technical jargon, learned in business schools and on trading floors, effectively masks the reality of what is happening: murder. The cold, neutral words of business and commerce are designed to make systems operate, even systems of death, with a ruthless efficiency.[34]

The people behind the windows and those of us with arms locked in a circle on the concrete outside, did not speak the same language. Profit. Trade. Speculation. Globalization. War. National security. These are the words they use to justify the snuffing out of tiny lives, acts of radical evil. The glass tower before us is filled with people carefully selected for the polish and self-assurance that come with having been formed in institutions of privilege. Their primary attributes are a lack of consciousness, a penchant for deception, aggressiveness, a worship of money, and an incapacity for empathy or remorse.

It is always the respectable classes, the polished Ivy League graduates, the prep school boys and girls who grew up in Greenwich, Connecticut, or Short Hills, New Jersey, who are the most susceptible to evil. To be intelligent, as many are, at least in a narrow, analytical way, is morally neutral. These respectable citizens are inculcated in their elitist ghettos with "values" and "norms," including pious acts of charity used to justify their privilege, and a belief in the innate goodness of American power. They are trained to pay deference to systems of authority. They are taught to believe in their own goodness, unable to see or comprehend—and are perhaps indifferent to—the cruelty inflicted on others by the exclusive systems they serve. And as norms change, as the world is steadily transformed by corporate forces into a small cabal of predators and a vast herd of human prey, these elites seamlessly replace one set of "values" with another. These elites obey the rules. They make the system work. And they are rewarded for this. In return, they do not question.

We seemed to have lost, at least until the advent of the Occupy Wall Street movement, not only all personal responsibility but all capacity for personal judgment. Corporate culture absolves all of responsibility. This is part of its appeal. It relieves all from moral choice. There is an unequivocal acceptance of principles such as unregulated capitalism and globalization as a kind of natural law. The steady march of corporate capitalism requires a passive acceptance of new laws and demolished regulations, of bailouts in the trillions of dollars and the systematic looting of public funds, of lies and deceit. The corporate culture, epitomized by Goldman Sachs, has seeped into our classrooms, our newsrooms, our entertainment systems, and our consciousness. This corporate culture has stripped us of the right to express ourselves outside of the narrow confines of the established political order. We are forced to surrender our voice. Corporate culture serves a faceless system. It is, as Hannah Arendt wrote, "the rule of nobody and for this very reason perhaps the least human and most cruel form of rulership."[35]

Those who resist—the doubters, outcasts, artists, renegades, skeptics, and rebels—rarely come from the elite. They ask different questions. They seek something else: a life of meaning. They have grasped Immanuel Kant's dictum, "If justice perishes, human life on Earth has lost its meaning."[36] And in their search they come to the conclusion that, as Socrates said, it is better to suffer wrong than to do wrong. This conclusion makes a leap into the moral. It refuses to place a monetary value on human life. It acknowledges human life, indeed all life, as sacred. And this is why, as Arendt points out, the only morally reliable people are not those who say "this is wrong," or "this should not be done," but those who say "I can't."

"The greatest evildoers are those who don't remember because they have never given thought to the matter, and, without remembrance, nothing can hold them back," Arendt wrote. "For human beings, thinking of past matters means moving in the dimension of depth, striking roots and thus stabilizing ourselves, so as not to be swept away by whatever may occur—the Zeitgeist or History or simple temptation. The greatest evil is not radical, it has no roots, and because it has no roots it has no limitations, it can go to unthinkable extremes and sweep over the whole world."[37]

There are streaks in my lungs, traces of the tuberculosis I picked up around hundreds of dying Sudanese during the famine I covered as a foreign correspondent. I was strong and privileged and fought off the disease. They were not and did not. The bodies, most of them children, were dumped into hastily dug mass graves. The scars I carry within me are the whispers of these dead. They are the faint marks of those who never had a chance to become men or women, to fall in love and have children of their own. I carried these scars to the doors of Goldman Sachs. I placed myself at the feet of these commodity traders to call for justice because the dead, and those dying in slums and refugee camps across the planet, cannot make this journey. I see their faces. They haunt me in the day and come to me in the dark. They force me to remember. They make me choose sides.

There were times when I entered the ring as a boxer and knew, as did the spectators, that I was woefully mismatched. Ringers—experienced boxers in need of a tune-up or a little practice—would go to the clubs where semi-pros fought, lie about their long professional fight records, and toy with us. Those fights became about something other than winning. They became about dignity and self-respect. You fought to say something about who you were as a human being. These bouts were punishing, physically brutal, and demoralizing. You would get knocked down and stagger back up. You would reel backward from a blow that felt like a cement block. You would taste your blood on your lips. Your vision would blur. Your ribs, the back of your neck, and your abdomen would ache. Your legs felt like lead. But the longer you held on, the more the crowd turned in your favor. No one, not even you, thought you could win. But then, every once in a while, the ringer would get overconfident. He would get careless. And you would find deep within yourself some new burst of energy, some untapped strength, and, with the fury of the dispossessed, bring him down. I have not put on a pair of boxing gloves for thirty years. But I feel this twinge of euphoria again in my stomach, this utter certainty that the impossible is possible, the realization that the mighty can fall.

ACKNOWLEDGMENTS

Eunice Wong, as she does with all my writing, edited, added passages, cut others, challenged and suggested ideas, and was my most steadfast and conscientious critic. This book would not be what it is without her. There were times when her editing was disconcerting, especially when she took my last chapter, printed it out, cut it up with a pair of scissors, and rearranged it on the living room floor. But once she had rearranged it the chapter was stronger and tighter. She also carried out major surgery with the Pine Ridge chapter. Much of the narrative of the book bears her imprint. She read and reread every sentence. I depend on her wisdom and her skills as an editor and a writer. That she is also beautiful, brilliant, a gifted stage actor, deeply compassionate, and as devoted and loving a mother as she is a wife makes our house a shelter from the storms of the world.

This book could not have been written without the generous support of the Lannan Foundation, The Investigative Fund of the Nation Institute, and the Wallace Global Fund, which provided the funds for our travel budget. We made numerous trips to Camden, New Jersey; West Virginia; Pine Ridge, North Dakota; Immokalee, Florida; and New York. The flights, hotels, and car rentals were costly, especially when we rented four-wheel drive vehicles in South Dakota and West Virginia. Gas alone around Pine Ridge cost us more than $50 a day. We would not have been able to make these trips without the Wallace Global Fund grant. The Lannan Foundation is the rock on which I build my work. I would not be able to survive as a writer without them. And The Nation Institute has been my home and my supporter since I left the *New York Times*.

During the two years we worked on this book, Joe Sacco and I encountered valiant and courageous people who resisted not because they could always win, but because it was right. They often knew that the forces they faced were so large and so powerful that defeat was almost assured. But from Pine Ridge to Camden to West Virginia to Immokalee to Zuccotti Park, they fought back. And the rise of a concerted, nationwide Occupy movement to resist corporate power gives us all a hope that did not exist before September 17, 2011.

We would especially like to thank Charlie Abourezk, who devoted tremendous amounts of time to help us on Pine Ridge, as well as Mike Red Cloud. We spent many hours with each of them, and they became good friends. Bill Means, Leonard Crow Dog, Jake Little, and Deborah Tobacco were also very generous in helping us navigate Pine Ridge. Father Michael Doyle in Camden, along with Lolly Davis, Brenda Hayes, and Dwight Ott, who for ten years covered Camden for the *Philadelphia Inquirer* and who took us around the city, were vital links. We would also like to thank Joe Balzano, who dropped his work to take us into Camden and was available for further questioning when we asked. In West Virginia, the Reverend Amanda Reed and the Reverend Jim Lewis devoted several days to helping us get to where we should go and see those we should see. It was only because of the respect so many people had for Jim and Amanda that doors were opened for us. Julian Martin, Allen Johnson, and the novelist Denise Giardina, whose lyrical and moving portrayals of working men and women in the coalfields are unsurpassed in contemporary fiction, were also very helpful. Larry Gibson was generous with his time and an inspiration to us, as he is to all who meet him. Ken Hechler was worth a book in himself. There are certainly few people alive today who knew Franklin Delano Roosevelt, Harry Truman, and Hermann Göring. And there are even fewer political figures with his integrity. We would like to thank Vivian Stockman and Susan Lapis, along with SouthWings, for flying us over the Appalachians, although the devastation we saw made us heartsick. There were several people at the Coalition of Immokalee Workers who were very helpful with the book, first and foremost Greg Asbed, who read through the chapter and provided invaluable criticism. Marc Rodrigues, Laura Germino, Gerardo Reyes-Chavez, and Lucas Benitez gave us much help and time, as well as advice to do our story. Professor Stephen Marini, over a dinner at Wellesley College, urged me to focus my writing on the corporate state. It was wise advice and has resulted in the last three books. Finally, we would like to thank all the occupiers who were camped out in Zuccotti Park, especially Zak Solomon, Sandy Nurse, John Friesen, and Ketchup. You made the last chapter possible. You completed the arch of the book. And you will write in your deeds the next part of this story.

I am grateful to Andy Breslau, Ruth Baldwin, Taya Grobow, and Jonathan Schell at The Nation Institute, as well as Roane Carey and Katrina vanden Heuvel at *The Nation* magazine. Carl Bromley at Nation Books, one of the finest editors in the business, was instrumental in forming the book. Michele Jacob and Dori Gelb are superb publicists who also care deeply about books. Patrick and Andy Lannan, along with Jo Chapman, at the Lannan Foundation have for years provided unwavering support. I am also deeply indebted to my former Eaglebrook School classmate and friend Randall Wallace.

John Timpane, as he always does, edited the final manuscript. There must be something he does not know, but I have yet to find out what it is. He is the filter through which I write, as adept with ideas as he is with line editing. And he even corrected my Spanish grammar.

Anton Woronczuk was my research assistant and saved me hours of work. He is dogged, smart, and reliable. Anton also transcribed many hours of transcriptions, as did

Chris Hohmuth and my son Thomas. Robert Scheer, who sets the gold standard for journalism and commentary, and Zuade Kaufmann, who publishes the Web magazine *Truthdig*, where I write a weekly column, along with the talented editor Tom Caswell, give me a weekly outlet and unqualified support. I would like to thank Ralph Nader, who knows more about corporate power and has been fighting corporations longer and more effectively than any other American, for his wisdom and friendship, along with Kevin Zeese, Margaret Flowers, Steve Kinzer, Peter Scheer, Kasia Anderson, Ann and Walter Pincus, Maria-Christina Keller, Lauren B. Davis, June Ballinger, Michael Goldstein, Gerald Stern, Anne Marie Macari, Tom Artin, the brilliant theologian James Cone, Ray Close, the Reverend Michael Granzen, the Reverend Karen Hernandez, Joe and Heidi Hough, Mark Kurlansky, Margaret Maurer, my mentor and former professor the Reverend Coleman Brown, to whom, along with my father, I dedicated my first book, Irene Brown, Sam Hynes, Sonali Kolhatkar, Francine Prose, Russell Banks, Celia Chazelle, Esther Kaplan, Noam Chomsky, Norman Finkelstein, John Ralston Saul, and Cornel West, who along with Noam and the late Howard Zinn is one of the few intellectuals in this country who matters. Dorothea von Moltke and Cliff Simms, friends in Princeton, fight to defend the printed word with valor and courage.

Lisa Bankoff of International Creative Management handled the contracts for the book and is, as she has been throughout the years, a joy to work with. Nicole Aragi, Joe's agent, was also of great assistance in helping to facilitate this joint project

Finally, I am, first and foremost, a father and a husband. And my four children, Thomas, Noëlle, Konrad, and Marina, along with Eunice, are the center of my universe. "Kiss and a hug!" Konrad will shout as he bursts through the door of my office. They are a balm to my soul. I don't want any of them to grow up too quickly. I hope they will always come home often.

NOTES

Introduction

1. James Gustave Speth, "We're Number One," *Yes Magazine*, March 22, 2011, http://www.yes magazine.org/people-power/on-american-superiority (accessed 26 Dec. 2011).

Chapter 1: Days of Theft

1. "2010 White Clay Year End Statistics," Nebraska Liquor Control Commission, http://www .lcc.ne.gov/Revenue Docs/2010 Whiteclay Year End Stats.pdf. The cans-a-day statistic was calculated using the figures provided by this source.

2. "Pine Ridge Indian Reservation Demographics (2009)," Red Cloud Indian School, www.red cloudschool.org/history/072409_PineRidge_FactSheet.pdf (accessed 23 Dec. 2011).

3. Ibid.

4. Ibid.

5. Nathaniel Philbrick, *The Last Stand: Custer, Sitting Bull, and the Battle of the Little Bighorn* (New York: Penguin, 2010), 138–139.

6. Evan S. Connell, *Son of the Morning Star: Custer and the Little Bighorn* (New York: History Book Club, 1984).

7. Philbrick, 258.

8. Ibid., 210.

9. Kingsley M. Bray, *Crazy Horse: A Lakota Life* (Norman, OK: University of Oklahoma Press, 2006), 192–195.

10. Connell, 330–332.

11. Herbert S. Klein, *Population History of the United States* (West Nyack, NY: Cambridge University Press, 2004), 159.

12. Sitting Bull, Tatanka Yotanka, "Behold, My Friends, the Spring Is Come," in Robert Blaisdell, *Great Speeches by Native Americans* (New York: Courier Dover, 2000), 166.

13. Ibid.

14. PBS.org. *New Perspectives on the West*. "Archives of the West, 1887–1914. The Dawes Act;

February 8, 1887," http://www.pbs org/weta/thewest/resources/archives/eight/dawes.htm (accessed 30 Jan. 2012).

15. Gregory J. Dehler, *The Encyclopedia of North American Indian Wars, 1607–1890: A Political, Social, and Military History*, ed. Spencer C. Tucker, vol. 1 (Santa Barbara, CA: ABC-CLIO, 2011), 229.

16. "Dawes Act."

17. Andrew Jackson, "To the Creek Indians," in Daniel Feller, Harold D. Moser, and Laura-Eve Moss, eds., *The Papers of Andrew Jackson, Volume 7: 1829* (Knoxville, TN: University of Tennessee, 2007), 112.

18. "Pine Ridge Indian Reservation Demographics (2009)."

19. Peter Matthiessen, *In the Spirit of Crazy Horse* (New York: Penguin, 1992), 316–369.

20. "Shannon County QuickFacts from the US Census Bureau," U.S. Census Bureau, modified December 23, 2011, http://quickfacts.census.gov/qfd/states/46/46113.html.

21. Donald R. Prothero, *After the Dinosaurs: Age of the Mammals* (Bloomington, IN: Indiana University Press, 2006), 151.

22. Richard Erdoes and Alfonso Ortíz, *American Indian Trickster Tales* (New York: Pantheon, 1985), 485–486.

23. Peter Nabokov, *Native American Testimony* (New York: Penguin, 1999), 117–118.

24. Mark Diedrich, *Sitting Bull: The Collected Speeches* (Rochester, MN: Coyote, 1998), 118.

25. Robert E. Gamer, *The Developing Nations: A Comparative Perspective* (Dubuque, IA: William C. Brown, 1988), 180–181.

26. Ward Churchill, *Since Predator Came: Notes from the Struggle for American Indian Liberation* (Oakland, CA: AK Press, 2005), 186.

27. Ian Frazier, *Great Plains* (New York: Picador, 1989), 117–118.

28. Matthiessen, 37–38.

29. Frazier, 145.

30. Churchill, 209–210.

31. Leonard Crow Dog and Richard Erdoes, *Crow Dog: Four Generations of Sioux Medicine Men* (New York: HarperCollins, 1995), 234–241.

32. Churchill, 214.

33. Matthiessen, 100.

Chapter 2: Days of Siege

1. "News in Brief," *Philadelphia Inquirer*, October 7, 2010, www.proquest.com (accessed 26 Dec., 2011).

2. Barbara Boyer and Darron Simon, "Camden Gang Slayings: Story of Frenzy, Brutality: A Year Later, Details of Carnage in a Rowhouse," *Philadelphia Inquirer*, February 21, 2011, A1. The fourteen-year old girl is now serving a twenty-year prison sentence for aggravated manslaughter. She avoided a life sentence by pleading guilty.

3. August Wilson, *Gem of the Ocean* (New York: Theatre Communications Group, 2006), 28.

4. Adam Liptak, "Inmate Count in U.S. Dwarfs Other Nations'," *New York Times*, April 23, 2008, A1.

5. Michelle Alexander, "Tomgram: Michelle Alexander, The Age of Obama as a Racial Nightmare," http://www.tomdispatch.com/archive/175215/ (accessed 26 Dec. 2011).

6. Imamu Amiri Baraka, *Tales of the Out and the Gone* (New York: Akashic Books, 2007), 31–32.

7. U.S. Department of Housing and Urban Development, Office of Community Planning and Development, "The 2011 Point-in-Time Estimates of Homelessness: Supplement to the Annual

Homeless Assessment Report December 2011, http://www.abtassociates.com/Reports/2011/The-2011-Point-in-Time-Estimates-of-Homelessness.aspx (accessed 26 Dec. 2011).

8. Sue Halpern, "Who Was Steve Jobs?" *New York Review of Books*, January 12, 2012, www.nybooks.com/articles/archives/2012/jan/12/who-was-steve-jobs/?pagination=false (accessed 12 Feb. 2012).

9. Charles Duhigg and Keith Bradsher, "How the U.S. Lost Out on iPhone Work," *New York Times*, January 21, 2012, www.nytimes.com/2012/01/22/business/apple-america-and-a-squeezed-middle-class.html/pagewanted=all (accessed 12 Feb. 2012).

10. Charles Duhigg and David Barboza, "The iEconomy; In China, the Human Costs That Are Built Into an iPad," *New York Times*, January 26, 2012.

11. Camden, which had forty-eight homicides by early December 2011, was named the second most dangerous city in America, second only to Flint, Michigan, according to the 2011 CQ Press City Crime Rankings. Camden was also named the second most dangerous city in 2010.

12. James Osborne, "Camden Agrees to Regional Police Force," *Philadelphia Inquirer*, December 9, 2011.

13. U.S. Census Bureau, 2005–2009 American Community Survey.

14. Ali Kokot, "Pa. Ranked 2nd in Black Homicide," *Daily Pennsylvanian*, February 2, 2011, http://thedp.com/index.php/article/2011/02/pa._ranked_2nd_in_black_homicide (accessed 26 Dec. 2011). Pennsylvania's lax guns laws are considered significant contributors to the high rate of homicide among the black population in the state.

15. Matt Katz, "Camden Rebirth: A Promise Still Unfulfilled," *Philadelphia Inquirer*, November 8, 2009, A1.

16. Ibid.

17. Eric Model, "Inmate Count In U.S. Dwarfs Other Nations'," *njnewsroom.com*, September 10, 2010, http://www.newjerseynewsroom.com/style/camden-was-once-a-hub-of-music (accessed 24 Dec. 2011).

18. Jeffery M. Dorwart, *Camden County, New Jersey: The Making of a Metropolitan Community, 1626–2000* (New Brunswick, NJ: Rutgers University Press, 2001), 143.

19. Ibid., 154.

20. U.S. Census Bureau, "Camden (city) QuickFacts from the US Census Bureau," *U.S. Census Bureau: State and County QuickFacts*, http://quickfacts.census.gov/qfd/states/34/3410000.html (accessed 26 Dec. 2011).

21. U.S. Census Bureau, "Table 18. Population of the 100 Largest Urban Places: 1950," http://www.census.gov/population/www/documentation/twps0027/tab18.txt (accessed 26 Dec. 2011). The calculation was made by comparing Census data.

22. Ethel A. Lawrence-Halley, "Biography of Ethel Robinson Lawrence," *The Richard C. Goodwin Lecture in Honor of Ethel Lawrence*, Rutgers University, Camden, http://goodwinlecture.rutgers.edu/lawrence.htm (accessed 26 Dec. 2011).

23. State of New Jersey Department of Education, "2010 NCLB Report," http://education.state.nj.us/rc/nclb/nclbreport.php?c=07;d=0680;s=030 (accessed 26 Dec. 2011).

24. CamConnect, "CamConnect Analysis of Camden's Municipal Expenditures," www.camconnect.org/datalogue/budget_expenditures.pdf (accessed 26 Dec. 2011).

25. Camden County Municipal Utilities Authority, "Welcome to the Camden County MUA," *Camden County MUA*, Camden County Municipal Utilities Authority, http://www.ccmua.org/?p=165 (accessed 26 Dec. 2011).

26. Katz, A1.

27. Dwight Ott, "Harmony in Camden, Now Faison and Primas Talk of Cooperation as the State

Takeover Gets Closer," *Philadelphia Inquirer*, http://articles.philly.com/2002–07–29/news/2535 6228_1_camden-mayor-gwendolyn-faison-state-takeover (accessed 26 Dec. 2011).

28. Katz, A1.

29. Richard Rys, "They Have No Choice," *Philadelphia Magazine*, May 15, 2006, http://www.philly mag.com/articles/feature_they_have_no_choice/page4 (accessed 26 Dec. 2011).

30. Josh Benson, "The Tale of the Tapes," *New York Times*, April 10, 2005, www.proquest.com (accessed 26 Dec., 2011).

31. Maureen Graham, "Informant Details Norcross Tape: John Gural Says the Democratic Leader Bragged about His Influence in a Secretly Recorded Chat," *Philadelphia Inquirer*, March 11, 2005, www.proquest.com (accessed 26 Dec., 2011).

32. Rys, 4.

33. Ibid.

34. Carl Mayer, "How NJ Corruption Works Caught on Tape," February 15, 2006, http://new jerseyuntouchables.blogspot.com/2006/02/how-nj-corruption—caught-on-tape.html (accessed 26 Dec. 2011).

35. James Osborne and Craig R. McCoy "Powerful Medicine: How George Norcross used his political muscle to pump up once-ailing Cooper Hospital," *Philadelphia Inquirer*, March 25, 2012.

36. Alan Guenther, "The Palmyra Tapes," *The Courier-Post*, February 16, 2003.

37. Rhys, 4.

38. Katz, A1.

39. Matt Katz, "How the Firms Know to Donate," *Philadelphia Inquirer*, November 08, 2009, www.proquest.com (accessed 26 Dec. 2011).

40. Ibid.

41. Troy Graham, "Sloan El Gets Term for Bribes," *Philadelphia Inquirer*, April 20, 2007, www.proquest.com (accessed 26 Dec. 2011).

42. James Cone, *The Cross and the Lynching Tree* (Maryknoll, NY: Orbis, 2011), 2.

43. Ibid., 2.

44. Ibid., 2.

Chapter 3: Days of Devastation

1. M. A. Palmer, et al., "Mountaintop Mining Consequences," *Science*, January 8, 2010, 148–149. The levels of selenium near mountaintop removal sites are high enough to cause reproductive failure in fish and birds.

2. Bureau of Labor Statistics, "U.S. Department of Labor, Career Guide to Industries, 2010–11 Edition, Mining," http://www.bls.gov/oco/cg/cgs004.htm (accessed 27 Dec. 2011). Mining jobs are expected to decline by 14.5 percent from 2008 to 2018.

3. Manuel Quinones, "Coal Industry Deploys Donations, Lobbying as Its Issues Gain Prominence," *New York Times*, October 13, 2011, http://www.nytimes.com/gwire/2011/10/13/13greenwire-coal -industry-deploys-donations-lobbying-as-it-45582.html (accessed 27 Dec. 2011). A Republican senator who received the most donations from the coal industry this year is quoted: "West Virginia jobs and every American's quality of life are at stake and I will strongly oppose any plan, Republican or Democrat, that makes war on fossil fuels and the working men and women whose families depend on the strength of these industries."

4. Bill McKibben, "Tomgram: Bill McKibben, Buying Congress in 2012," *TomDispatch.com*, January 5, 2012, http://www.tomdispatch.com/blog/175485/tomgram%3A_bill_mckibben%2C_buying _congress_in_2012 (accessed 7 Jan. 2012).

5. Jeff Goodell, *Big Coal: The Dirty Secret Behind America's Energy Future* (New York: Mariner, 2007), 4. The Powder River basin provides about forty percent of the coal burned in the United States.

6. Erik Reece, *Lost Mountain: A Year in the Vanishing Wilderness* (New York: Riverhead, 2006), 3.

7. U.S. Census Bureau, *2005–2009 American Community Survey*, http://factfinder.census.gov.

8. Geospatial and Statistical Data Center at University of Virginia, *Historical Census Browser*, http://fisher.lib.virginia.edu/collections/stats/histcensus/index.html (accessed 27 Dec. 2011).

9. Ibid. The national median home value is six times higher.

10. U.S. Census Bureau, *American FactChecker*, http://factfinder.census.gov (accessed 27 Dec. 2011).

11. Rob Goodwin, "Report from Citizens' Inspection of Coal River Mountain," *Coal River Mountain Watch*, http://www.crmw.net/crmw/content/report-citizens-inspection-coal-river-mountain (accessed 27 Dec. 2011).

12. Naomi Spencer and Rosa Lexington, "The Social Crisis in Appalachia Part 3: Environmental Disaster and Private Profit," *World Socialist Web Site*, July 27, 2010, http://wsws.org/articles/2010/jul2010/app3-j27.shtml (accessed 27 Dec. 2011).

13. Ronald Wright, *A Short History of Progress* (Toronto: House of Anansi, 2004), 102.

14. "Ocean life 'facing mass extinction,' " *Al Jazeera English*, June 21, 2011, http://www.aljazeera.com/news/americas/2011/06/20116216141857396.html (accessed 28 Dec. 2011).

15. Derrick Jensen, Aric McBay, and Lierre Keith, *Deep Green Resistance: Strategy to Save the Planet* (New York: Seven Stories, 2011).

16. Mike Pflanz, "World Water Day: Dirty Water Kills More People Than Violence, says UN," *Christian Science Monitor*, http://www.csmonitor.com/World/Africa/2010/0322/World-Water-Day-Dirty-water-kills-more-people-than-violence-says-UN (accessed 28 Dec. 2011).

17. Dr. Pieter Tans, NOAA/ESRL (www.esrl.noaa.gov/gmd/ccgg/trends/) and Dr. Ralph Keeling, Scripps Institution of Oceanography (scrippsco2.ucsd.edu/).

18. Ben Geman, "Amendment That Says Climate Change Is Occurring Fails in House," *The Hill*, December 28, 2011, http://thehill.com/blogs/e2-wire/e2-wire/154445-house-votes-down-climate-science-amendment.

19. Paul Bahn and John Flenley, *Easter Island, Earth Island* (London: Thames and Hudson, 1992), 211–212.

20. Ibid., 212–213.

21. Harry M. Caudill, *Night Comes to the Cumberlands: A Biography of a Depressed Area* (Ashland, KY: Jesse Stuart Foundation, 2001), 273.

22. Ibid., 275.

23. Ibid., 280.

24. Alison Knezevich, "Prescription Drug Abuse Takes Deadly Toll in W.Va.," *Charleston Gazette*, January 15, 2011, http://www.wvgazette.com/News/pillage/201101151175 (accessed 28 Dec. 2011).

25. Naomi Spencer, "Economic Transformation of Welch, West Virginia: From Mines to Prisons," *World Socialist Web Site*, August 3, 2010, http://www.wsws.org/articles/2010/aug2010/welc-a03.shtml (accessed 28 Dec. 2011).

26. Howard Zinn, *People's History of the United States* (New York: HarperCollins, 2010), 183.

27. Shirley Stewart Burns, Mari-Lynn Evans, and Silas House, *Coal Country: Rising Up Against Mountaintop Removal Mining* (San Francisco: Sierra Club, 2009), 231.

28. Ibid., 231–233.

29. Ibid., 232.

30. Ibid., 233.

31. Ibid., 233–234.

32. Ibid., 235–236.

33. Shirley Stewart Burns, *Bringing Down the Mountains: The Impact of Mountaintop Removal on Southern West Virginia Communities* (Morgantown, WV: West Virginia University Press, 2007), 111.

34. Shirley Stewart Burns, et al., *Coal Country*, 237–238.

35. "Massey Energy Company, Inc. Clean Water Act Settlement," U.S. Environmental Protection Agency, http://www.epa.gov/compliance/resources/cases/civil/cwa/massey.html (accessed 31 Dec. 2011).

36. "25 Miners Dead in WV Coal Mine Explosion, Massey Energy Mine Cited for Hundreds of Safety Violations," *Democracy Now!*, April 6, 2010, http://www.democracynow.org/2010/4/6/25_miners_dead_in_wv_coal.

37. Sabrina Tavernise and Clifford Krauss, "Mine Owner Will Pay $209 Million in Blast That Killed 29 Workers," *New York Times*, December 6, 2011, A16.

38. Adam Liptak, "Trip to Europe Has Repercussions in West Virginia." *New York Times*, Jan 15, 2008, www.proquest.com (accessed 28 Dec. 2011).

39. Jeff Goodell. *Big Coal*, 45.

40. Jeff Goodell, "The Dark Lord of Coal," *Rolling Stone*, Nov. 29, 2011.

41. Lon Savage, *Thunder in the Mountains: The West Virginia Mine War 1920–21* (Pittsburgh, PA: University of Pittsburgh Press, 1990), 19–24.

42. Ibid., 70.

43. Ibid., 165–166.

Chapter 4: Days of Slavery

1. In 2000, the U.S. Department of Labor described farmworkers as "a labor force in significant economic distress," citing "low wages, sub-poverty annual earnings, [and] significant periods of un- and underemployment" to support its conclusions. In 2008, the USDA reaffirmed the Department of Labor's findings from 2000. It reported that farmworkers remain "among the most economically disadvantaged working groups in the U.S." and that "poverty among farmworkers is more than double that of all wage and salary employees."

2. "Background Statistics: Market-fresh Tomatoes," United States Department of Agriculture Economic Research Service (last modified June 10, 2008), http://www.ers.usda.gov/News/tomato coverage.htm.

3. U.S. Bureau of Labor Statistics, "All Charts, Census of Fatal Occupational Injuries, 2010." U.S. Department of Labor, http://www.bls.gov/iif/oshwc/cfoi/cfch0009.pdf, 16.

4. Coalition of Immokalee Food Workers," CIW 101," http://www.ciw-online.org/101.html#facts (accessed 1 Jan. 2012).

5. Barry Estabrook, *Tomatoland: How Modern Industrial Agriculture Destroyed Our Most Alluring Fruit* (Kansas City, MO: Andrews McMeel, 2011), 75.

6. Coalition of Immokalee Food Workers. "CIWNews: CIW at the 2011 Future of Food Conference, Georgetown University, Washington, D.C.," http://www.ciw-online.org/CIW_at_future_of_food.html.

7. Ibid.

8. "Ending WalMart's Rural Stranglehold," The United Food and Commercial Workers, http://www.ufcw.org/docUploads/AG%20Consolidation%20White%20Paper2%2Epdf?CFID=13478539&CFTOKEN=85387754.

9. "CIW at the 2011 Future of Food Conference."

10. Estabrook, 25.

11. Geoffrey M. Calvert, et. al, "Acute Pesticide Poisoning Among Agricultural Workers in the

United States, 1998–2005," *American Journal of Industrial Medicine* 51 (2008): 883–898, doi:10.1002/ajim.20623. "The rates provided should be considered low estimates of the magnitude of acute pesticide poisoning among agricultural workers."

12. "CDC-NIOSH Publications and Products-Impact: NIOSH Pesticide Poisoning Monitoring Program Protects Farmworkers (2012–108)," Center for Disease Control and Prevention, http://www.cdc.gov/niosh/docs/2012–108 (accessed 2 Jan. 2012).

13. Estabrook, 27–28.

14. Ibid., 25.

15. David Ricardo, *On Wages* (1817), excerpted, Fordham University, Internet History Sourcebooks, http://www.fordham.edu/halsall/mod/ricardo-wages.asp (accessed 1 Jan. 2012).

16. John Bowe, "Nobodies," *The New Yorker*, April 21, 2003, 122.

17. Estabrook,74.

18. Ron Field, *The Seminole Wars 1818–58* (New York: Osprey, 2009), 3.

19. Howard Zinn, *A People's History of the United States* (New York: HarperCollins, 2010), 146.

20. Tommy Rodriguez, *Visions of the Everglades* (Bloomington, IN: AuthorHouse, 2011), 29.

21. Historical Census Browser, http://mapserver.lib.virginia.edu (accessed 27 Jan. 2010).

22. Paul Ortiz, *Emancipation Betrayed: The Hidden History of Black Organizing and White Violence in Florida from Reconstruction to the Bloody Election of 1920* (Berkeley, CA: University of California Press, 2006), 61.

23. Leon F. Litwack, *Trouble in Mind: Black Southerners in the Age of Jim Crow* (New York: Vintage, 1999), 290.

24. Ibid., 272.

25. Matthew Mancini, *One Dies, Get Another: Convict Leasing in the American South, 1866–1928* (Columbia, SC: University of South Carolina Press, 1996), 3.

26. Estabrook, 98.

27. "CIW 101."

28. Edward R. Murrow and Fred W. Friendly, producers, *Harvest of Shame*, CBS News, November 26, 1960.

29. Coalition of Immokalee Workers, Florida Modern-Day Slavery Museum pamphlet.

30. Barry Estabrook, "Politics of the Plate: The Price of Tomatoes," *Gourmet*, March 2009, http://www.gourmet.com/magazine/2000s/2009/03/politics-of-the-plate-the-price-of-tomatoes (accessed 1 Jan. 2012).

31. Estabrook, *Tomatoland*, 10.

32. Ibid., 92–93.

33. United States District Court. Middle District of Florida, Fort Myers Division, Case 2:07-cr-00136-JES-DNF. Document 130, July 16, 2008, www.news-press.com/assets/pdf/A411691592.PDF (accessed 2 Jan. 2012).

34. "Congressional Testimony: Coalition of Immokalee Workers, Government Reform Committee," Robert F. Kennedy Center for Justice & Human Rights, http://www.rfkcenter.org/node/244 (accessed 2. Jan 2012).

Chapter 5: Days of Revolt

1. Chris Bryant, "Leipzig Reclaims Its Role in Liberation," *Financial Times*, October 9, 2009, http://www.ft.com/intl/cms/s/0/1124a04a-b469–11de-bec8–00144feab49a.html (accessed 6 Jan. 2012).

2. Victor Sebestyen, *Revolution 1989: The Fall of the Soviet Empire* (New York, Vintage, 2010), 338–339.

3. Ibid., 122.

4. Dan Fishers, "A Martyr Is Vindicated in Prague Square: Czechoslovakia: 10,000 Gather to Remember the Ultimate Sacrifice of Jan Palach," *Los Angeles Times*, January 17, 1990, http://articles.latimes.com/1990–01–17/news/mn-97_1_ultimate-sacrifice (accessed 3 Jan. 2012).

5. Paul Avrich, *Anarchist Portraits* (Princeton, NJ: Princeton University Press, 1988), 231.

6. Rudolf Rocker, *The London Years* (London: Robert Anscombe & Co. for the Rudolf Rocker Book Committee, 1956), 90.

7. Andy Kroll, "Mayors and Cops Traded Strategies for Dealing With Occupy Protesters," *Mother Jones*, November 26, 2011, http://motherjones.com/mojo/2011/11/occupy-protest-coordinate-crackdown-wall-street.

8. Jenna Johnson, "One Trillion Dollars: Student Loan Debt Builds Toward Yet Another Record," *Washington Post*, October 19, 2011.

9. Kamlesh Bhuckory, "Stiglitz Expects 2 Million U.S. Foreclosures This Year," *Bloomberg News*, February 9, 2011.

10. Sheldon Wolin, *Democracy Incorporated: Managed Democracy and the Specter of Inverted Totalitarianism* (Princeton, NJ: Princeton University Press, 2008), 2.

11. Ibid., 13.

12. Ibid., 18.

13. Robert Pear, "Obama to Ask for $1.2 Trillion Increase in Debt Limit," *New York Times*, December 27, 2011. At the time this article was published, the federal debt was $15.1 trillion.

14. Jason deParle, Robert Gebeloff, and Sabrina Tavernise, "Older, Suburban and Struggling, 'Near Poor' Startle the Census," *New York Times*, November 18, 2011, http://www.nytimes.com/2011/11/19/us/census-measures-those-not-quite-in-poverty-but-struggling.html (accessed 6 Jan. 2012).

15. Peter Finn and Greg Miller, "Anwar al-Awlaki's Family Speaks Out Against His Son's Death in Airstrike,"*Washington Post*, http://www.washingtonpost.com/world/national-security/anwar-al-awlakis-family-speaks-out-against-his-sons-deaths/2011/10/17/gIQA8kFssL_story.html. His sixteen-year-old son, Abdulrahman al-Awlaki, was killed in a U.S. airstrike on October 14, 2011.

16. Sebestyen, 386–387.

17. Adam Michnik, *Letters from Freedom* (Berkeley, CA: University of California Press, 1999), 146–147.

18. Alessandro Tinonga and Gaston Lau, "The Struggle Continues in Oakland," *socialistworker.org*, November 16, 2011 (accessed 3 Jan. 2012).

19. Václav Havel, "The Power of the Powerless," Václav Havel, 5.10.1936–18.12.2011, http://www.vaclavhavel.cz/showtrans.php?cat=clanky&val=72_aj_clanky.html&typ=HTML (accessed 13 Feb. 2012).

20. Havel as president exemplified Julian Benda's assertion in *The Treason of the Intellectuals* that we must choose between two sets of principles—justice and truth or privilege and power. The more concessions one makes to privilege and power, the more it diminishes one's capacity to fight for justice and truth. This understanding should have been heeded by Havel, who as president served systems of state power and supported the invasion and occupation of Iraq. Havel's positions as a politician tarnished all he had fought for as an outsider and a dissident. The same can be said of Nelson Mandela, who, once in office, bowed to the demands of foreign investors and international banks and abandoned the African National Congress's thirty-five year-old socialist economic policy, known as the Freedom Charter, which called for the nationalization of mines, banks, and monopoly industries.

21. Jonathan Mirsky, "Liu Xiaobo's Plea for the Human Spirit," *New York Times*, December 30, 2011, http://www.nytimes.com/2012/01/01/books/review/liu-xiaobos-plea-for-the-human-spirit.html.

22. Timothy Garton Ash, *The Magic Lantern: The Revolution of '89 Witnessed in Warsaw, Budapest, Berlin, and Prague* (New York: Random House Digital, 1993), 78.

23. Karl Marx, "The Eighteenth Brumaire of Louis Bonaparte," http://www.marxists.org/archive/marx/works/1852/18th-brumaire/ch01.htm (accessed 6 Jan. 2012).

24. Carolyn Jones, "Berkeley Tree-sitters Finally Down to Earth," *San Francisco Chronicle,* September 10, 2008, http://articles.sfgate.com/2008–09–10/news/17157077_1_tree-sitters-uc-berkeley-training-center (accessed 3 Jan. 2012).

25. Marx, "Eighteenth Brumaire."

26. Avrich, 9–10.

27. Suzanne Goldenburg, "US Eco-activist Jailed for Two Years," *Guardian*, July 27, 2011, http://www.guardian.co.uk/world/2011/jul/27/tim-dechristopher-jailed-two-years.

28. Fran Spielman, "Downtown Will Be on Lockdown During NATO, G-8 Summit," *Chicago Sun-Times*, January 12, 2012.

29. Shanthi Bharatwaj, "Bank Foreclosures to Surge in 2012: RealtyTrac," *MainStreet*, January 4, 2012, http://www.mainstreet.com/article/real-estate/foreclosure/bank-foreclosures-surge-2012-real tytrac (accessed 7 Jan. 2012).

30. Peter King, "1 in 5 Predicted to Default," *mortgageloan.com*, September 21, 2011, http://www.mortgageloan.com/1–5-predicted-default-8856 (accessed 6 Jan. 2012).

31. Susan Heavey, "Study Links 45,000 U.S. Deaths to Lack of Insurance," Reuters, September 17, 2009, http://www.reuters.com/article/2009/09/17/us-usa-healthcare-deaths-idUSTRE58G6W520090917 (accessed 6 Jan. 2012).

32. Aparna Mathur and Matt Jensen, "Tracking the Unreported (15.6%) Unemployed," *Real Clear Markets*, January 4, 2012, http://www.realclearmarkets.com/articles/2012/01/04/tracking_the_unreported_156_unemployed_99440.html (accessed 7 Jan. 2012). The authors note that the official unemployment rate of 8.6 percent masks an actual unemployment rate that is closer to 15.6 percent. This is because the Bureau of Labor Statistics takes the number of unemployed people and divides it by the number of people in the labor force. The disparity in the percentages occurs because of those who are included and those who are excluded officially from the labor force. The Bureau of Labor Statistics measures the labor force as those who are employed or who have actively looked for work within the last four weeks. The official rate, the authors point out, excludes workers who have decided to stop looking for employment. It also excludes those who have part-time work but seek a full-time job. The Bureau of Labor Statistics, aware of the disparity, publishes an alternative measure of the unemployment rate based on an analysis of the Current Population Survey, a household survey. This measure, referred to as the "U-6 rate," includes those who have looked for work in the last twelve months rather than the last four weeks. It also includes people who opted to work part-time even though they seek full-time jobs. The U-6 rate moved from 8.8 percent in December 2007 to 17.4 percent in October 2009 and 15.6 percent in November 2011. More than 5.7 million Americans had been unemployed by the end of 2011 for more than twenty-seven weeks, or forty-three percent of all unemployed.

33. William Shakespeare, *Coriolanus*, 3.3.148–167, in *The Riverside Shakespeare*, ed. G. Blakemore Evans and J. J. M. Tobin (Boston, Houghton Mifflin, 1997).

34. Commodity index investing, as Matt Taibbi does a good job of laying out in his fine book *Griftopia*, was originally designed as a space for two main parties—those producing, like farmers who grow corn, and those purchasing, like cereal companies in need of corn—to buy and sell a particular commodity in large quantities. But it also allowed each party to buy futures contracts as a form of protection. If a cereal company's success next year depends on corn being at $3 a bushel, it might buy six months worth of futures contracts guaranteeing corn at $3 a bushel, so that if there's a spike in price and corn goes up to $3.20, which it can't afford, the business doesn't collapse. The same is true for farmers. If a farmer anticipates a glut during which the price of corn might sink down to, let's say,

$2.50 a bushel, he'll buy futures contracts so that he can keep selling corn at $3 a bushel. The third party—composed of speculators—ensures that business runs smoothly. Say there's a shortage of demand. Companies aren't buying enough from the corn supply. A speculator will come in and buy the remaining futures contracts, hold on to them, and sell them later at a slightly higher price when there's more demand. Speculators ease periods of stagnancy, and keep everyone happy. Too much speculative involvement, however, destroys the market. This is what prompted Franklin Roosevelt's Commodity Exchange Act (CEA) of 1936, which prevented speculators from manipulating the prices of day-to-day commodities. Speculators only want the prices of commodities to go up. It's how they make a profit. But farmers rely on a steady price. So does the cereal company. When prices swell, the farmer loses money because he sells less, the cereal company loses money because corn is more expensive, and finally the consumer loses money because food is more expensive.

Goldman Sachs in 2003 convinced the government to lift the position limits Roosevelt had set up in the CEA, despite the evident danger. It argued that, like the farmer or the cereal company, it was at the whim of fluctuating prices, that position limits discrimination against the speculators who took on the same risk. The government conceded, allowing Goldman Sachs to buy up all the futures contracts and generate an artificial commodities bubble. So from 2003 to 2008, the commodities index market increased by a factor of twenty-five, from $13 billion to $317 billion. And prices increased two hundred percent. International relief agencies estimated that one hundred million additional people starved during the summer of 2008 because of an increase in food prices. See Taibbi's chapter "Blowout: The Commodities Bubble," in *Griftopia* (New York: Spiegel & Grau, 2010), 124–155.

35. Hannah Arendt, *Responsibility and Judgment* (New York: Random House Digital, 2009), 31.

36. Ibid., 52.

37. Ibid., 95.

BIBLIOGRAPHY

Agee, James and Walker Evans. *Let Us Now Praise Famous Men: Three Tenant Families.* Boston: Houghton Mifflin, 1988.

Archer, William R. *Images of America: McDowell County.* Portsmouth, NH: Arcadia Publishing, 2005.

Avrich, Paul. *Anarchist Portraits.* Princeton, NJ: Princeton University Press, 1988.

_____. *The Russian Anarchists.* Princeton, NJ: Princeton University Press, 1967.

Arendt, Hannah. *Responsibility and Judgment.* New York: Schocken Books. 2003.

_____. *The Origins of Totalitarianism.* San Diego: Harcourt, 1976.

Bahn, Paul and John Flenley. *Easter Island, Earth Island.* London: Thames and Hudson, 1992.

Benda, Julien. *The Treason of the Intellectuals.* New Brunswick, NJ: Transaction Publishers, 2009.

Berman, Morris. *Dark Ages America: The Final Phase of Empire.* New York: W.W. Norton & Company, 2006.

_____. *Why America Failed: The Roots of Imperial Decline.* New York: John Wiley & Sons, 2011.

Biggers, Jeff. *Reckoning at Eagle Creek: The Secret Legacy of Coal in the Heartland.* New York: Nation Books, 2010.

Blizzard, William C. *When Miners March.* Oakland, CA: PM Press, 2010.

Bowe, John. "American Slaves Today." *The New Yorker* (April 21, 2003): 106–33.

Bray, Kingsley M. *Crazy Horse: A Lakota Life.* Norman, OK: University of Oklahoma Press, 2006.

Brinton, Crane. *The Anatomy of Revolution.* New York: Vintage, 1965.

Brown, Joseph Epes. *The sacred pipe.* Norman, OK: University of Oklahoma Press, 1953.

Buecker, Thomas R. *Fort Robinson and the American West, 1874–1899.* Norman, OK: University of Oklahoma Press, 1999.

Burns, Shirley Stewart, Mari-Lynn Evans, and Silas House. *Coal Country: Rising Up Against Mountaintop Removal Mining.* San Francisco: Sierra Club Books, 2009.

Burns, Shirley Stewart. *Bringing Down the Mountains: The Impact of Mountaintop Removal on Southern West Virginia Communities.* Morgantown, WV: West Virginia University Press, 2007.

Camus, Albert. *The Plague, The Fall, Exile and the Kingdom, and Selected Essays.* New York: Everyman's Library, 2004.

_____. *Resistance, Rebellion, and Death.* Trans. Justin O'Brien. New York: Alfred A. Knopf, 1961.

Caudill, Harry M. *Night Comes to the Cumberlands: A Biography of a Depressed Area.* Ashland, KY: Jesse Stuart Foundation, 2001.

Chaliand, Gérald. *Revolution in the Third World: Myths and Prospects.* New York: Viking Press, 1977.

Churchill, Ward. *Since Predator Came: Notes from the Struggle for American Indian Liberation.* Reprint. 1995. Oakland, CA: AK Press, 2005.

Cockburn, Andrew. "21st Century Slaves." *National Geographic* (September 2003): 10–24.

Cone, James. *The Cross and the Lynching Tree.* Maryknoll, New York: Orbis Books, 2011.

Connell, Evan S. *Son of the Morning Star: Custer and the Little Bighorn.* New York: History Book Club, 1984.

Crow Dog, Mary. *Lakota Woman.* New York: HarperCollins, 1991.

Deloria, Jr., Vine. *Custer Died For Your Sins.* Norman, OK: University of Oklahoma Press, 1988.

Diedrich, Mark. *Sitting Bull: The Collected Speeches.* Rochester, MN: Coyote Books, 1998.

Dorwart, Jeffery M. *Camden County, New Jersey: The Making of a Metropolitan Community, 1626–2000.* New Brunswick, NJ: Rutgers University Press, 2001.

Erdoes, Richard and Alfonso Ortíz. *American Indian Trickster Tales.* New York: Pantheon Books, 1985.

Estabrook, Barry. *Tomatoland: How Modern Industrial Agriculture Destroyed Our Most Alluring Fruit.* Kansas City, MO: Andrews McMeel, 2011.

Field, Ron. *The Seminole Wars 1818–58.* New York: Osprey, 2009.

Fletcher, Alice C. *Lakota Ceremonies.* Kendall Park, NJ: Lakota Books, 1993.

Flood, Reneé Sansom. *Lost Bird of Wounded Knee: Spirit of the Lakota.* New York: Da Capo, 1998.

Frazier, Ian. *Great Plains.* New York: Farrar Straus and Giroux, 1989.

_____. *On The Rez.* New York: Picador, 2000.

Freese, Barbara. *Coal: A Human History.* New York: Penguin, 2004.

Gamer, Robert E. *The Developing Nations: A Comparative Perspective.* Dubuque, IA: William C. Brown, 1988.

Genovese, Eugene D. *Roll, Jordan, Roll: The World Slaves Made.* New York: Random House, 1976.

Giardina, Denise. *Storming Heaven: A Novel.* New York: Random House, 1987.

_____. *The Unquiet Earth: A Novel.* New York: Random House, 1992.

Goddard, Harold C. *The Meaning of Shakespeare.* Vol. 1. Chicago: Chicago University Press, 1951.

_____. *The Meaning of Shakespeare.* Vol. 2. Chicago: Chicago University Press, 1954.

Goodell, Jeff. *Big Coal: The Dirty Secret Behind America's Energy Future.* New York: Mariner, 2007.

Gorn, Elliot J. *Mother Jones: The Most Dangerous Woman in America.* New York: Hill and Wang, 2001.

Green, Jerome A. *Washita: The U.S. Army and the Southern Cheyennes, 1867–1869.* Norman, OK: University of Oklahoma Press, 2004.

Hardoff, Richard G. *The Death of Crazy Horse: A Tragic Episode in Lakota History.* Lincoln, NE: University of Nebraska Press, 1998.

House, Silas, and Jason Howard. *Something's Rising: Appalachians Fighting Mountaintop Removal.* Lexington, KY: University Press of Kentucky, 2009.

Jackson, Helen. *A Century of Dishonor.* New York: Indian Head Books, 1994.

Johnson, Chalmers. *The Sorrows of Empire: Militarism, Secrecy, and the End of the Republic.* New York: Henry Holt, 2004.

Jones, Mary Harris. "Mother," in Mary F. Parton, Meridel LeSueur, Clarence Darrow, and Fred Thompson. *The Autobiography of Mother Jones.* Chicago: Charles H. Kerr, 2005.

Kindleberger, Charles P. and Aliber, Robert. *Manias, Panics, and Crashes.* Hoboken, NJ: John Wiley & Sons, 1978.

Klein, Herbert S. *Population History of the United States.* West Nyack, NY: Cambridge University Press, 2004.

Korten, David C. *When Corporations Rule the World.* San Francisco: Berrett-Koehler Publishers, 1995.

Krader, Lawrence. *The Ethnological Notebooks of Karl Marx.* Assen, Netherlands: Van Gorcum, 1974.

Lasch, Christopher. *The Culture of Narcissism: American Life in an Age of Diminishing Expectations.* New York: W.W. Norton, 1979.

_____. *The New Radicalism in America 1889–1963: The Intellectual as a Social Type.* New York: W.W. Norton, 1965.

_____. *The True and Only Heaven: Progress and Its Critics.* New York: W.W. Norton, 1991.

Litwack, Leon F. *How Free Is Free?: The Long Death of Jim Crow.* Cambridge, MA: Harvard University Press, 2009.

_____.*Trouble In Mind: Black Southerners in the Age of Jim Crow.* New York: Vintage, 1999.

MacDonald, Dwight. *Against the American Grain: Essays on the Effects of Mass Culture.* London: Victor Gollancz, 1963.

_____. *The Memoirs of a Revolutionist: Essays in Political Criticism.* New York: Farrar, Straus and Cudahy, 1957.

_____. *The Root Is Man.* Brooklyn, NY: Autonomedia, 1995.

Macgregor, Gordon, Royal B. Hassrick, and William Earl Henry. *Warriors Without Weapons; A Study of the Society and Personality Development of the Pine Ridge Sioux.* Chicago: University of Chicago Press, 1946.

Magnuson, Stew. *The Death of Raymond Yellow Thunder.* Lubbock, TX: Texas Tech University Press, 2008.

Marshall III, Joseph M. *The Day the World Ended at Little Bighorn: A Lakota History.* New York: Penguin Books, 2008.

_____. *The Journey of Crazy Horse: A Lakota History.* New York: Penguin Books, 2005.

Marx, Karl. *The Economic and Philosophic Manuscripts of 1844.* New York: International Publishers Co., Inc., 1964.

_____. *The Ethnological Notebooks of Karl Marx: Studies of Morgan, Phear, Maine, Lubbock.* Assen: Van Gorcum, 1972.

Mason, David. *Ludlow.* Pasadena, CA: Red Hen Press, 2007.

Matthiessen, Peter. *In the Spirit of Crazy Horse.* New York: Penguin Books, 1992.

Maynard, Lee. *Crum: The Novel.* Morgantown, WV: Vandalia, 2001.

McKibben, Bill. *Eaarth: Making Life on a Tough New Planet.* New York: St. Martin's Press, 2011.

Mellman, Seymour. *The Permanent War Economy: American Capitalism in Decline.* New York: Simon & Schuster, 1985.

Mills, C. Wright. *The Politics of Truth: Selected Writings of C. Wright Mills*, ed. John H. Summers. New York: Oxford University Press, 2008.

_____. *The Power Elite.* New York: Oxford University Press, 1956.

Moffat, Charles H. *Ken Heckler: Maverick Public Servant.* Charlestown, WV: Mountain State Press, 1987.

Moorhead, Alan. *The Fatal Impact: The Invasion of the South Pacific, 1767–1840.* Sydney, Australia: Mead & Beckett, 1987.

Nabokov, Peter. *Native American Testimony: A Chronicle of Indian-White Relations from Prophecy to the Present, 1492–2000.* New York: Penguin, 1999.

Niebuhr, Reinhold. *Beyond Tragedy: Essays on the Christian Interpretation of History.* New York: Scribner's, 1965.

Neihardt, John G. *Black Elk Speaks.* Albany, NY: State University of New York Press, 2008.

Noble, David F. *America by Design: Science, Technology, and the Rise of Corporate Capitalism.* New York: Alfred A. Knopf, 1977.

Ortiz, Paul. *Emancipation Betrayed: The Hidden History of Black Organizing and White Violence in Florida from Reconstruction to the Bloody Election of 1920.* Berkeley: University of California Press, 2006.

Peltier, Leonard. *Prison Writings: My Life is My Sun Dance.* New York, St. Martin's Press, 1999.

Philbrick, Nathaniel. *The Last Stand: Custer, Sitting Bull, and the Battle of the Little Bighorn.* New York: Penguin, 2010.

Polanyi, Karl. *The Great Transformation: The Political and Economic Origins of Our Time.* Boston: Beacon Press, 1944.

Pollard, Sidney. *The Idea of Progress: History and Society.* London: C.A. Watts, 1968.

Pommersheim, Frank. *Broken Landscape: Indians, Indian Tribes, and the Constitution.* New York: Oxford University Press, 2009.

Popper, Karl. *The Open Society and Its Enemies: The Spell of Plato.* Princeton, NJ: Princeton University Press, 1966.

Powers, Thomas. *The Killing of Crazy Horse.* New York: Alfred A. Knopf, 2011.

Powers, William K. *Lakota Cosmos: Religion and the Reinvention of Culture.* Kendall Park, NJ: Lakota Books, 1998.

Prothero, Donald R. *After the Dinosaurs: Age of the Mammals.* Bloomington, IN: Indiana University Press, 2006.

Redfield, Robert. *The Primitive World and Its Transformations.* Reprint of the 1953 ed. Ithaca, NY: Cornell University Press, 1989.

Reece, Erik. *Lost Mountain: A Year in the Vanishing Wilderness: Radical Strip Mining and the Devastation of Appalachia.* New York: Penguin Group, 2006.

Reinhardt, Akim D. *Ruling Pine Ridge: Oglala Lakota Politics from the IRA to Wounded Knee.* Lubbock, TX: Texas Tech University Press, 2007.

Ricker, Eli Seavey, and Richard E. Jensen. *Voices of the American West: The Indian Interviews of Eli S. Ricker, 1903–1919.* Lincoln, NE: University of Nebraska Press, 2005.

Rodriguez, Tommy. *Visions of the Everglades.* Bloomington, IN: AuthorHouse, 2011.

Rocker, Rudolf, *The London Years.* London, AK Press,1956.

Sansom Flood, Renée. *Lost Bird of Wounded Knee: Spirit of the Lakota.* LaVergne, TN: Da Capo Press, 1998.

Saul, John Raulston. *The Unconscious Civilization.* New York: Free Press, 1995.

_____. *Voltaire's Bastards: The Dictatorship of Reason in the West.* New York: Vintage, 1992.

Savage, Lon. *Thunder in the Mountains: The West Virginia Mine War 1920–21.* Pittsburgh, PA: University of Pittsburgh Press, 1990.

Sebestyen, Victor. *Revolution 1989: The Fall of the Soviet Empire.* New York: Vintage. 2010.

Sellers, Randall Sean. *"'Del pueblo, para el pueblo': The Coalition of Immokalee Workers and the Fight for Fair Food."* Master's Thesis. University of Texas. May 2009.

Shakespeare, William. *The Riverside Shakespeare,* 2d edition., ed. G. Blakemore Evans and J. J. M. Tobin. Boston: Houghton Mifflin, 1997.

Shapiro, Tricia. *Homegrown Resistance to Mountaintop Removal, for the Future of Us All.* Baltimore, MD: AK Press, 2010.

Sitting Bull and Mark Diedrich. *Sitting Bull: The Collected Speeches.* Rochester, MN: Coyote, 1998.

Slotkin, Richard. *Gunfighter Nation: The Myth of the Frontier in Twentieth-Century America.* New York: Atheneum, 1992.

_____. *Regeneration Through Violence; The Mythology of the American Frontier, 1600–1860.* Norman, OK: University of Oklahoma Press, 1973.

_____. *The Fatal Environment: The Myth of the Frontier in the Age of Industrialization, 1800–1890.* New York: Atheneum, 1985.

Standing Bear, Luther. *Land of the Spotted Eagle.* Lincoln, NE: University of Nebraska Press, 2006.

Stewart, Kathleen. *A Space on the Side of the Road.* Princeton, NJ: Princeton University Press, 1996.

Taibbi, Matt. *Griftopia: Bubble Machines, Vampire Squids, and the Long Con That Is Breaking America.* New York: Spiegel & Grau, 2010.

United States of America. *Trafficking in Persons Report*. 10th ed. [Washington, D.C.]. Office of the Under Secretary for Democracy and Global Affairs, June 2010.

Utley, Robert M. *Frontier Regulars: The United States Army and the Indian, 1866–1891*. Lincoln, NE: University of Nebraska Press, 1973.

_____. *The Lance and the Shield: The Life and Times of Sitting Bull*. New York: Henry Holt, 1993.

_____. *The Last Days of the Sioux Nation*. Binghamton, NY: Vail-Ballou Press, 1963.

Wagner, Sally Roesch. *Sisters in Spirit: Haudenosaunee (Iroquois) Influence on Early American Feminists*. Summertown, TN: Native Voices, 2001.

Walker, James R. *Lakota Society*. Lincoln, NE: University of Nebraska Press, 1982.

Walker, James R., Raymond J. DeMallie, and Elaine A. Jahner. *Lakota Belief and Ritual*. Lincoln, NE: University of Nebraska Press, 1991.

Weisman, Alan. *The World Without Us*. New York: Thomas Dunne / St. Martin, 2007.

Woodruff, Paul. *Reverence: Renewing a Forgotten Virtue*. Oxford: Oxford University Press, 2001.

Wright, Ronald. *Stolen Continents: Conquest and Resistance in the Americas*. Toronto: Penguin Canada. 2003.

_____. *A Short History of Progress*. Toronto: House of Anansi, 2004.

Zinn, Howard. *A People's History of the United States*. New York: HarperCollins, 2010.

INDEX